Stanley Cavell and Film

Series Editors:
Lúcia Nagib
Professor in Film at the University of Reading

Tiago de Luca
Associate Professor in Film & Television Studies at the University of Warwick

Advisory Board:
Martine Beugnet, Université Diderot Paris
Thomas Elsaesser, University of Amsterdam
Catherine Grant, Birkbeck University
D.N. Rodowick, The University of Chicago
Ágnes Pethő, Sapientia University
David Martin-Jones, University of Glasgow
Philip Rosen, Brown University
Laura U. Marks, Simon Fraser University

Film Thinks is an original book series that asks: how has film influenced the way we think? The books in this series are concise, engaging editions written by experts in film history and theory, each focusing on a past or present philosopher, thinker or writer whose intellectual landscape has been shaped by cinema. *Film Thinks* aims to further understanding and appreciation, through sophisticated but accessible language, of the thought derived from great films. Whilst explaining and interpreting these thinkers' ideas and the films at their origin, the series will celebrate cinema's capacity to inspire and entertain – and ultimately to change the world. Aimed at film fans as well as specialists, *Film Thinks* is devoted to knowledge about cinema and philosophy as much as to the pleasure of watching films.

Published and forthcoming in the *Film Thinks* series:

Adorno and Film: Thinking in Images
By James Hellings

Georges Didi-Huberman and Film: Politics of the Image
By Alison Smith

Noël Carroll and Film: A Philosophy of Art and Popular Culture
By Mario Slugan

Roland Barthes and Film: Myth, Eroticism and Poetics
By Patrick ffrench

Slavoj Žižek and Film: A Cinematic Ontology
By Christine Evans

Stanley Cavell and Film: Scepticism and Self-Reliance at the Cinema
By Catherine Wheatley

Queries, ideas and submissions to:
Series Editor: Professor Lúcia Nagib – l.nagib@reading.ac.uk
Series Editor: Dr Tiago de Luca – T.de-Luca@warwick.ac.uk
Senior Commissioning Editor at Bloomsbury: Anna Coatman – Anna.Coatman@bloomsbury.com

Stanley Cavell and Film

Scepticism and Self-Reliance at the Cinema

Catherine Wheatley

BLOOMSBURY ACADEMIC
LONDON • NEW YORK • OXFORD • NEW DELHI • SYDNEY

BLOOMSBURY ACADEMIC
Bloomsbury Publishing Plc
50 Bedford Square, London, WC1B 3DP, UK
1385 Broadway, New York, NY 10018, USA
29 Earlsfort Terrace, Dublin 2, Ireland

BLOOMSBURY, BLOOMSBURY ACADEMIC and the Diana logo
are trademarks of Bloomsbury Publishing Plc

First published in Great Britain 2019
Paperback edition first published 2021

Copyright © Catherine Wheatley, 2019

Catherine Wheatley has asserted her right under the Copyright,
Designs and Patents Act, 1988, to be identified as Author of this work.

For legal purposes the Acknowledgements on p. viii constitute
an extension of this copyright page.

Cover design: Charlotte Daniels

All rights reserved. No part of this publication may be reproduced or
transmitted in any form or by any means, electronic or mechanical,
including photocopying, recording, or any information storage or retrieval
system, without prior permission in writing from the publishers.

Bloomsbury Publishing Plc does not have any control over, or responsibility for,
any third-party websites referred to or in this book. All internet addresses given
in this book were correct at the time of going to press. The author and publisher
regret any inconvenience caused if addresses have changed or sites have
ceased to exist, but can accept no responsibility for any such changes.

A catalogue record for this book is available from the British Library.

A catalog record for this book is available from the Library of Congress.

ISBN: HB: 978-1-7883-1025-3
PB: 978-1-3501-9135-8
ePDF: 978-1-3501-1323-7
eBook: 978-1-4411-2382-4

Series: Film Thinks

Typeset by Integra Software Services Pvt. Ltd.

To find out more about our authors and books visit
www.bloomsbury.com and sign up for our newsletters.

Contents

List of Figures	vi
Acknowledgements	viii
Introduction	1
1 A Life in Movies	5
2 Everything Matters	29
3 Screening Scepticism	61
4 Acknowledgement, Other Minds	95
5 Self-Reliance	137
6 Perfectionism, Friendship, Education	181
7 Love's Work	215
Postscript: The End. The Beginning	251
Notes	254
Bibliography	287
Index	299

List of Figures

1. Wittgenstein's imagined duck-rabbit (University of Berkeley, www.ocf.berkeley.edu). — 25
2. The famous packed cabin sequence from *A Night at the Opera*: In the world of the Marx Brothers, to honk is to speak, which is how Cavell can claim that in their world 'nothing goes without saying'. *A Night at the Opera* (Sam Wood, 1935). — 50
3. Deeds lies on his bed in *Mr Deeds Goes to Town*. Here, the camera's attention to the ordinary asks us to linger on this moment, to turn and return, to respond to it. *Mr Deeds Goes to Town* (Frank Capra, 1936). — 55
4. Alfred Hitchcock's *Psycho* (1960) diagnoses modernity's obsession with 'the phony psychological explanations we give ourselves to ward off knowledge'. *Psycho* (Alfred Hitchcock, 1960). — 89
5. Buster Keaton's *Sherlock Junior* (1924): 'it's as if every lie ever told by a photographer's backdrop or prop … had suddenly come to life'. *Sherlock Junior* (Buster Keaton, 1924). — 92
6. In the finale of *The Awful Truth*, Jerry returns to Lucy's room three times, building into the scene an 'acceptance of repetition' that entails the 'acceptance of human relatedness'. *The Awful Truth* (Leo McCarey, 1937). — 124
7. Instead of the festival of marriage *The Awful Truth* closes with a shot of a cuckoo clock, which implies that the festivity of marriage will play out over the days and nights to come. *The Awful Truth* (Leo McCarey, 1937). — 124
8. *Adam's Rib*: 'Vive le difference!' *Adam's Rib* (George Cukor, 1949). — 126

List of Figures

9 The myth of the Fall: in *The Awful Truth* Lucy handles an orange – a substitute for the apple Eve hands Adam. *The Awful Truth* (Leo McCarey, 1937).   131

10 *It Happened One Night*: The couple are embarking upon an endless journey towards something better and something endlessly out of reach. *It Happened One Night* (Frank Capra, 1934).   133

11 Garbo, according to Cavell: 'the greatest, or the most fascinating, cinematic image on film of the unknown woman'. *Queen Christina* (1933, dir. Rouben Mamoulian).   154

12 Bette Davis: in her demeanour is a refusal to accept a world that is second-rate. *Now, Voyager* (1942, dir. Irving Rapper).   156

13 The controversial ending of *Stella Dallas*. *Stella Dallas* (King Vidor, 1937).   166

14 Lucy sings for Jerry in *The Awful Truth*. *The Awful Truth* (Leo McCarey, 1937).   172

15 Paula confronts her tormentor in *Gaslight*: her speech is like a 'mad aria'. *Gaslight* (George Cukor, 1944).   174

16 *The Philadelphia Story*: the husband as moral model. *The Philadelphia Story* (George Cukor, 1941).   197

17 Félicie in *Conte d'hiver*: 'She exists, as her thoughts exist; she loves; she counts herself happy.' *Conte d'hiver* (Éric Rohmer, 1993).   201

18 *The Band Wagon*: Fred Astaire walks 'the walk of a man who is known to move in dance exactly like no other man'. *The Band Wagon* (Vincente Minnelli, 1953).   228

19 *The Band Wagon*: the beginning of the shoeshine dance. *The Band Wagon* (Vincente Minnelli, 1953).   230

20 *The Band Wagon*: as Astaire exits the scene, Daniels is left on his knees (Vincente Minnelli, 1953).   231

Acknowledgements

Could a greater miracle take place than for us to look through each other's eyes for an instant?

– *Walden, Or Life in the Woods*

Fittingly for a work about a man who spent much of his life thinking about teaching, this book began life in the classroom. My first debt of thanks is to Sarah Cooper, for encouraging me to take over her module Thinking Cinema and devote it to studying the works of Stanley Cavell, as well as to the students who have borne with me over the eight years that I have been teaching it and without whose conversation this book would undoubtedly have taken a very different shape. My colleagues in the department of Film Studies at King's College London have been a great source of ideas, inspiration and encouragement. I am thankful for the stimulating and supportive environment they provide, as well as their ongoing friendship.

Thanks to Eugenie Brinkema, William Brown, Catherine Constable, Andrew Klevan, Richard Rushton, Eva Sancho Rodriguez, William Rothman, David Sorfa, Ben Tyrer and Ginette Vincendeau for advice, coffees, kind words and moral support. Also to Fiona Handyside, Stephen Mulhall, David Rodowick, Daniele Rugo and Kyle Stevens, who were generous enough to let me read and watch work in progress that has informed this book. Anna Backman Rogers invited me to present my own work in progress at the Film-Philosophy conference she hosted in Gothenburg in July 2018. John Ó Maoilearca very kindly took the time to read and offer detailed feedback on an early draft of the book. Lucy Bolton has been the model of intellectual and spiritual friendship. To paraphrase Cavell, the academic life is a life whose texture is a weave of cares and commitments in which one is bound to become lost and to need the friendly and credible words of others in order to find one's way. These individuals, and the other scholars who make up the Film-Philosophy community, are a constant source of inspiration and guidance.

A supportive editor is worth her weight in gold. I am grateful to the series editors Lúcia Nagib and Tiago de Luca for encouraging me to submit a proposal to the Film Thinks series, to Maddy Hamey-Thomas for her graciousness and forebearing as I worked through various iterations of the book, and her judiciousness when wielding her editorial pen. (I once accidentally told her I loved her at the end of the phone call; Freud might, I think, have had something to say about that.) My thanks also go to Rebecca Barden and Anna Coatman for steering the project through its final stages. And of course to the two anonymous reviewers whose careful reports have hopefully helped me to improve the book in important ways. Manuscript reviewing is often a thankless task: I do hope you read this and see how much I appreciate your time and effort.

Love is the subject of this book's final chapter; in a sense it is the thread that runs throughout the whole work, arising out of three of Cavell's central themes: what it is to be a friend, what it is to be a spouse and what it is to be a mother. During the writing of this book I've been learning about all three. The book would never have existed had my children's grandparents not rallied round to provide unpaid childcare to allow me to read, write, watch films and attend conferences. Jennifer and Malcolm Parry, Ann and Les Wheatley: thank you, thank you.

My greatest debt of gratitude goes to Christopher Parry (if Cavell is right that bickering is the surest proof of a strong marriage, I think we've got it nailed), and to Esther, Daniel and Felix Parry, who every day are teaching me to view the world through someone else's eyes. This book is for them.

Introduction

The impact of movies is too massive, too out of proportion with the individual worth of ordinary movies, to speak politely of involvement. We involve the movies in us. They become further fragments of what happens to me, further cards for the shuffle of my memory, with no telling what place in the future. Like childhood memories whose treasure no else appreciates, whose content is nothing compared with their unspeakable importance for me.
– Stanley Cavell

Memory is the most faithful of films.
– André Bazin

Imagine the scene. The year is 1933. It is a balmy summer day in downtown Atlanta. A seven-year-old boy stands, clasping his mother's hand, before a fabulous picture palace edged with gilt. Domes and minarets arise from its white brick exterior. He enters a vast lobby and from there, a viewing space suggesting a Middle Eastern courtyard overarched by a night sky with visible stars and moving clouds. His mother, a pianist with the pit orchestra, leaves him alone in the dressing room used by the vaudeville performers who share the stage with the moving pictures. It is a room lined with the old-fashioned, lightbulb-lined mirrors so familiar to us from black-and-white movies featuring would-be starlets. Here the boy will encounter an adolescent girl of such crushing beauty that, when she starts to undress, he flees the room. Later, waiting for his mother to drive him home, the boy finds a place in the back of the theatre from which to watch the cartoon that is playing. This turns out not to be a piece of humorous fun but rather shows a frightened crowd of people in a street shown running from a black bird who sweeps down and covers them with a black cloth on which the word DEPRESSION is written in huge blurry white letters. Then a drawing fills the screen. It is of a face that the young boy recognizes, from a picture in his house, as that of President Roosevelt. The audience breaks into rapturous applause.[1]

Another scene, some fifteen years later. A mahogany-walled classroom in Juilliard. A young man, in his early twenties, gazes out the window. We cut to 42nd Street in its last hurrah, the late 1940s, before it becomes overrun with porn theatres and before it is reconstructed. Cinema hoardings advertise repertory films and reruns. A montage of film posters shows Spencer Tracy in *Dr Jekyll and Mr Hyde*, Ronald Reagan in *King's Row*, Paul Muni in *I Am a Fugitive from a Chain Gang*, Katherine Hepburn in *Stage Door*, Margaret Sullavan in *Three Comrades*, Ronald Coleman in *Lost Horizon*, Carole Lombard in *To Be or Not to Be*, Margo in *Winterset* and Ann Harding in *Peter Ibbotson*.

Jump forward another ten years to the mid-1950s. The man is now in his thirties. He hunches over a desk, surrounded by papers and philosophy books with long, weighty titles: *A Treatise of Human Nature*, *Groundwork of the Metaphysics of Morals*, *Tractatus Logico-Philosophicus*. He seems frustrated: perhaps he is suffering from writer's block? Suddenly, he pushes back his chair and stalks purposefully out of the room. We cut to a darkened auditorium and a series of shot/reverse-shots of the scholar's rapt face and the images on screen, which are taken from Bergman's *Smiles of a Summer's Night*. The credits come up and the young man dashes out of the theatre. A final scene shows him back in his garret, writing furiously, passionately. A close-up on a hand-scrawled page reveals that what he has written down is his thoughts on the film that he has just seen. The journal entry reads: 'Seasons of Love: Bergman's *Smiles of a Summer Night* and *The Winter's Tale*'.

These excerpts from the life of Stanley Cavell, imaginary reconstructions of events that he has described in interviews and his autobiographies, are in a sense cinematic memories. That is, they are memories that have the vividness of scenes from films, but they are also memories of cinema and of its lasting impact on the emotional and intellectual life of one person. As Cavell tells us in the opening line of *The World Viewed*, 'movies are strand over strand with memories of my life'.[2] Just so, his life is strand over strand with Cavell's philosophy, which is, as we will see, unusually autobiographical, threaded with personal anecdotes, studded with scenes from his childhood and adolescence. Cavell's work is deeply engaged with the question of what it might mean to live a philosophical life, with 'why philosophy, of a certain ambition, tends to intersect with the autobiographical', and it is equally bound up with matters of human experience, an experience that can only ever be subjective, bounded by our own point of view. 'How does one communicate this experience?' Cavell asks, time and again; 'Why does it matter that we try?' Katrina Forrester puts it beautifully when she writes that, for Cavell, philosophy is therapeutic: bound up (or interchangeable) with literature, psychoanalysis and care of the self.[3]

Cavell understands philosophy 'as a willingness to think not about something other than what ordinary human beings think about, but rather to think undistractedly about things that ordinary human beings cannot help thinking about'.[4] He has spent a career, one that spans over fifty years, struggling with what exactly that entails. Throughout that time, and even before, before philosophy was a concept that had even entered Cavell's vocabulary, film has played a pivotal role in shaping his thinking and his impressions of the world. Quite how it did so, and why it matters, is the subject of this book.

1

A Life in Movies

By my way of thinking the creation of film was as if meant for philosophy – meant to reorient everything philosophy has said about reality and its representation, about art and imitation, about greatness and conventionality, about judgement and pleasure, about scepticism and transcendence, about language and expression.

– Stanley Cavell, *Contesting Tears*

Stanley Cavell was born Stanley Goldstein in Atlanta, Georgia, in 1926, the only son of two immigrants. His mother, a professional pianist of local repute, played on the radio, at the vaudeville and during intermissions at the Fox Movie Theatre. His father was a shopkeeper-cum-pawnbroker and – importantly – a consummate raconteur (but also, in the words of Cavell's mother, 'a serious man'). The young Cavell seems to have been quite fascinated by his mother, who often worked late and who he suspected had sacrificed a career as a concert pianist to raise him. She recurs as a touchpoint throughout much of his work (as, too, does his father, but in a rather different, less poetic manner) and is, perhaps, the prototype of the Unknown Woman who Cavell writes about in relation to Hollywood melodramas of the 1940s and 1950s, a subject considered in detail in Chapter 5 of this book.

But back to young Stanley, growing up during the Great Depression, following his parents as they moved, several times, between Atlanta and Sacramento, California. According to Cavell, his family would go to the films 'quite religiously'. In fact they attended twice a week, an activity that must have afforded a small amount of consistency amidst a rather peripatetic childhood.[1] Cavell was by his own admission a precocious child and was skipped two grades at school during first grade, a custom that he describes as 'absolutely destructive' to his social and psychological life. School was particularly painful: the young Stanley's clothes were never quite right; he failed to understand the jokes being made at his expense. Tellingly, perhaps, one of the few positive experiences he recounts comes courtesy of a young English teacher who gave the class as a writing assignment the reviewing of a film: *Hold Back the Dawn* starring Charles Boyer and Olivia de Havilland (Mitchell Leisen, 1941). The teacher's praise for Cavell's work seems to have had a lasting effect, informing his imagination 'of the permanent effects an act of acknowledgement may have'.[2]

His adolescence was thus isolating, 'helplessly lonely' in his own words, the only respite coming from cinema and – via his involvement in a band – music, and sometimes the two together, as when he would visit the cinema with his bandmate Bob Thompson: 'looking forward as much to the conversation afterward as to the film'.[3] He was only sixteen when he headed off to Berkeley in 1943 to take his BA in Music, shortly after taking the decision to change his name to Cavell, an anglicization of his family's original Russian name, Kavelieruskii (changed at Ellis Island).[4] Cavell graduated in 1947. But when he moved to New York to study composition at Juilliard the following year, he felt too old to begin a career as a composer. Unmoved by his classes and sensing that music was not lost to him but would no longer be his career, he started 'playing hooky' by going to at least two films a day, a practice that would prove formative.

In 1948, he returned to California to enrol as a student at UCLA, first in psychology, then in philosophy. Here he met a visitor from Harvard, Morton White, who suggested that Cavell apply to Harvard. At Harvard, he attended a series of lectures given by the Oxford-based philosopher J.L. Austin. He describes the encounter with Austin – who came to Harvard to deliver a series of lectures in 1955 – as the decisive encounter of his life, describing the moment as one where 'I found the beginning of my own intellectual voice'.[5] Cavell put this voice to the test in dialogue with colleagues and fellow philosophers such as White, Thomas Kuhn and Bernard Williams. Friendship was, and continued to be, important to Cavell as a means of developing his ideas about what philosophy should be and how one should live a philosophical life. Important, too, was the meeting of minds constituted by the best marriages. Cavell met Marcia Schmid, who was to be his first wife and the mother of Cavell's daughter Rachel, around the same time as he embarked upon his path towards becoming a professional philosopher. Their short-lived marriage ended in divorce in 1961 for reasons that Cavell, in his 2010 memoir, fails to fully fathom but which had to do, he senses, with the fact that although 'we seemed to share everything, friendship, philosophy, music … Our minds were not freely given'.[6] Such a failure to give freely of oneself to another, to meet as equals on some common ground, is a failure that Cavell understands as both personally and philosophically devastating. The question of what makes for a successful marriage is one that lies at the heart of his work on screwball comedy, to which we will turn in Chapter 4. Happily for Cavell, in 1964, shortly after accepting a tenured position at Harvard, he met Cathleen Cohen, a student reporter for the *Harvard Crimson*, and the pair were married in 1967. They were still married at the time of Cavell's death in 2018 and have two sons, Benjamin (born 1976) and David (born 1984).

It was while struggling to write his PhD thesis (finally submitted in 1961) that Cavell, at the end of his tether one night, saw Bergman's *Smiles of a Summer Night* and hurried home to dash off an essay describing its effect upon him. Around this time he began, once more, to visit the cinema, watching films regularly again: now some Godard, Fellini, Resnais, Antonioni.[7] Upon his appointment at Harvard, Cavell was assigned a general philosophy course to teach, 'Ideas of Man and the World in Western Thought'. The reading list he inherited features all the canonical classics: Machiavelli's *The Prince*, Luther's *Preface to the Letter of St. Paul to the Romans*, Descartes's *Meditations* and Locke's *Second Treatise of Government*; Hume's *Dialogues on Natural Religion*, Kant's *Groundwork of the Metaphysics of Morals*, Mill's *On Liberty* and Nietzsche's *The Birth of Tragedy* (many of which will pop up, in various manners, throughout Cavell's later work). But Cavell, determined to drag the course into the twentieth century, and determined not to let the twentieth century be represented by works of philosophy that lacked 'influence' or 'value', opted to end with a film, which in his words worked 'pedagogical wonders'. So when he was asked to also deliver a course in philosophical aesthetics, he opted to focus on film here, too. Cavell explains his motivation for this – at the time – rather unorthodox decision in his autobiography, *Little Did I Know*:

> I found little charm in analytical aesthetics. I had never been convinced by the ways I had managed to bring that strain of contemporary English-speaking philosophy and the individual arts into the classroom together, let alone my writing. Individual works in the arts never seemed for my taste to talk back sufficiently to philosophy … to make philosophy look at its own limitations, its own dependence on literary conditions. What the best or most influential literary critics in English (T.S. Eliot, William Empson, I.A. Richards, Kenneth Burke, R.P. Blackmur, Robert Penn Warren, Paul Goodman) had been saying about works of literature remained to my mind incomparably more interesting, and indeed intellectually more accurate, than the competing provisions of analytical philosophy [...] Art historians (for example, Panofsky, Wölflinn) supplied their own philosophy that philosophers whom I knew did not improve upon. The analysis of music was, in my experience … done best by composers, and in any case assumed a basic knowledge of harmony and classical forms that would have left nonmusicians out of the picture. It was from this sense of pedagogical impasse that I came to the idea of experimenting

with what could be said about film, a field in which new work, by directors and writers in France and Italy and Sweden and Japan, had brought new consciousness and interest to the international art of cinema, at a time when American film seemed to shrink before the competition of television.[8]

Historical context

Cavell's work on film arises, then, from a very specific context. Firstly, it comes out of a philosophy department. It is the work of a philosopher who is interested in film (rather than, say, a film scholar who is interested in philosophy). His approach to the subject is indeed rather ironic given Cavell's own insistence in the above passage that it is the experts in literature, art and music who write best about their subjects, rather than interlopers from his own discipline. This irony has not been lost on Cavell's critics, a point to which I will return when I come to consider the reception of Cavell's work. Secondly, it emerges from a North American, academic, context at a time when comparatively little intellectual work on film had been written in or translated into English. In both his autobiography and his writing on film Cavell himself acknowledges that figures such as Sergei Eisenstein, Walter Benjamin, Erwin Panofksy and André Bazin had already written 'fresh and free' treatments of film, but they were hardly well known amongst US scholars (Bazin's *What Is Cinema?* was not translated into English by Hugh Gray until 1967). In fact the only other American writer on film Cavell refers to in his first essays on film is the critic James Agee, although there were others working in the field – Andrew Sarris's 'Notes on the Auteur Theory' was published in 1961, for example. Thirdly, Cavell begins writing on film at a point when, as he notes, the American cinema, or at least Hollywood cinema, was in the doldrums, while the European cinemas, including the French New Wave and Italian Neorealism, were enjoying a golden age. Finally, if the seed that was to grow into Cavell's extensive writing on film was born with his late-night scribblings on *Smiles of a Summer Night*, it was nurtured and took root in a classroom at Harvard, where Cavell was facing 'fellow citizens of mine' to whom 'anything could be said that I found it worth saying and felt that aspirants to democracy should gladly hear, on the condition that I took pains sufficient to say it, as talent allowed, lucidly and provocatively'.[9]

Each of these factors would have an impact on Cavell's approach to film as well as to his selection of particular movies. But it is perhaps just as important that Cavell's first thorough-going engagement with film, inspired in part by a restiveness with philosophy's avoidance of human experience, coincided with the festiveness that marked the move to a new, permanent job and the start of his academic career in earnest (as well as, of course, the beginning of a new love affair). Cavell's first engagement with film is marked by a sense of giddiness, of possibility – a brave new world opening up. It certainly presaged a glut of productivity. Cavell published his first book, *Must We Mean What We Say?*, in 1968, and two years later *The World Viewed: Reflections on the Ontology of Film* was released. One year after that came yet another book: on the philosopher Henry David Thoreau, *The Senses of Walden*. Thoreau, though widely read at the time, had yet to receive any extended attention, so Cavell was breaking ground on two fronts: by writing the first serious book produced within the context of North American academia, and the first serious book on Thoreau. The two interests would eventually collide, as I will examine in greater detail by and by, in Cavell's subsequent books on film: *Pursuits of Happiness: The Hollywood Comedy of Remarriage* (1981) and *Contesting Tears: The Hollywood Melodrama of the Unknown Woman* (1996), as well as in *Cities of Words: Pedagogical Letters on a Register of the Moral Life* (2005), a book that weaves philosophy and philosophical accounts of literature with studies of films to provide a moral articulation of a democratic society. Cavell has also written essays on television and video and on specific films, many of which are gathered together in a collection edited by his former student William Rothman, called *Cavell on Film* (2005). While these works do not form a strict and unified system, there are deep connections between them.[10] There are also connections between them and Cavell's philosophical work broadly, and it will be one aim of this book to sketch out some of these connections.

The avoidance of Cavell

At the time of its release, *The World Viewed* was not particularly well received. Responses ranged from polite bafflement to Leo Braudy's damning review of it as a 'little book designed to make anyone interested in good film criticism very unhappy'.[11] Today, it has become something of a truism that Cavell is overlooked and underappreciated by the scholarly community, and in particular the Film Studies community. Several articles and at least one entire book[12] exist devoted to examining the question of why it is that Cavell's work has been, to borrow a term from Garrett Stewart, 'avoided' for so long.[13] Or, as Russell B. Goodman puts it, why it is that while Cavell is a major figure within several disciplines, people 'don't quite know how to use' his work.[14] Michael Fischer's 1989 book *Stanley Cavell and Literary Skepticism* investigates the grounds of neglect in the specifically literary reception of Cavell, which he believes stems from the neoscepticism at its base.[15] Stephen Melville, writing in 1993, locates the disregard for Cavell on four fronts, by which he is positioned as 'a maverick figure within the American philosophic academy, an obscure register of mainstream contemporary film theory, an odd man out with respect to the current literary theoretical orthodoxy, and, I imagine, a figure of retrograde enthusiasms to a community of Americanists largely in flight from New Critical canonization'.[16] Timothy Gould's

1998 book *Hearing Things* perhaps gets to the crux of the problem, however, suggesting that perhaps the biggest obstacle facing readers of Cavell is not methodological, but stylistic.[17]

Cavell is considered notoriously difficult to read, and with good reason. On the one hand, he is committed to the ordinary, and to communicating his ideas as clearly and lucidly as possible, always with an eye to encouraging his reader to better understand how he sees the world. To write – to write for someone – is in short to attempt to overcome the problem of scepticism, an issue that goes to the heart of Cavell's philosophy. For Cavell, then, much is at stake in the act of writing. But there is a sense in which his writing constantly struggles under this effort. In Garrett Stewart's words, 'Cavell's diction is straightforward enough, no technical argot, and the syntax much of the time cadenced not unlike speech, but it all comes at us with a heft and velocity that transfigures the ordinary.'[18] Numerous critics point to the opening paragraph of *The Claim of Reason*, which consists of just two sentences, one of which is two hundred words long, as an example of such laboriousness.[19] One adjective used time and again is 'dense'; another is 'weighty'. Every word seems so carefully chosen, every subclause (and there are many!) so laboured, so deliberate. The burden transfers itself to the reader, who in turn finds herself struggling under its load.

Hand in hand with Cavell's idiosyncratic prose style goes a deliberate lack of distinct or rigorous argument, a lack that springs from Cavell's commitment to finding words adequate to convey an experience (of philosophy, of theatre, of art, of film), rather than to persuade his interlocutor of the rightness of a position. As Cavell explains in *Themes out of School*, 'I look for the conviction of others in what I say only to the extent that I can manifest my own conviction by it.'[20] Robert Sinnerbrink thus conceptualizes Cavell's writing on film as 'romantic film-philosophy': a form of criticism that, rather than attempting to impose philosophical paradigms upon a work of art, instead, *respond*s to film as a way of thinking, allowing film itself to be philosophically self-reflective. Cavell's work, Sinnerbrink, says, offers a way of relating philosophy and film in which both are profoundly transformed, an idea I will spend some time thinking about in Chapter 7 of this book.[21]

Some critics, Leo Braudy among them, question whether in this case what Cavell is doing can even be called philosophy. How can Cavell eschew argument or 'theory' and still be regarded as engaging in philosophical work? In Cavell's writing, Braudy practically spits, 'subjects are brought up, dropped, and resummoned to serve the demands of a logic no doubt rooted in the author's psyche, but little in evidence on the page'.[22] He compares reading Cavell's *The World Viewed* to having to 'hack' and 'slash' one's way through a 'thicket' of style, a metaphor taken up – intentionally or not – by Anthony Kenny, who in a later review of *The Claim of Reason* dismisses the book as a 'misshapen, undisciplined amalgam of ill-assorted parts', one that 'could have been much better had it been pruned of dead wood and over-exuberant foliage'.[23] As Sinnerbrink astutely surmises, what these and other negative reviews of Cavell's work criticize is not so much poor argument as something excessive, self-indulgent. There is *too much* in Cavell's writing: too much complexity, idiosyncrasy, ambiguity, interruption, irony, reflexivity and, of course, too much autobiography.[24] In short: too much Cavell. As those who have spent any time reading Cavell will testify, after a while, one comes to feel one knows him – not the author as a product of the text but Stanley Cavell, the man himself. This effect is rather disarming, and for some, evidently rather infuriating. To paraphrase Leo Braudy, it is difficult not to take Cavell's writing personally.

But such emphasis on the personal is strategic for Cavell, who in placing the partiality of his own experience front and centre invites his reader to do the same, thus transforming a monologue into a conversation. Stephen Mulhall reframes the problem of Cavell's style by arguing that the very feature that readers find most annoying can in fact instruct us in how to read him. Mulhall describes *The Claim of Reason* as a modernist text written in the absence of philosophical conventions that we can take for granted, 'a half-built edifice whose form acknowledges both its origin in ruins and the completion it foreshadows'.[25] We might think of it like this: if Cavell's writing doesn't read like the stripped back, logical progression of professional philosophy, it may bear at least some resemblance to film criticism. Not the academic criticism with which many readers will be familiar – ideological, structuralist or formalist – but rather popular criticism, which is centred around the subjective opinion of the individual assessing the film. We read these reviews before seeing the film, wanting to know what our esteemed critic thought, to gauge whether it might be worth seeing too. And we read them afterwards to test our opinions against their own. In this much, the experience of reading a film review is a time-delayed version of the conversations that we share with our fellow filmgoers once the titles come up (the sort of conversations that Cavell himself so enjoyed as a young man). Just so, Cavell sees criticism as a practice that involves accounting for his own experience of movies, taking responsibility for his responses. And what this practice produces is not the last word, but the opening gambit in a conversation. As the epigraph to *The Claim of Reason*, taken from Emerson's 'Address Delivered before the Senior Class in Divinity College, Cambridge, Sunday Evening, 15 July 1838', reads, 'Truly speaking, it is not instruction, but provocation, that I can receive from another soul.'

There is a final explanation as to why Cavell has languished, at times, in something of a critical hinterland, which is that his work lacks, for want of a better word, modishness. As Garrett Stewart has pointed out, Cavell's approach to his subject matter, whether philosophy, literature, film or any of the other arts, is never quite of the zeitgeist, be that the current interest in postcolonialism, race, subaltern studies, globalization, cultural hybridity, queerness and pluralist identity politics; or before that, New Historicism; or before that, deconstruction; and before that still, semiotics.[26] Often Cavell's work has been eclipsed or swallowed up by louder, more trendy or more politicized voices: Derrida, Foucault and Lacan are the names that Stewart offers up, but we might well add Žižek, Butler, and the name with whose Cavell's is most often lumped, at least within Film Studies, Gilles Deleuze (more on whom later).

Cavell might justifiably be criticized for his (lack of) politics. His heteronormative, patriarchal portrait of what marriage is and can be has long troubled feminist writers such as Tania Modleski. So too have ill-judged asides such as the following, from *Disowning Knowledge*: 'Then are we to conclude that the issue of scepticism does not arise for women? (I do not want to answer this question now to expose the apparently more general question whether philosophy as such arises for women).'[27] As Garrett Stewart points out, such a comment may be partially justifiable in the context of a one-sided anxiety in *The Winter's Tale* – a play which turns around the question of paternity and whether one's children are knowably one's own – but the gendering of the sceptic's pain leads Cavell into somewhat exclusionary waters nonetheless.[28] And when he repeats the formula in *Pursuits of Happiness* in relation to Hollywood comedies – where the male protagonist is repeatedly seen to assist in the 'creation of the woman' by overcoming his own doubts about her suitability as a match – it seems openly paternalistic, to say the least. Cavell only adds fuel to the feminist fire when, in seeking to clarify his position, he apparently appropriates the female voice, speaking 'for' the female characters of melodrama in his later book *Contesting Tears*. Likewise Cavell's defence of what has been seen as a quite problematic portrayal of race in Vincent Minnelli's in *The Band Wagon* has led several critics to take him to task for what appears to be an at best naive view of America's history of racial discrimination.[29] I will expand upon these critiques in Chapters 5 and 7 of this book.

Equally if not more problematic in the political climate in which I write is Cavell's allegiance to a particular brand of American liberal humanism, what Stewart refers to as the 'heroic individualism' propounded by Cavell's favoured authors, Emerson and Thoreau.[30] The political associations of this type of humanism, which opens out onto democracy and by implication capitalism, are to say the least rather unpalatable to the academy's current generation of largely left-leaning politicized readers. Stewart eloquently summarizes the problem with reference to the title of Cavell's book on Emerson, *Conditions Handsome and Unhandsome*: 'the most unhandsome facts of economic determinism would be found by its critics to disfigure [Cavell's] very topic, occluding a class- and race-based problem of other bodies as well as (and before) other minds.'[31]

Of course it does not help in this respect that Cavell is a white, male professor at an Ivy League university in the world's most prosperous nation. Not only is he vested with huge amounts of cultural capital and what is referred to today as 'privilege', but the objects that he most usually chooses to write about reflect this special status: opera, modern art, Shakespeare. Not forgetting the mainstream Hollywood films he so enjoys, which, while popular and therefore arguably more 'democratic' than the other media Cavell discusses, are nonetheless populated almost exclusively with white, wealthy characters, tearing about in expensive cars at golf clubs or taking lengthy cruises. However overlooked his work may have been, however humble his origins, Cavell is hardly a marginal figure. Indeed, at times his determination to cast himself as the misunderstood outsider calls to mind an academic version of Ryan Gosling's mournful jazz musician with his somewhat muddled views on revolution and traditionalism in *La La Land* (Damien Chazelle, 2016). Cavell's autobiography, for example, works to suggest that he is – has always been – out of sync with his peers, somehow born of the wrong time. And perhaps this is fair. He was, after all, too young for high school and undergraduate study; too old for grad school. As Forester astutely points out, injury prevented him from taking part in the main struggle of his own age, the Second World War; by the time the Civil Rights movement and Vietnam War came around in the 1950s and 1960s, he was past the usual age of rebellion and yet unwilling to accept an establishment role. It's telling that when students occupied the University Hall, Cavell's role was to 'translate' the demands of the student body into academic language for presentation to the Philosophy Faculty. In terms of his work, Cavell describes his intellectual adventure as taking place 'primarily in the company of those younger than the members of my own generation' (including his wife Cathleen) and agrees with a friend's characterization of *The Claim of Reason* (Cavell's magnum opus, the centrepiece around which the rest of his work is arranged) as 'a book for the next generation'.[32]

Cavell and Film Studies

The Claim to Reason was first published in 1979. We are now at least one generation removed from its original recipients, and Cavell, whose work was for so long met with 'silence or dismay' by his contemporaries, now finds himself feeling as if he has 'outslept Rip van Winkle', and reversing his experience, has awakened to find that 'a surprising number recognize me and know where I have been'.[33]

Cavell's current status lies beyond mere recognition, however. Today, he is considered to be one of America's foremost philosophers: a brilliant, idiosyncratic writer and thinker whose work spans philosophy of mind, philosophy of language, epistemology, ethics, aesthetics and politics. He is a significant figure in Cultural Studies and American Studies. He has written on psychoanalysis, the question of the animal, literature, opera, modern art. And of course, film. Over a vast body of publications spanning all of these subjects and others besides, he has endeavoured to show that philosophy ought not to be the rarified pursuit of a privileged handful of professional philosophers but rather is innately bound up with our daily lives, including the books and movies which are part of those lives. In addition to the numerous books, journal editions and articles written about his work, there is a periodical devoted solely to him and his work: *Conversations: The Journal of Cavellian Studies*. Nowadays the complaints against him are best and, most often, phrased by his champions: few and far apart are genuine detractors of Leo Braudy's ilk. And in France, the country that famously birthed a generation of cinephiles enraptured of classic American cinema, his work has found a very warm reception indeed. Perhaps Cavell was never really out of sync, but merely out of place.

Cavell's is one of two names most commonly cited in association with what is referred to as 'the philosophical turn' in Film Studies, the other being Gilles Deleuze.[34] In his eloquent and very detailed discussion of this turn, D.N. Rodowick characterises it as the consequence of a broader move away, a 'retreat', from theory, with its unilateral pronouncements and explanations, and towards a more piecemeal approach to cinema, that involves, amongst other things, a reinvigoration of historical research, more sociologically rigorous reconceptualizations of spectatorship and the film audience, and the placement of film within a broader context of visual culture and electronic media. In the late 1990s, Film Studies was becoming increasingly empirical, even scientific (as in the marriage of cognitivism and neuroscience) in its approach to film. Partly as a response to this empiricism, a body of work rose up that returned to the notion of film as an art form, one made by men and women, and which was engaged in the intertwining projects of evaluating our styles of knowing with the examination of our modes of existence and their possibilities of transformation. Rodowick singles out Deleuze and Cavell as 'exemplars of the twinned projects of ethical and epistemological evaluation […] the two contemporary philosophers with the strongest commitment to cinema, yet with distinctly original conceptions of the specificity of cinema and of philosophical expression to film'.[35] And yet while countless books have been written elucidating, commenting upon and extending Deleuze's relationship to film and film theory, there exists relatively little literature devoted exclusively to Cavell's writings on film or indeed the impact of film on his broader body of work. Why might this be? A number of answers present themselves.

First is Cavell's somewhat problematic relationship to a dominant philosophical divide. On one side of that divide is analytic philosophy, a term used to refer to a philosophical practice characterized by an emphasis on argumentative clarity and precision, formal logic, conceptual analysis and, to a lesser degree, maths and science; it is associated with Anglo-American figures such as Bertrand Russell, Ludwig Wittgenstein and G.E. Moore. On the other side is continental philosophy, a set of nineteenth- and twentieth-century philosophical traditions from mainland Europe, which includes the following movements: German idealism, phenomenology, existentialism (and its antecedents, such as the thought of Kierkegaard and Nietzsche), hermeneutics, structuralism, post-structuralism, French feminism, psychoanalytic theory, and the critical theory of the Frankfurt School and related branches of Western Marxism.[36] While Cavell's training and leaning towards Wittgenstein place him within a lineage of analytic philosophers, his rather poetic writing style aligns itself more readily with continental philosophy, as do his concerns with historicism, contingency, transformation (and therefore human agency) and metaphilosophy: thinking about the precise nature of philosophy itself. On the whole, where Film Studies has availed itself of philosophy, it has tended towards the continental tradition – through the work of Deleuze, but also Heidegger (in phenomenology), Levinas (ethics), Foucault (semiotics) and the Frankfurt School (the culture industry). Since Cavell's ambivalent relation to both the continental and the analytic models means he falls between two stools, it is therefore rather tricky to know how to take him.

The second explanation is that in addition to the usual reasons for the avoidance of Cavell – the mannered prose, the political ambivalence, the perceived uncoolness – there is the problem of Cavell's breadth of knowledge and reference. More than once an individual has remarked to me that he or she felt it wasn't possible to read Cavell without having first read Austin and Heidegger, and Wittgenstein and Nietzsche, and Emerson (of course!) and Thoreau and Kant and so forth. Cavell is not deliberately esoteric; indeed he seems to have perceived this problem and attempted to broach it in *Cities of Words*, a book that 'pairs' a philosopher (or writer) with a film (say, Emerson and *The Philadelphia Story* (George Cukor, 1940), or Ibsen and *Stella Dallas* (King Vidor, 1937)) in order to better elucidate the connections between them. Still, to continue Braudy's analogy, the forest of references and allusions can be a daunting prospect. Áine Kelly describes it especially well when she describes Cavell's work as 'challenging, complex, intricate, intractable, obstinate, testing and tough – and that's for the reader with more than a passing familiarity with the writings of Cavell's chosen philosophical forebears'.[37]

The problem is only made worse when Cavell turns away from whatever film he is writing about in order to engage in an extended philosophical aside, indulging what Noël Carroll has termed a 'penchant for philosophical ascent' that can lead to logical fallacy. Carroll describes how, within Cavell's work (and in particular *Pursuits of Happiness*), 'a topic will emerge in the discussion of a film that will prompt Cavell to think about the issue per se, often in terms reminiscent of existential psychology, and then Cavell will return to the film, suggesting that his remarks are something that can be attributed to the film'.[38] Carroll admires Cavell, and sees much that is of value in his work, but finds that he often wanders too far from the works with which he is ostensibly concerned and occasionally subjects them to a kind of wilful misreading.

Cavell's marriage of textual explication and philosophizing resembles the type of allegorical reading that is called, in some circles, application. But how beneficial is this combination of tasks to either explication or philosophising? We are most comfortable with allegorical readings when the truths hidden in the story pre-exist the text in question, preferably in another text. But when, as in Cavell's account of *The Awful Truth*, the proposed theme appears to be only fleetingly related to the film and the idea at hand seems to be something just discovered by Cavell, one asks how this film could possibly be expressing it.[39]

So while it is no longer the case that, as William Rothman has it, 'within the field of film study the potential usefulness of Cavell's writings – and the potential usefulness of philosophy, as he understands and practices it – remains generally unrecognised',[40] Cavell nonetheless remains a somewhat divisive, elusive figure for Film Studies. My hope is that this book – while by no means serving as a substitute for a thorough engagement with Cavell's writing – might offer a series of entry points to his work for scholars of film hitherto put off his work either by its scale or by its philosophical denseness.

As such, the present work situates itself alongside Rothman's own books, *Reading Cavell's The World Viewed: A Philosophical Perspective on Film* (written with Marian Keane) and *Cavell on Film*, as a work devoted in part to illuminating the importance of Cavell's work to the practice of film study in America and throughout the world. Rothman studied under Cavell and has been the most consistent advocate for, commentator upon and exegete of Cavell's work on film for the last twenty years. Alongside these two books he has published numerous articles on Cavell's writing about film, including a thirty-two-page essay on Cavell's relationship to film, television and opera in Richard Eldridge's edited collection *Stanley Cavell* which constitutes a very useful overview of Cavell's approach to the medium. A similarly dense overview of Cavell's filmic interests appears in Stephen

Mulhall's 1994 *Stanley Cavell: Philosophy's Recounting of the Ordinary*. This twenty-three-page section (entitled 'Cinema: Photography, Comedy, Melodrama') offers a brief but useful outline of how Cavell's philosophical themes are picked up within his film writing. Likewise, Russell Goodman's edited collection *Contending with Stanley Cavell* features one lucid, intelligent essay on film, 'Guessing the Unseen from the Seen: Stanley Cavell and Film Interpretation', in which Andrew Klevan explicates Cavell's film writing with reference to a specific film, *It's a Wonderful Life* (1946, Frank Capra).

Within volumes on Cavell, then, film usually merits a chapter. And within volumes on film, theory and philosophy, Cavell increasingly merits one too. *The Routledge Companion to Film and Philosophy* features another introduction to Cavell by Rothman. In Felicity Colman's collection *Film, Theory and Philosophy: The Key Thinkers*, Rex Butler offers an encyclopaedia-style synthesis of Cavell's work on film. In their exemplary undergraduate guide to theory, *What Is Film Theory?*, Richard Rushton and Gary Bettinson pair Cavell with Deleuze in their short chapter on film and philosophy, as does Robert Sinnerbrink in both his 2011 book *New Philosophies of Film: Thinking Images* and his 2017 book *Cinematic Ethics*. Still, the writing about Cavell and film is surprisingly limited. The essays collected in Rupert Read and Jerry Goodenough's edited collection *Film as Philosophy: Essays in Cinema after Wittgenstein and Cavell* are symptomatic of a tendency to 'use' Cavell to perform readings of individual films, as in Nancy Bauer's 'Cogito Ergo Film: Plato, Descartes and *Fight Club*' and Simon Critchley's 'Calm: On Terrence Malick's *The Thin Red Line*', or else to engage with films and genres he has discussed, finessing, as it were, Cavell's own arguments, as in Stuart Klawan's 'Habitual Remarriage: The Ends of Happiness in *The Palm Beach Story*'.

Despite this growing body of work, then, Cavell remains undertaught and his writing under-anthologized, at least within the Film Studies context, as more than one commentator has pointed out.[41] It is difficult to select one chapter or article of his to stand for the body of his work. Sampling him in a Film Studies department course on screwball comedy, for example, potentially puts the class in contact with Wittgenstein, Emerson and so forth, just as introducing Cavell in a philosophy course might bring along Shakespeare, Ibsen or Preston Sturges. An excerpt from Cavell thoroughly studied thus risks eclipsing a course. Given insufficient attention, on the other hand, it slides past many students, unaccustomed to Cavell's unique way of expressing himself. As Daniel Morgan points out, the reprinting of Chapters Three through Six of *The World Viewed* in Leo Braudy and Marshall Cohen's much-taught anthology *Film Theory and Criticism*, while undoubtedly responsible in no small measure for establishing Cavell as part of the film theoretical tradition and thereby to some extent legitimizing him as a film critic, may also have had the deleterious effect of narrowing many people's understanding of his approach down to these three short and largely unrepresentative chapters.[42] In this context, and with only these chapters reprinted, Cavell is positioned as a direct inheritor of a line of thinking that emerges from Panofsky and Bazin and continues through Siegfried Kracauer's *Theory of Film*, according to which film emerges at the end of the nineteenth century as a technological solution to an increasing demand for realism across the arts. Cavell certainly contributes to this reading, calling Panofsky and Bazin 'the two continuously intelligent, interesting and to me useful theorists'.[43] However he also diverges from the same tradition in a number of important ways, as we will see in Chapter 3 of this book, and one should not be too hasty to group the three thinkers together.

This book's approach: Aspects and acknowledgement

This book is aimed in part at redressing this situation by providing a detailed, full-length study of Cavell's work that places film front and centre. In the chapters that follow, I shall investigate how Cavell's interest in film intersects with and informs his broader philosophical concerns with matters of the ordinary, scepticism, acknowledgement, moral perfectionism and self-reliance. In so doing, I approach Cavell from the perspective of a film scholar. I should stress, however, that this book, while hopefully providing a useful introduction to those unfamiliar with Cavell's writing about film, is not a complete or systematic account. Cavell's work is particularly rich and, in equal parts, fascinating and infuriating; many different paths are possible through his books.

For my own part, while I engage in detail with what is so important about the body of films particularly associated with Cavell – the 'remarriage comedies' and 'unknown women melodramas' made during Hollywood's golden age (in particular in Chapters 4 and 5) – I have also attempted to move beyond them somewhat in order to trace the other references to film that litter Cavell's work: references to Chaplin and Keaton, Greta Garbo and Ingmar Bergman, Italian neorealism and contemporary North American cinema. Sometimes the areas of thought and filmic examples I choose to focus on are as coincident with my own interests as with Cavell's. In other words, I have tried where possible to be faithful to the spirit of Cavell's writing, but not always the letter. The book discusses what Cavell has to say *about* film, of course, but it also examines what Cavell says *in the light of* film. It poses a number of central questions. 'How has film shaped Cavell's philosophy?' 'How do the film books reflect and expand upon concerns already present within Cavell's early work?' 'What, in short, does film – *all* film – teach Cavell, about how best to live in the world?'

In focussing on one aspect of Cavell's work, I am naturally ignoring others or at least according them a lesser significance than other readings might do. Of literature, music and modern art, I will make little mention here. Philosophy, on the other hand, plays a central role, but this role has to do with its usefulness to film and how we think about the medium. In this much, I am inspired by Cavell's remark, in *Pursuits of Happiness*, that while 'this book is primarily devoted to the reading of seven films … if my citing of philosophical texts along the way hinders more than they help you, skip them. If they are as useful as I take them to be they will find a further chance with you'.[44]

I am equally inspired by Cavell's formulation, taken from Wittgenstein, on the matter of *seeing as*. In Part II of *Philosophical Investigations*, Wittgenstein discusses figures that can be seen and understood in two different ways, using the famous example of the 'duck-rabbit', an ambiguous image that can be seen as either a duck or a rabbit. Often one can see something in a straightforward way – seeing that it is a rabbit, perhaps. But, at other times, one notices a particular aspect – seeing it *as* something. When one looks at the duck-rabbit and sees a rabbit, one is not interpreting the picture as a rabbit but rather reporting what one sees. One sees the picture as a rabbit. One might equally see it as a duck. Importantly the two things are not separate pictures but aspects of one figure which together they constitute.

Figure 1 Wittgenstein's imagined duck-rabbit (University of Berkeley, www.ocf.berkeley.edu).

Seeing Cavell's writing as being about film, inspired by film, above all does not preclude seeing it as philosophical or literary, or musical, for that matter. Quite to the contrary. As William Rothman suggests in his introduction to *Cavell on Film*, to understand what Cavell has to say about film is to understand Cavell's philosophical concerns more broadly. Taken together, Rothman argues, Cavell's thoughts on movies ranging from *A Night at the Opera* (Sam Wood, 1935) through *Mr Deeds Goes to Town* (Frank Capra, 1936) and *The Birds* (Alfred Hitchcock, 1963), from Jean-Luc Godard's *Hail, Mary* (1985) and Eric Rohmer's *Tale of Winter* (1992) to *Groundhog Day* (Harold Ramis, 1993) and *American Beauty* (Sam Mendes, 1999), 'reflect and illuminate the major developments that have shaped Cavell's thinking over the years'.[45] These include the central themes of ordinariness and ordinary language, scepticism and its overcoming, genre and gender, self-reflection and self-reliance and the outlook on morality that he calls moral perfectionism. But what if we go beyond Rothman's claim and argue that films don't just mirror but rather *are* some of the major developments that have shaped Cavell's writing over the years?

Throughout this book, my main objective is to demonstrate the centrality of film to Cavell's work in a way that I hope will guide non-initiates along one path through Cavell's film writing, while simultaneously allowing those who are familiar with it to perhaps see certain aspects afresh. With this in mind, the chapters that follow will move through Cavell's work mostly chronologically, tracing the references to film that pepper the philosophy books proper and examining the overlaps between these books and the books more overtly dedicated to film. Key concepts will arise organically at various points throughout the work, but in the interests of clarity I have decided to focus on one conceptual or philosophical principle in detail in each chapter alongside the works where this theme receives its fullest treatment. So it is that Chapter 2 introduces readers to ordinary language philosophy as practised by Wittgenstein and

Austin and taken up by Cavell in *Must We Mean What We Say?*; Chapter 3 places it into conversation with the discussion of cinematic ontology that Cavell offers in *The World Viewed*; while Chapter 4 discusses how *The World Viewed* and *Pursuits of Happiness* tackle the problem of subjectivity and solipsism outlined in *The Claim of Reason*. In Chapter 5, I turn to the question of self-reflection and self-reliance developed from Thoreau and Emerson and put to the test in the films that make up *Contesting Tears*' case studies. And in Chapter 6, I examine how *Cities of Words* explicitly links the notion of self-reliance to Cavell's later concern with moral perfectionism, which receives its fullest treatment in *Conditions Handsome and Unhandsome*. Throughout I hold it as a truth that Cavell is not merely interested in the philosophical ideas that are exemplified or illustrated by particular films but in the philosophical ideas that arise from the encounter between the film viewer and the film. Hence this book's subtitle: scepticism and self-reliance *at* the cinema, not in the cinema.

Conclusion: Friendship, marriage … love?

Cavell's writings on film are born of

> a sense of gratitude for the existence of the great and still enigmatic art of film, whose history is punctuated, as that of no other, by works, small and large, that have commanded the devotion of audiences of all classes, of virtually all ages, and of all the spaces around the world in which a projector has been mounted and a screen set up.[46]

The films that he is most passionately interested in, meanwhile, all 'concern a quest for transcendence, a step into an opposite or transformed mood'. They give 'access to another world'.[47]

Cavell conceives of the relationship between film and philosophy as a marriage and conceives of marriage, as we shall see, not as a happy ending but as a constant process of overcoming one's gripes and grumbles and of recommitting, daily, anew, to sharing one's life with another and to accepting to share theirs.

In the book's final chapter, 'Love's Work', I comment at length on the relationship between Cavell's philosophy, his film writing and love – a theme that is often tacit within Cavell's work. What place does love hold within a body of works concerned with the relationship between us and ourselves, between ourselves and others, between ourselves and the world? I believe it is a central place and that for Cavell philosophy, film, writing and reading are all – or at least have the potential to be – acts of love.

These acts of love are also acts of faith: thrown out into the world with little premonition of whether they will be well or ill received. According to Cavell it took twenty years for him to begin to learn of print reactions to the essays in *Must We Mean What We Say?*, twenty years during which he had no idea as to whether his words had taken effect. He compares his work to 'passionate utterances', contrasting these with Austin's performative utterances: 'You characteristically know clearly, even immediately, whether your declaration of a promise or your warning or your acceptance of marriage has taken effect,' he writes. But it's 'easy to remain doubtful about your expressions of love or anger or irony,'[48] an unease only heightened by the time lag between expression and reception. How do we know that we have made ourselves comprehensible to friends? To strangers? With great difficulty. But, as Cavell muses, this is yet what writing should strive for: 'to make friends of strangers and strangers of friends, modifying needless distances and needy intimacies.'[49] With this quote in mind, what follows is written in the spirit of friendship.

2

Everything Matters

WOMAN (*knocking on door*): Did you want a manicure?
GROUCHO: No. Come on in.
JOHN LANGSHAW AUSTIN (*during a lecture at Columbia University*): Although a double negative in English implies a positive meaning, there is no language in which a double positive implies a negative.
SIDNEY MORGENBESSER (*in audience*): Yeah, right.

In an illuminating interview with Andrew Klevan that took place in 2005, Cavell ruminates on the impact on his subsequent work of his time studying under J.L. Austin. Cavell explains to Klevan that 'the question about Austin's importance to me, and Wittgenstein's several years later, is a question about philosophy's importance to me altogether'. These two philosophers encouraged Cavell to

> think about anything I was interested in, as very much opposed to almost all the rest of philosophy that I was working at, where I felt to match the tone, the strictures, the agenda, the conventions of professional philosophy dictated a certain kind of response, a certain kind of research paper, a certain kind of sequence of chapters for a dissertation, that both gave me a subject but deprived me of having any say in the subject.[1]

In short, Austin and Wittgenstein allowed Cavell to see philosophy neither as the preserve of the privileged few nor as a way of thinking about certain circumscribed topics. Rather, they opened philosophy up and out so that all kinds of topics might be thought about in a manner considered 'philosophical': including the subject of film.

Austin, a philosopher of language, was particularly interested in the subject of excuses: considerations that mitigate or extenuate the slips or mishaps or lapses in actions so familiar in everyday life. Cavell offers Klevan one of his favourite examples from Austin, which turns around the difference between doing something by mistake or by accident:

> First story. There are two donkeys, mine and my neighbour's, in a field there beyond the fence. I take a sudden dislike to my donkey and decide to shoot it. I take careful aim at one of the donkeys, fire, and the donkey that I aimed at drops. I walk over to the fence and discover to my horror that it's my neighbour's donkey. Have I done this by mistake or by accident? [Wait before answering, he tells Klevan].
>
> Second story. Same two donkeys; same sudden dislike. This time I take careful aim and just as I fire the donkeys shift and to my horror I realise that I have shot my neighbour's donkey. I run up to it but it's dead. Now have I done that by mistake or by accident?[2]

What is the appeal of this pair of stories for Cavell? Firstly, they teach us something about how we use language and how we fail to use it. Ask a group of people (a classroom of students, say) whether there is a difference between doing something by mistake or by accident, and there will be little consensus, says Cavell, but ask them again after telling this story, and there will be little doubt that in the first instance, a donkey has been shot by mistake; in the second it was shot by accident. This much seems commonsensical. So what we have learned by listening to, or reading, these examples, is something we perhaps already knew but were not able to express: we needed Austin's example in order to articulate the difference. Secondly, the example takes the form of a narrative. It is even, although Cavell does not explicitly acknowledge it as such, somewhat cinematic, reading a little like a screenplay starring Chaplin, or Keaton, or Laurel and Hardy.[3] And perhaps these figures come to mind in particular because, thirdly, both the dying donkeys and the words they illustrate are rather banal, even absurd. To paraphrase Cavell himself, that propositions of such ludicrousness can be seen to illustrate, even to explore, philosophical sublimities is surely part of his fascination with so-called popular movies.[4] Cavell sees cinema as having a special relationship to the ordinary or the uneventful. In film, he claims, 'everything matters'.[5]

This chapter looks at how Cavell's interest in ordinary language philosophy anticipates his work on film. At the same time, it asks how that work on language is already informed by film. Austin earns no explicit mention within *The World Viewed*; Wittgenstein gets a few but hardly seems a central figure, at least not to the reader unfamiliar with his philosophy. For its part, *Must We Mean What We Say?* makes reference to only three filmmakers. Two of these – René Clair and Michaelangelo Antonioni – Cavell mentions within the same sentence. The third, Federico Fellini, receives somewhat lengthier treatment, and I shall come back to Cavell's treatment of his 1954 *La Strada* in due course. Still, Cavell's discussion of that film, which is mostly limited to questions of authorship and allusion, occupies only seven of the book's 353 pages.

Nonetheless, Cavell's first book on film was in preparation at the same time as Cavell was writing the later essays of *Must We Mean What We Say?* (and while he was forming the idea of writing a book about Thoreau's *Walden*), and the seeds of Cavell's future observations on film's power to evoke the everyday – such a crucial feature of his later work – are embedded beneath his musings on literature, language and modern art. Thus, in Cavell's own words, he was 'gathering the implications of Austin's and Wittgenstein's work in allowing contemporary philosophical access to the achievements of Beckett and Kierkegaard and Shakespeare and Thoreau' and he counts this access as 'essential' to the writing of *The World Viewed*.[6] It is a central aim of this chapter to trace how, exactly, Cavell moves from Austin to Shakespeare to cinema, and how *Must We Mean What We Say?* paves the way for Cavell's later work on film.

Ordinary language philosophy

Austin's influence on Cavell cannot be overstated. Like Wittgenstein he is hugely responsible for shaping Cavell's thought, and his work in what Cavell calls – for want of a better term – ordinary language philosophy resonates throughout Cavell's writing on film. With that in mind, it is worth spending some time on a brief (and necessarily schematic) description of what ordinary language philosophy as practised by Austin and Wittgenstein is, before going on to see how it emerges in Cavell's work.

Along with other thinkers such as Gilbert Ryle and P.F. Strawson, Austin and Wittgenstein were working in the early twentieth century on questions of how words are ordinarily used in order to elucidate meaning and by this means avoid philosophical confusions. Both are therefore grouped together under the moniker of 'ordinary language philosophers'. Neither, in fact, was particularly enamoured of the term, with Austin in particular preferring to think of himself as a 'linguistic phenomenologist'.[7] Nonetheless, there are a number of key differences between them in terms of how they approached language and what they had to say about it.

Wittgenstein, the older of the pair, was concerned throughout his work with the nature of language and the world. In his early work, the *Tractatus Logico-Philosophicus*, first published in 1921, he proposes that the structure of reality determines the structure of language. This structure provides the limits of what can be said meaningfully and therefore what can be thought. The limits of language, that is, are the limits of philosophy. Much of philosophy involves the attempt to say the unsayable, but for Wittgenstein 'what can we say at all can be said clearly'.[8] Anything beyond that – religion, ethics, aesthetics, the mystical – cannot be discussed. They are not in themselves nonsensical, but any statement about them must be, because they use language in an attempt to transcend the limits of language, trying to go beyond what meaningfully can be said: they attempt to speak of matters that the final remark of *Tractatus* asks us to 'pass over in silence'. 'What can be said' consists only of the propositions of natural science. As Wittgenstein writes towards the end of the *Tractatus*:

> The correct method in philosophy would really be the following: to say nothing except what can be said, i.e. propositions of natural science – i.e. something that has nothing to do with philosophy – and then, whenever someone else wanted to say something metaphysical, to demonstrate to him that he had failed to give a meaning to certain signs in his propositions.[9]

For clarity's sake, we should note that Wittgenstein, in describing ethical, aesthetic and religious discourse as 'nonsensical', was not renouncing them as useless. Rather, in making a fundamental distinction between, on the one hand, the language of natural science and, on the other, that of ethics, aesthetics and religion, he saves the latter from any sort of reduction to or translation into the former. But while the early Wittgenstein was concerned with the logical relationship between propositions and the world, believing that by providing an account of the logic underlying that relationship he would be able to set out an all-encompassing philosophic system, the later Wittgenstein rejected many of the conclusions of the *Tractatus* in the *Philosophical Investigations* (first published 1956). Here he argues instead that it is language that gives us our conception of reality; that there is not a uniform structure to language but rather that it has various forms that exhibit only loose interconnections. Thus, while both his philosophies are concerned with language and its limits, the earlier philosophy is a coherent, well-structured and orderly whole, while the later work is, in the words of Diane Collinson and Kathryn Plant, 'piecemeal and written as a series of remarks, descriptions, questions and conjectures that invite the reader to engage in working towards an understanding that is not dominated by any guiding theory'.[10]

What emerges from this later work is a conception of philosophy that sees it as quite distinct from the systematized procedures of science, and as an activity of *clarification*, rather than the setting out of a thesis or theory. In the *Philosophical Investigations*, Wittgenstein remarks of philosophical problems that they are

> not empirical problems; they are solved, rather, by looking into the workings of our language, and that in such a way as to make us recognise those workings: in spite of an urge to misunderstand them. The problems are solved, not by giving new information, but by arranging what we have always known. Philosophy is a battle against the bewitchment of our intelligence by means of language.[11]

Whereas in the *Tractatus*, then, Wittgenstein bases everything on the idea that meaning and lack of meaning depend on the formal relationship in which a proposition stands to objective reality, in the *Investigations*, meaning is seen as a function of how we use words. Human purposes and the forms of life in which human beings engage are what give language its meanings. The later Wittgenstein sees language as a natural human phenomenon, and philosophy's task as that of assembling reminders of our actual use of language in order to abolish the puzzlement it sometimes produces. Wittgenstein argues that philosophical problems are 'bewitchments' that arise from philosophers' misguided attempts to consider the meaning of words independently of their context, usage and grammar, what he called 'language gone on holiday'. He claims that philosophical questions arise when language is forced from its proper home into a metaphysical environment, where all the familiar and necessary landmarks and contextual clues are removed: an environment he compares to frictionless ice. Where conditions are perfect for a philosophically and logically perfect language, Wittgenstein argues, all philosophical problems can apparently be solved without the muddying effects of everyday contexts. But it is precisely this lack of friction, of everyday context, that undermines language. On the frictionless ice of abstraction, language can in fact do no work at all.

Wittgenstein therefore argues that philosophers must leave the frictionless ice and return to the 'rough ground' of ordinary language in use. The *Investigations* explores the idea that the meaning of a word depends on its use and that there are many different ways of using words. In particular, Wittgenstein rejects the assumption that there must be something common to all uses of language and turns attention to the notion of language games, arguing that the meaning of words is constituted by the function they perform in any given language game. He writes of the speaking of language as being 'as much a part of our natural history as walking, eating, drinking, playing' and claims that just as there are rules for games, so there are rules for language, but that just as different games have different rules, so there are differing language games.

A language with no rules would be no use at all, as we need to agree on some elements to communicate. Language is thus a question of consensus, at least in some measure, even at the same time as the meanings of words might be private or subjective. Wittgenstein takes the example of the word 'pain'. On the one hand, this refers to a personal experience that cannot be shared and so may hold different meanings for different people. But on the other hand, we as human beings all come to know what it is to have a sensation that we call pain. How is this the case? Wittgenstein relates words to the spontaneous, natural, preverbal sensations of a child: a child who is hurt cries out, and then adults talk to him so that he gradually learns exclamations and, eventually, ways of speaking about what he has experienced.

Natural pain behaviour – the crying out – has been changed into what Wittgenstein describes as 'new pain-behaviour', in which a linguistic expression of pain is added to, or replaces, the natural expression. What Wittgenstein is particularly concerned to show is that in the case of a sensation such as pain, meaning cannot be taught by pointing to an object that is pain. The method is a different one, and we need to break with the idea that language always functions in only one way: an idea that will prove to be very important to Cavell both in his work on language and, later, in his work on film.

Austin shared Wittgenstein's concern that the language of philosophy was divorced from language as it is ordinarily used in the world. Guy Longworth explains Austin's position succinctly when he writes, 'In short, it mattered to Austin that, in attempting to make out positions and arguments, philosophers should meet ordinary standards of truth, accuracy and so forth.'[12] The challenge to philosophy, as Austin saw it, was therefore twofold. Firstly, philosophy ought to make use of an ordinary vocabulary in order to make claims that are, according to ordinary standards, true, or ought to do the serious work required to set up an appropriate technical vocabulary and then use it to say things that are by appropriate standards true. Secondly, when approaching a general question, philosophers should find connections between those general, often rarified concerns and the more specific claims or judgements we ordinarily make. (Although Cavell deviates from Austin in some ways, this is, as we shall see, precisely the methodology that he uses throughout his work.) It is worth quoting Austin's own summary of his view of language and its importance to philosophy:

> First, words are our tools, and, as a minimum, we should use clean tools: we should know what we mean and what we do not, and we must forearm ourselves against the traps that language sets us. Secondly words are not (except in their own little corner) facts or things: we need therefore to prise them off the world, to set them apart from and against it, so that we can realize their inadequacies

and arbitrariness, and can re-look at the world without blinkers. Thirdly, and more hopefully, our common stock of words embodies all the distinctions men have found worth drawing, and the connexions they have found worth making, in the lifetimes of many generations: these surely are more likely to be more sound, since they have stood up to the long test of the survival of the fittest, and more subtle, at least in all ordinary and reasonably practical matters, than any that you or I are likely to think up in our armchairs of an afternoon – the most favoured alternative method.[13]

As we can see from the above quote, Austin is not opposed to theory or certain strands of philosophy in the same way as Wittgenstein is. He simply holds that before philosophizing – at least on some topics – we should think carefully about the words we use to speak on that topic and about how we use them. Since there are plenty of words in the world already, words that have been created to deal with the world as it is experienced ordinarily, Austin spurns neologisms, a practice continued by Cavell and one that accounts for an important distinction between Cavell's work and Deleuze's, for example.

Austin also parts ways with Wittgenstein in moving away from questions of truth. In fact Austin describes the question of whether something can be said to be true or false as one of the few cases where the language we have might not be adequate to the task. In part this is because truth is often contingent on context (hence, to say that something is true, we usually have to outline the circumstances in which it is true). There are various degrees of success in making statements and the statements fit the facts always 'more or less loosely'.[14] But it is also to do with Austin's belief that sentences or statements can be used to perform a variety of different linguistic acts.

Austin pointed out that we use language to *do* things as well as to *assert* things: that the utterance of a statement like 'I promise to do so-and-so' is best understood as doing something – making a promise – rather than making an assertion about anything. Hence the name of one of his best-known works: *How to Do Things with Words* (based on a series of lectures given at Harvard in 1955, at which Cavell was in attendance). Prior to Austin, the attention of linguistic and analytic philosophers had been directed almost exclusively to statements, assertions and propositions – that is to the way in which language states some fact, which it must do either truly or falsely. In *How to Do Things with Words*, however, Austin argues that sentences with truth values form only a small part of the range of utterances. Grammarians have known this for a long time, he says: there are, after all, besides statements, also questions and exclamations and commands or wishes or concessions. After introducing several of these kinds of sentences – which he asserts are neither true nor false – he turns to one particular kind, which he calls performative utterances or just 'performatives'.

The action which takes place when a 'performative utterance' is issued belongs to what Austin later calls a speech act. For example, if you say 'I name this ship the Queen Elizabeth,' and the circumstances are appropriate in certain ways, then you will have done something special, namely you will have performed the act of naming the ship. Other examples include: 'I take this woman to be my lawfully wedded wife,' used in the course of a marriage ceremony, or 'I bequeath this watch to my brother,' as occurring in a will, or, 'I bet you sixpence it will rain tomorrow.' In all four cases the sentence is not being used to describe or state what one is 'doing' but being used to actually 'do' it.[15]

Initially, Austin characterizes performatives by two features. Firstly, though they may take the form of a typical indicative sentence, performative sentences are not used to describe (or 'constate') and are thus not true or false; they have no truth value. And secondly, to utter one of these sentences in appropriate circumstances is not just to 'say' something but rather to perform a certain kind of action. He goes on to say that when something goes wrong in connection with a performative utterance it is, as he puts it, 'infelicitous', or 'unhappy', rather than false (he gives as one example the naming of the ship: it's all very well me smashing a bottle on the side of a ship and declaring it to be called HMS Austin, but if I haven't been chosen to name the ship the statement means nothing).

After numerous attempts to find more characteristics of performatives, and after having met with many difficulties, Austin makes what he calls a 'fresh start', in which he considers 'more generally the senses in which to say something may be to do something, or in saying something we do something'. For example: I turn to you and ask, 'Is the cat on the mat?', to which you reply 'Yes'. In posing this question, and eliciting an answer, I perform what Austin now terms a *locutionary* act: the production of a sentence that can be classified by its phonetic, grammatical and lexical characteristics, up to sentence meaning (the phatic act). Austin contrasts the locutionary act with the illocutionary act: an act classifiable by not just its content but also its force – examples would be stating, warning, promising. This in turn is contrasted with the perlocutionary act, an act classifiable by its consequential effects upon the feelings, thoughts, or actions of the audience or of the speaker: persuading someone, encouraging someone, amusing someone. The way in which Austin produces this taxonomy is by testing out language, using synonyms and paraphrases, turning words about until he has exhausted their possibilities and seen all of their aspects.

Like Wittgenstein, Austin connects questions of language to the question of what we can know about other people. In the essay 'Other Minds', Austin criticizes Cartesian sceptical responses to the question of whether we can know that person S feels X (with X being, for example, pain). Such sceptics work, he claims, from the following three assumptions:

(1) We can know only if we intuit and directly feel what he feels.
(2) It is impossible to do so.
(3) It may be possible to find strong evidence for belief in our impressions.

Although Austin agreed with (2), quipping that 'we should be in a pretty predicament if I did', he found (1) to be false and (3) to be therefore unnecessary. The background assumption to (1), Austin claims, is that if I say that I know X and later find out that X is false, I did not know it. Austin believes that this is not consistent with the way we actually use language. He claims that if I was in a position where I would normally say that I know X, if X should turn out to be false, I would be speechless rather than self-corrective. He thus draws an equivalence between speech acts and knowledge of other minds. According to Austin believing is to knowing as intending is to promising – knowing and promising are the speech-act versions of believing and intending, respectively. In effect, as Longworth puts it, for Austin, 'if you know, you can't be wrong'.[16]

Austin explains the distinction between knowing and believing by pointing to how we might differently challenge the statements 'I know' and 'I believe'. When person S states he knows something, he might be challenged to explain how he knows this, Austin says, but if he states he believes something, he might be asked why. The consequences of failing to meet those challenges are also different: in the first case, it might turn out that S didn't, after all, know; in the second, S ought not to believe, but that might not stop him from believing. The potential overcoming of the problem of scepticism that Austin attempts will prove to be very important to Cavell, especially when it comes to the writing of *The Claim of the Reason*. I will return to the question of overcoming scepticism in Chapter 3 of this book. For now it is enough to say that Austin and Wittgenstein argue in different ways for paying attention to specific cases of communication without seeking to generalize them and that early in Cavell's academic career, he perceives that the real breakthrough of ordinary language philosophy lies in its opposition to the then-dominant idea that it would be necessary to reduce language to a set of unchanging rules in order to explain how it worked.

Cavell, ordinary language philosophy and the arts

The subject of *Must We Mean What We Say?* is the question of how our words and actions mean. Cavell proposes a series of what he called criteria or principles, insisting that the meaning of any particular work or action must be determined each time anew in different circumstances. Speech and actions follow, alter or even make up their rules depending on what they are wanting to say and to whom they are wanting to say it. Each instance of communication is not a matter of obeying a preexisting rule but of a negotiation with the prevailing conditions of language and the attempt to make oneself understood within them. This is perhaps his unique contribution to ordinary language philosophy: he extends it to an explicit philosophical self-consciousness, a precursor of the self-reliance that we will consider in detail in Chapter 5 of this book.

Ordinary language philosophy allows Cavell a methodology for thinking about a range of subjects. Cavell appreciates the practice whereby in Austin's hands other words, compared and distinguished, tell what a given word is about. 'To know why they do, to trace how these procedures function … hints at an explanation for our feeling that what we learn will not be new empirical facts about the world, and yet illuminating facts about the world.'[17] So it is that when Austin seeks to define the difference between doing something by mistake and doing it by accident, what transpires is a characterization of what a mistake is and what an accident is. When he asks what the difference between being sure and being certain is, what he uncovers is a survey 'of the complex and mutual alignments that are necessary to successful knowledge.'[18] And when he asks for the difference between belief and knowledge, 'what comes up is a new sense and new assessment of human limitations, or human responsibilities, of human knowledge, and so on'.[19] For Cavell, the goal of ordinary language philosophy is clarity, achieved by 'mapping the fields of consciousness lit by the occasions of a word, not through analysing it or replacing a given word by others'.[20]

From here, Cavell draws a direct line to the practice of aesthetic criticism. In a chapter of *Must We Mean What We Say?* entitled 'Aesthetic Problems of Modern Philosophy', Cavell argues that by registering differences between words, and from there coming to understand something more about the significance of these words to us, an ordinary language philosopher makes claims that are closer to aesthetic judgement than empirical judgements. He connects the ordinary language philosopher's process of comparing and contrasting words to the art critic's purpose in comparing and distinguishing works of art. He explains that in this crosslight, 'the capacities and salience of an individual object in question are brought to attention and focus'. In making critical claims about art works, he writes, at some point we are compelled to say: 'Don't you see, don't you hear, don't you dig?' The best critic will know the best points, claims Cavell, 'because if you do not see something, without explanation, then there is nothing further to discuss'. At some point, the critic will have to say: 'This is what I see. Can you see it too?'.[21]

When making a claim as to what we ordinarily say and mean, such a philosopher thus turns to the reader, as an art critic does, not to convince without proof but to get the reader to prove something, test something against himself or herself. The philosopher is saying, 'Look and find out whether you can see what I see, wish to say what I wish to say'.[22] Even when others are convinced, though, the philosopher's judgements remain, essentially, subjective. So the problem for philosopher and critic alike is not to discount but to include his or her subjectivity, 'not to overcome it in agreement, but to master it in exemplary ways'.[23] Cavell succinctly expresses his position to the reader in the closing passages of the essay, where he writes: 'Philosophy, like art, is, and should be, powerless to prove its relevance; and that says something about the kind of relevance it wishes to have. All the philosopher, this kind of philosopher, can do is to express, as fully as he can, his world, and attract our undivided attention to our own.'[24]

Must We Mean What We Say? therefore moves from a reflection on ordinary language philosophy as practised by Wittgenstein and Austin to a proposal for a new mode of philosophical criticism. This mode of criticism is self-critical, 'a mode of criticism whose subject and object is philosophy itself'.[25] In a twinned pair of essays, 'Music Discomposed' and 'A Matter of Meaning of It', Cavell applies the method of ordinary language philosophy to art in general and modern art in particular, testing out definitions of what constitutes 'art', 'theatre', 'literature', 'music' and 'sculpture' with a particular emphasis on questions of the artist's intention and the audience's response.

Viewed from the present moment and from the perspective of Film Studies, in which auteur and spectatorship theory flourishes, such an emphasis hardly seems radical. But at the time Cavell was writing, the critical establishment was mainly concerned with 'the object itself' (in particular, Cavell mentions formalism's focus on the details of the artwork itself). Cavell states that he is 'far less sure that any such philosophical theory is correct than I am that when I experience a work of art I feel that I meant to notice one thing and not another; that the placement of a note or rhyme or line has a purpose, and that certain works are perfectly realised, or contrived, or meretricious'.[26] That is, he knows very well that there 'are people recognisable as artists, and all produce works which we acknowledge, in some sense, to call for and warrant certain kinds of experience'.[27] The very fact that there is such an activity as criticism and a recognizable group of people whose profession it is to discuss the arts, that is, critics, is indicative of the fact that art incites response and reflection. And it is of course common practice amongst these critics to ask why a work of art is as it is (we might ask, for example, why Shakespeare follows the murder of Duncan in *Macbeth* with a scene which begins with the sound of knocking). For Cavell, theory denies this puzzlement that is internal to our experience and avoids the perspective of self-reflection that philosophy is capable of providing. He cites Wittgenstein's exhortation that philosophy must 'do away with all explanation, and description alone must take its place', as a guiding principle.[28]

In short, what Cavell wants to ask is why this thing (this play, this painting, this sonata) *is as it is*, how it *means what it does*. He feels that it is insufficient to answer this question by having recourse to only what he calls the 'sources of organisation': the rhyme schemes, scansion patterns, Baroque structures and so forth that the New Critics had recourse to.[29] This is not just a question of meaning for Cavell but also one of intention and, by extension, of ethics. A work of art is created *by* someone *for* someone and as such forges a relationship between creator and recipient, one which has moral implications. The recipient of a poem, for example, has a responsibility in listening; its author has a responsibility in speaking, knowing he is being listened to. When we listen to a poem, says Cavell, we have a choice: to accept these words or reject them. 'What is called for is not merely our interest, nor our transport – these may serve as betrayals even now. What is called for is our acknowledgement that we are implicated, or our rejection of the implication.'[30]

The question that poses itself at this juncture is how to establish intention in a work of art. In order to think this through, Cavell turns for the first time in his work to an extended discussion of a film: Fellini's *La Strada*. Upon viewing *La Strada*, Cavell sees an evident connection between the film's narrative and the myth of Philomel, a minor figure in Greek mythology to whom Shakespeare makes frequent allusion. Philomel is raped and mutilated by her sister's husband, Tereus, who cuts out her tongue, but she obtains her revenge by weaving a tapestry telling of her abuse and is transformed into a nightingale. Gelsomina, the heroine of *La Strada*, who is sold to the brutish Zampanò, 'is virtually speechless, she is rudely forced, she tells her charge by playing the trumpet, one tune over and over which at the end fills the deserted beach and whose purity at last attacks her barbarous king'.[31]

Two questions arise from this connection that Cavell makes. Firstly, the philosopher, with his fascination for Shakespeare, sees Philomel in Gelsomina, but what of those who aren't familiar with the myth: have they missed something? And secondly, and more pertinent to Cavell's concerns here, what about Fellini: did he mean this allusion? Cavell admits that his conviction of the relevance is so strong that, if he asked Fellini, he would not so much be looking for a confirmation of his view as enquiring as to whether Fellini had recognized this fact about his work. This leads Cavell to ask what the relation might be between what one knows (or knew) and what one intends. We might think back here to the sorry soul who shot his friend's donkey. What did he *know* he was doing? What did he *intend* to do?

Cavell tests the limits of knowledge and intention against one another to see how the two terms might relate. Either Fellini did or did not know of the connection with the Philomel story. If he did know, and he did make the allusion deliberately, then it was intended. And if he did not know, then it follows that he did not intend the connection. That much is straightforward. But suppose, for example, that he did know of the story, and he does now acknowledge the relevance but hadn't thought of it until it was pointed out to him. For Cavell, it makes sense to say Fellini intended (that is to say, Fellini can have intended) the reference to Philomel if he knew the story and now sees its relevance to his own, whether or not the story occurred to him at the time. Everything depends on how the relevance is, or is not, acknowledged. Cavell imagines Fellini's acknowledgement of the relevance as coming with a sharp sense of recognition, a sense of clarification. From here he draws two further points:

1. Fellini doesn't have to have in fact been aware of the connection, but he must be able to become aware of it in a particular way.
2. An artist is a person who knows how to do something, to make something and who spends his life learning how to do it better.

> Just as Babe Ruth might not be aware, exactly, of how he bends his knees when swinging at a pitch, so Fellini might not be aware of an allusion to Philomel. But it does not follow that their actions are unintentional. On the other hand if Babe Ruth were tugging his cap habitually before swinging, this would not be intentional.

Cavell concludes that 'intending to do something is internally related to wanting something to happen, and discovering an intention is a way of discovering an explanation. That one is locating intention is what accounts for the fact that a piece of criticism takes place.'[32]

Cavell thus positions Fellini's intentional but unwitting allusion to Philomel as a rediscovery of the myth of Philomel: a discovery for himself and in himself, of the feelings and wants which originally produced it. 'I do not wish to claim that everything we find in a work is something we have to be prepared to say the artist intended to be put there,' he writes. 'But I am claiming that our not being so prepared is not the inevitable state of affairs; rather, it must be exceptional (at least in successful works of art) – as exceptional as happy accidents, welcome inadvertencies, fortunate mistakes, pure luck.'[33] What counts is what is *there*, Cavell admits, 'but everything that is there is something a man has done.'[34] In fine, we don't necessarily find out about intention by asking the filmmakers, or by researching studio documents, or by conducting any other investigations outside the work itself but by *looking further into the work*.[35]

Though Fellini features as little more than a cypher in this discussion, Cavell's inclusion of him as a film director and an artist here is the opening gambit in a career-long discussion of what it means for things to be in film and on film; where these things come from, how we see them and what – and why – they mean. This discussion of intention, which opens onto questions of acknowledgement and, from there, responsibility, is also one of the earliest moments in which ethics enters Cavell's philosophical purview. He writes:

> The artist is responsible for everything that happens in his work – and not just in the sense that it is done, but in the sense that it is meant. It is a terrible responsibility; very few men have the gift and the patience and the singleness to shoulder it. But it is the more terrible, when it is shouldered, not to appreciate it, to refuse to understand something meant so well.[36]

It is hard to read these words, written at the very beginning of Cavell's career, without feeling a pang of sympathy for a man who would spend a lifetime of writing feeling often under-appreciated, occasionally misunderstood. What Cavell is setting out here is an agenda for the writing and reading of philosophy as well as the creation of art. He sees it as the duty of the philosopher to pay attention to what is being communicated to them and the terms on which it is being communicated. One must avoid 'applying' a theory to the object – let's say the film. And one must avoid writing or talking about using language and words that are not the kind of language and words that we use every day. We should say what we mean, not what some theory gives us to say. As he summarizes in 'The Avoidance of Love':

> The issue is one of placing the words and experiences with which philosophers have always begun in alignment with human beings in particular circumstances who can be imagined to be having those experiences and saying and meaning those words. This is all that 'ordinary' means in the phrase 'ordinary language philosophy'.[37]

'Nothing goes without saying': From the Marx Brothers to Mr Deeds

In explaining the importance of ordinary language for his work, Cavell has recourse to notions of humanness, community, communication and meaningfulness. He adopts from Wittgenstein and Austin 'a conception of the author as a someone who brings us back to our human existence'.³⁸ Language, that is, puts us in contact with the world.

The importance attached to ordinary language on this account forges the connection between philosophy and movies. As Cavell puts it in *Pursuits of Happiness*, film words mimic everyday conversation (at least in the main).³⁹ Film gives us back our ordinary words. Of course other art forms use language too, but movies have a strong connection to our everyday lives and the events that punctuate them. Because of their origins in vaudeville and nickelodeons, movies moreover are a more democratic art form and thus available to ordinary men and women in a way that certain other arts are not.

Although Cavell makes no further explicit mention of film in *Must We Mean What We Say?*, a couple of later pieces of film criticism are instructive in clarifying the relationship between ordinary language philosophy and film (and writing about film) as distinct from the other arts (and writing about the other arts). In the first, the films of the Marx Brothers offer us philosophical examples – not unlike the donkey story – of how language can be slippery and multivalent, subject to twists of intention or interpretation. The publication in 1994 of scripts of several of their films – *Monkey Business* (1931), *Duck Soup* (1933) and *A Day at the Races* (1937) – occasioned an essay on their use of language, first published in *The London Review of Books*. Cavell's guiding intuition here is that 'it is essential to the Brothers' sublimity that they are thinking about words, to the end of words, in every word – or in Harpo's emphatic case, in every absence of words'.⁴⁰ He continues: 'Marx Brothers films, as unmistakably revealed in these scripts, are extensively explicit about their intentions. Their pun-crammed air, well recognised as a medium of social subversion, also presses a standing demand to reach some understanding – which is incomparably better avoided than faked.'⁴¹

The Marx Brothers consistently foreground questions of intention and interpretation through their use of puns. 'Keep out of this loft!', someone barks at them, to which Chico replies, 'Well, it's better to have loft and lost than never to have loft at all.' Here we understand the intention of the first speaker, as well as the intended misinterpretation by Chico (as if to underline the purposefulness of this misinterpretation, Groucho pats his brother on the shoulder and tells him 'Nice work!'). Such reflexivity – a repeated trope within the Marx Brothers' craft – lets us know, says Cavell, 'that they know that we know that we may fall to imagining that they don't know what they're doing.'[42] That is, this reflexivity shores up their deliberateness. Intention is also highlighted in set pieces such as Chico's peddling Groucho a tip on a horse by selling him a code book, then a master code book to explain the code book, then a guide required by the master code, then a sub-guide supplementary to the guide: a scene which Cavell wittily describes in appropriately punning terms as 'a scrupulous union, or onion, of semantic and monetary exchanges and deferrals to warm the coldest contemporary theorist of signs.'[43]

It is in the character of Groucho, however, that Cavell sees the importance of interpretation as being most cannily and consistently emphasized. He offers as an example the famous packed cabin sequence from *A Night at the Opera* (simultaneously an image of the squalor of immigrant crowding and of the immigrant imagination of luxury.) Outside an overfull cabin in which his brother Harpo is sleeping, Groucho stands in the corridor, trying to order food for himself and his brothers. After each item he orders, Chico's voice from within the cabin appends, 'And two hard-boiled eggs', which, after Groucho dutifully repeats it, is punctuated by a honk from within, to which Groucho effortlessly responds by adding 'Make that three hard-boiled eggs'. Succinctly put, Cavell understands the relationship between Groucho and Harpo here as one of well-placed trust: Harpo has faith that Groucho will understand what he wants and interpret his honks correctly. In the world of the Marx Brothers, to honk is to speak, which is how Cavell can claim that in their world 'nothing goes without saying'.[44]

Cavell demonstrates the power of ordinary language, the intention behind and the importance – and subjectivity – of interpretation in a heavily autobiographical reading of *Monkey Business*'s climatic scene.

GROUCHO:	A fine sailor you are.
CHICO:	You bet I'm a fine sailor … my father was-a partners with Columbus.
GROUCHO:	Columbus has been dead for four hundred years.
CHICO:	Well, they told me it was my father ….
GROUCHO:	I'll show you a few things you don't know about history. Now look … [Drawing a circle on a globe] Now there's Columbus.
CHICO:	That's-a Columbus Circle
GROUCHO:	Now, Columbus sailed from Spain to India looking for a short cut.
CHICO:	Oh, you mean strawberry short cut.

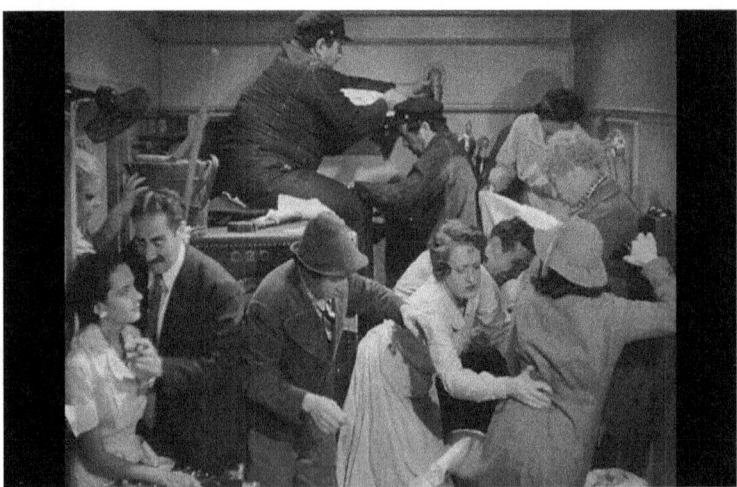

Figure 2 The famous packed cabin sequence from *A Night at the Opera*: In the world of the Marx Brothers, to honk is to speak, which is how Cavell can claim that in their world 'nothing goes without saying'. *A Night at the Opera* (Sam Wood, 1935).

Cavell, born Goldstein, the son of an immigrant father who never fully shook the feeling that something might perhaps be discovered to be wrong with his 'papers', reads the sequence, which opens in the captain's cabin of a ship bearing the brothers to America, as a commentary on the experience of immigration. 'It is some mimesis of the shattered tiles of facts and interpretations, the urgent emplacement of which had to prepare masses of arrivals for citizenship, learning who their fathers are, the fathers of their new country, and searching to put new and old names to unheard-of objectives.'[45]

Cavell finds the richness of meaning that runs through the Marx Brothers' films rewarding. It enacts, for him, an unexpected understanding of Wittgenstein's comparison, in *Philosophical Investigations*, of language learning as being something like as if a child came into a strange country and did not understand its language, only that of where he was born. There is something about the Marx Brothers' use, and non-use, of language, that highlights its weird logic, its frequent non-literalism, its playfulness and strangeness. The array of implications that they wrest from language reveals its inherent democracy: that is, the fact that the meaning of words is neither fixed nor unilateral. The brothers 'steal back' sense from the world and thereby 'show that there are still, ordinary words, beyond and between us'[46] whose meanings are as much ours as anyone else's.

It is worth restating that Cavell is writing here not of the Marx Brothers' films but of their scripts. These scripts, to Cavell's mind, 'release the words and deeds from a confinement to film, or to what we think of as a film' and align them with, for example, Bergson or Brecht or Beckett. In short, these are words written on a page, not delivered by a person and not captured on film. The example of the Marx Brothers can illuminate something about language and its use, then, but not something about the peculiar relationship between ordinary language and cinema. Across several readings of *Mr Deeds Goes to Town* (Frank Capra, 1936), however, Cavell connects ordinary language as it is – or again, is not – spoken, with cinematic ontology in a way that opens up questions of the medium and its specificity. Here, Cavell shows how film itself functions as a kind of language – an intentional way of communicating something that we must work to interpret. He also argues that film, of all the arts, has a privileged relationship to the ordinary, an important theme within *The World Viewed*. In particular, Cavell is concerned here with the movies' ability to capture motion and in particular with the very ordinary fact that 'human beings are more or less nervous, that their behaviour is fidgety'.[47]

Cavell focuses in particular on the film's climactic courtroom scene, in which Deeds is on trial, charged with insanity (a charge cooked up by Deeds's lawyers, who are trying to get their hands on $20,000,000 inheritance that Deeds is determined to give away to those in greater need of it). Deeds's response to the accusations against him is to become completely silent, refusing to utter a word even in his own defence. His muteness causes distress to Mary 'Babe' Bennett, a reporter who has pretended to be in love with Deeds in order to extract a series of sensational newspaper stories which hold him up to ridicule and who has, it now seems, fallen for him for real. Babe finally speaks out passionately in defence of Deeds. And when he sees the true strength of her feelings, Deeds in turn breaks his silence to defend himself.

A small but vital part of the case against Deeds is the fact that he plays the tuba at odd hours. In his speech to the court Deeds recasts this idiosyncrasy as a type of fidgeting: an action that each human being performs under certain recurrent conditions. He looks around the courtroom and points out a man twitching his nose, a woman cracking her knuckles, the judge filling in the letter Os in his notes, the court-mandated psychiatrist doodling in his pad. As he indicates each of these individuals, the camera illustrates their gestures in close-up, 'as if it is setting up exhibits for Mr Deeds's case'.[48] Cavell points out that Deeds, who quotes directly from Henry David Thoreau elsewhere in the film, seems here to be echoing Ralph Waldo Emerson's belief, expressed in his essay 'Behaviour', that the body's movements show us something – albeit unwittingly – about the mind within it:

> Nature tells every secret once. Yes, but in man she tells it all the time, by form, attitude, gesture, mien, face and parts of the face, and by the whole action of the machine. The visible carriage or action of the individual, as resulting from his organisation and his will combined, we call manners. What are they but thought entering the hands and feet, controlling the movements of the body, the speech and behaviour? … The power of manners is incessant – an element as unconcealable as fire.[49]

Cavell does not make a case that Deeds's speech is a deliberate allusion to Emerson on the part of the film's writers or director. What matters to him is, rather, that for Deeds and Emerson alike, our behaviour gives us away. *All* our behaviour – not just that which is deliberate, purposeful, remarkable – but also that which is incidental, careless or fidgety. Cavell points out that Deeds has a particular name for the condition that causes universal fidgetiness, and that name is thinking. 'Everyone does silly things when they think,' he declares. He uses the word 'think' or 'thinking' repeatedly, each time emphasizing a further idiosyncrasy. For Deeds, and Cavell after him, fidgetiness is not merely evidence of Wittgenstein's claim, in the *Investigations*, that 'the human body is the best picture of the human soul', but more than this, fidgetiness is proof of thought itself. As such, Cavell argues, Deeds's perception of fidgetiness is a strange, silly, yet absolutely coherent continuation of Descartes's *cogito*: I think, therefore I am, and this thinking is expressed externally as fidgeting. Fidgeting proves the existence of the human: not only to others but more importantly to himself.[50] Or, as Cavell puts it in a later essay on *Mr Deeds*, in Descartes the proof of my existence was that my thinking cannot doubt itself;

after Emerson – and Deeds – the proof of my embodied thinking is that it cannot be concealed.[51]

Deeds is in some way – Cavell isn't really clear how – *aware* that the camera is there and that the camera can offer proof of his thoughtfulness. He thus enters into a kind of contract with the camera, Cavell argues, whereby he offers himself up for scrutiny, and in return the camera, an emblem of perpetual visibility, affirms his existence. The price, for Deeds, played by the beautifully awkward, notoriously shy actor Gary Cooper, is perpetual embarrassment. (Cavell points to one scene in which Deeds clatters clumsily away from Babe's house after presenting her with a poem he has written, described by Cavell as 'a solo of awkwardness that cinematically registers the falling of an American in love'.[52]) But he is also able to use this affinity to his advantage, as when, in the courtroom, he seems to direct its gaze towards the various forms of fidgeting taking place in the courtroom, while he, in voice-over, narrates their revelation of thinking.

It is cinema's unique power to capture the incidental or ordinary behaviour of human beings that proves their existence, to bear witness to that proof through its attentiveness to 'the most apparently insignificant repetitions, turnings, pauses, and yieldings of human beings'.[53] For Cavell, Deeds's evidence for the connection between fidgeting and thought – and crucially the connection between fidgeting and rational (if not intentional) thought – is not being presented to the judge and jury – or at least not only to them – but also to us, the film's viewers, whose attention it draws towards these ordinary details. In the interview with Klevan, Cavell refers to certain filmic moments as 'nothing shots': pauses or breaks in the narration in which little happens, and yet – in part as a result of this inaction – our attention is drawn to small gestures or aesthetic choices that we might not otherwise have noticed.[54] He and Klevan see one such example in a shot of Deeds lying on his bed talking to Babe Bennett on the phone. Klevan describes the scene: 'He has his right calf and ankle resting on the knee of the other leg, and he's playing with his foot while he's talking to her. The camera is behind his head so that most of his face is obscured (this shot is repeated a number of times). Then when the phone call is over you see him playing his trusty tuba and his face is even more hidden than in the previous version of the shot.' He asks: 'Why did they think to execute it like that … like that?'[55] For Cavell, the answer is less important than the fact that we are momentarily stopped. The camera's attention to the ordinary asks us to linger on this moment, to turn and return, to respond to it. It asks us, that is, to practise philosophical criticism, a practice to which we will return in Chapter 7 of this book.[56]

Cavell admits that some will be unwilling to grant this degree of seriousness to Deed's courtroom lecture on silliness and thinking. Such detractors may wish to protect their use of the serious, he concedes, by suggesting that Deeds's words are at best a parody of philosophy, not the thing of philosophy itself. Cavell is not unsympathetic towards this position since he judges that in the modern era one is at perpetual

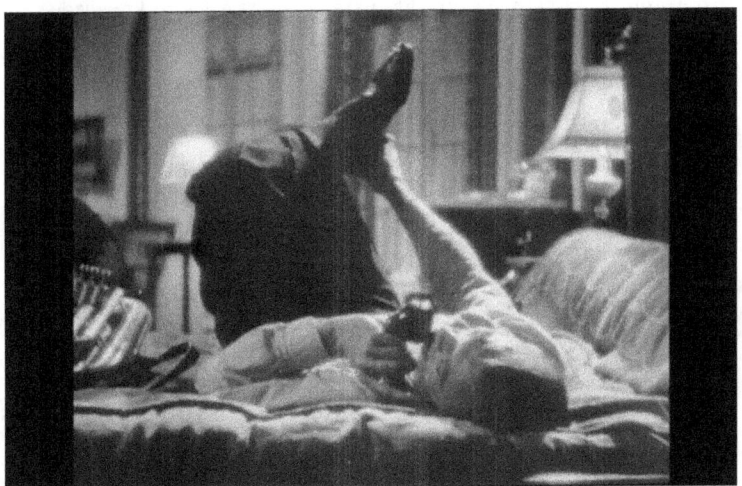

Figure 3 Deeds lies on his bed in *Mr Deeds Goes to Town*. Here, the camera's attention to the ordinary asks us to linger on this moment, to turn and return, to respond to it. *Mr Deeds Goes to Town* (Frank Capra, 1936).

risk of seriousness sliding into parody. Nonetheless, he argues, there is something deeply invidious in arguing that just because Deeds risks parody, he lacks authority over his own experience. 'To dismiss Deeds as too silly for philosophical thought is to deny him a voice in defining what silliness is, a concept essential to his explicit view of the human. And if we deny him this voice, how are we different to the corrupt prosecution, who would exercise an analogous denial by having him declared insane?'[57] Cavell draws a direct line from those who would dismiss Deeds to those who dismiss film more broadly as incapable of thinking seriously, of 'doing' philosophy. It is as if Deeds epitomizes Cavell's description, in 'The Thought of Movies', of film's power to draw our attention to what he calls 'the physiognomy of the ordinary', to make the unseen familiarity of things be seen anew:

> I understand it to be, let me say, a natural vision of film that every motion and station, in particular every human posture and gesture, however glancing, has its poetry, or you may say its lucidity ... Any of the arts will be drawn to this knowledge, this perception of the poetry of the ordinary, but film, I would like to say, democratizes the knowledge, hence at once blesses and curses us with it. It says that the perception of poetry is open to all, regardless as it were of birth or talent, as the ability is to hold a camera on a subject, so that a failure to perceive, to persist in missing the subject ... is ascribable only to ourselves, to failures of our character; as if to fail to guess the unseen from the seen, to fail to trace the implications of things – that is, to fail the perception that there is something to be guessed and traced, right or wrong – requires that we persistently coarsen and stupefy ourselves.[58]

Conclusion: A modern medium

The World Viewed expands these thoughts, explaining in greater detail what is at stake in such coarsening and stupefying. Before turning to that work in earnest, though, I would like to make a brief detour by way of the modern and the place of cinema in relationship to it. Cavell's reading of *Mr Deeds* begins to show us how he thinks about film as a form of language and a form of art that has a special interest in the ordinary. But it also raises for him the important topic of the relationship between the serious and the popular in modern culture, via a narrative strand in which Deeds is made president of an opera association.[59] When it transpires that the opera is losing money, Deeds suggests that it may be putting on the wrong kind of shows – the implication being, for Cavell at least, that film might be the right kind of show. In an article entitled 'Opera in (and as) Film', Cavell thus poses question: what is it that film offers in the place of opera?[60]

The answer has to do with inheritance – a central theme of *Mr Deeds* – and of opera's origins in the first decade of the seventeenth century, a historical juncture that Cavell sees as the beginning of the modern age. Cavell characterizes the modern as

> a moment in which history and its conventions can no longer be taken for granted; the time in which music and painting and poetry (like nations) have to define themselves against their pasts; the beginning of the moment in which each of the arts becomes its own subject, as if its immediate task is to establish its own existence. The new difficulty which comes to light in the modernist situation is that of maintaining one's belief in one's own enterprise, for the past and the present become problematic together.[61]

Rex Butler sums this all up by saying that for Cavell, 'modernism' in society and culture – a period marked not only in the performing arts by the birth of opera but also in philosophy by Descartes's *Meditations* and in literature by the plays of Shakespeare – is indicative of a questioning of conventions in the form of tradition. That is, prior to the modern age there was a set of conventions that were commonly agreed upon and which were taken to define an art form. But after modernism these criteria are placed into doubt – in part by the artists who once would have upheld them. In the absence of any universally agreed criteria for judgement, individual artists have to establish the criteria by which their work is to be judged through the artwork itself.'[62] We are brought back, then, to questions of intention. In the essay 'Music Decomposed' from *Must We Mean What We Say?*, Cavell addresses the problem of the potential 'fraudulence' of so-called new music written by figures such as Arnold Schoenberg, Ernst Krenek and John Cage, insofar as without the recognized rules of tonality there is simply no way of knowing in advance what constitutes a successful piece of music. It is always possible that the composer has failed to communicate their intention or indeed has nothing to say at all. This is also the problem raised with respect to the visual arts in 'A Matter of Meaning It'. The artist is entirely responsible for what they do in their work in the absence of preexisting conventions that they can directly follow. But this does not mean that the artist can avoid or circumvent convention. Rather, as Cavell puts it, 'the task of the modernist artist, as of the contemporary critic, is to find what it is his art finally depends upon'.[63] In *Must We Mean What We Say?* Cavell takes up these issues through a reading of two plays. In 'The Avoidance of Love: A Reading of King Lear', he traces the tragic consequences of Lear being unable to acknowledge the love of his daughter Cordelia. And in 'Ending the Waiting Game: A Reading of Beckett's Endgame', he examines the way in which Beckett's play dramatizes at once the irreducible ambiguity of everyday language and the equally irreducible desire to communicate despite the ambiguity – a point to which I shall return in Chapter 4.

But what about film? Where does that stand? Well, we have already seen that Cavell is able to consider Fellini alongside Shakespeare and Arnold in considering the question of intention and the modern arts. But in the same chapter he also claims that film is 'relatively free of the ideologies that we have constructed for the major arts'.[64] It is significant, moreover, that having devoted several pages to considering the development of other arts in their classical and modern periods, he turns to film not because he sees a continuity but because there is something different about it, which allows him to test his case in less muddy waters. Here he rather leaves this assumption hanging, but it will merit greater consideration in *The World Viewed*, where Cavell takes up the matter of modernism once more and expands on the relationship between Beckett's play and this brave new medium. So let us turn, now, to that work, to examine the place of the everyday within it and how that ultimately opens onto questions of scepticism.

3

Screening Scepticism

What's true? What's false? In case you haven't noticed, the world has pretty much given up on the old Enlightenment idea of piecing together the truth based on observed data. Reality is too complicated and scary for that. Instead, it's way easier to ignore all the data that doesn't fit your preconceptions and believe all data that does. I believe what I believe, and you believe what you believe, and we'll agree to disagree. It's liberal tolerance meets dark ages denialism. It's very hip right now.

– Nathan Hill, *The Nix*

Film, the latest of the great arts, shows philosophy to be the often invisible accompaniment of the ordinary lives that film is so apt to capture.

– Cavell, *Cities of Words*

The World Viewed opens with Cavell's notoriously baffling statement that the pages that follow constitute a 'metaphysical memoir': 'not the story of a period of my life but an account of the conditions it satisfies'.[1] What does Cavell mean by this, exactly? Metaphysics – the branch of philosophy concerned with the nature of existence, being and the world – asks questions like: 'What is the nature of reality?', 'How does the world exist, and what is its origin or source of creation?', 'Does the world exist outside the mind?' Such questions are bound up with the ordinary – with our experience of being in the world – but as Cavell knows all too well, they are often annexed off from the daily lives of men and women, deemed to be the preserve of the professional philosopher.

Being the good ordinary language philosopher that he is, Cavell is more interested in what the ordinary can tell us about the world than what professional philosophers might have to say about it, and in particular he is interested in what light the ordinary practice of film-going might cast on such questions. By the time he sits down to write *The World Viewed*, movie-going has been for Cavell a weekly practice for roughly twenty-five years. During his doctoral research, it offered relief from that rarified philosophical sphere that he inhabited at work in the university. Films returned Cavell to the ordinary world. At the same time, the best films were able to transport him, to offer him experiences that felt somehow heightened – *extraordinary*. *The World Viewed* attempts to account for this discovery of the extraordinary in the ordinary through an examination of Cavell's experience of film-going and film-viewing. It is a memoir because, as with all Cavell's work, it is deeply personal, bound up in the lived experience of this individual and with his memories of those experiences. It is metaphysical because it connects this experience to broader speculations about the nature of experience: asking how we connect with films and what this might reveal about our connection – or the lack of it – with the world we live in.

It is a given for Cavell that movies are important. They are important *to him*. And judging by their popularity, he supposes, they are important to others too. But *why* is this, he asks. A first answer presents itself in the matter of their accessibility. Many of the arts – music, painting, sculpture, poetry – are, to Cavell's mind, as elitist as philosophy, inaccessible to all but those privileged individuals fortunate to have received an education in these subjects. But everyone can enjoy films: 'rich and poor, those who care about (other) art and those who live on the promise of art, those whose pride is education and those whose pride is power or practicality – all care about movies, await them, respond to them, talk about them, hate some of them, are grateful for some of them'.[2] And more than this, film as an art form and film-going as a practice have no internal hierarchy of value, at least not according to Cavell.[3] He writes vividly of film's democratic pleasures:

> The movie seems naturally to exist in a state in which its highest and its most ordinary instances attract the same audience (anyway until recently). Anyone ought to be able rise to the occasion of recognition at the end of *City Lights*, to the eloquence of Garbo's moods, to the intelligence and manliness of Olivier's *Richard the Third*, to the power of justice in Henry Fonda's young Lincoln, to Carole Lombard's wit, to Emil Jannings' despair, to Marilyn Monroe's doomed magnetism, to Kim Stanley's sense of worthlessness, to the mutual pleasure and trust William Powell and Myrna Loy give one another, to Groucho's full and calm acceptance of Harpo's raging urgencies, to the heart-breaking hesitations at the center of an Astaire routine. And the highest sensibility must thrill at the knowledge with which Fonda interrupts the mythical question – 'Say, what's your name, stranger?' – looking around straight into Walter Brennan's eyes, dropping it as he walks out, 'Earp. Wyatt Earp'; and hate and fear Basil Rathbone's courtly villainies or Richard Widmark's psychotic killers or Lee Marvin's Liberty Valance, at once completely gratified and perfectly freed of guilt at their lucid and baroque defeats; and participate in the satisfaction of one of Kirk Douglas's or Burt Lancaster's rages. Merely to think of the way Bette Davis makes her entrance in *Jezebel* – bursting into view on a rearing horse, her elegant riding habit amplifying the dash with which she dismounts, then jamming the point of her whip back into the side folds of her skirt to free her boot for the step into the house where she knows she is awaited with dazzled disapproval – merely to think of the way, in *Now, Voyager*, her restoration to sanity is signaled by an opening shot on her sheer-stockinged ankles and legs, released from the thick, shapeless, dark cotton wrappings and health shoes into which her wicked mother had charmed her – these moments provide us with a fair semblance of ecstasy.[4]

This passage offers several hints as to film's peculiar appeal for Cavell and how it motivates the writing of *The World Viewed*. The first has to do with the films and stars listed: throughout *The World Viewed* and beyond, into Cavell's books on individual genres (*Pursuits of Happiness* and *Contesting Tears*) and films (*Cities of Words*), Cavell shows a predilection for a certain type of film: North American, specifically Hollywood, productions made during the first half of the twentieth century and starring some of the biggest names of the time. Cavell makes little mention of Eisenstein, Buñuel, French surrealism or German expressionism, an omission which some critics are hasty to point out.[5] But this preference is not incidental: the Hollywood cinema as Cavell describes it is cinema's standard bearer, the norm from which all other cinemas are the exception, an assumption that Cavell unpacks later in the book.

The second point that we should note is in those parentheses: the situation that Cavell describes has existed *until recently*. Something changes for Cavell around the time that he starts writing *The World Viewed*. He writes that his 'natural relation' to movies has broken,[6] a rupture that he part attributes to the emergence in ordinary US cinemas of a new type of cinema – European post-war productions made by the likes of Bergman, Antonioni, Fellini, Godard, Resnais, Truffaut and so on – and in part to the fact that Hollywood films themselves are changing. Films such as *The Children's Hour* (William Wyler, 1961), *The Graduate* (Mike Nichols, 1967) and *Rosemary's Baby* (Roman Polanski, 1968) have more in common with the new waves of European cinema than with their American predecessors, Cavell feels, and provide an altogether different experience for their viewers. In his 'Concluding Remarks Presented at Paris Colloquium on *La Projection du Monde*', he describes that experience as an 'original relation to film, some pretheoretical trust' being broken, 'causing a stronger sense of discontinuity than ... any development since the advent of the talkie'.[7] Cavell doesn't yet ask the question of *why* this change to the movies themselves has occurred, but it, too, will become an important concern later in *The World Viewed*, as we will see.

The third point that arises from Cavell's description of the power of Hollywood cinema has to do with the audiences watching these films. What emerges most strongly from Cavell's description is the responsiveness of spectators, who 'rise to the occasion' of these films, whose sensibilities 'thrill' until they resemble 'ecstasy'. Hollywood film has – had – a power to move its spectators, and *The World Viewed* is as much about the experience of film-viewing as it is about the films themselves. More than this, it is about the lasting impressions of films on their viewers and about the sharing of these impressions with other, like-minded viewers. Cavell describes his experiences of films that he has cared about as 'lined with fragments of conversations and responses of friends I had gone to the movies with'.[8] Other experiences of art – reading a book, for example – do not to his mind engender similar feelings of companionship. Reading is a solitary activity, and books are timeless (there will always be twelve-year-olds and there will always be copies of *The Count of Monte Cristo* handy) but film screenings are fleeting.

At least this is the case in 1971, before the advent of VHS, DVD or video-on-demand. By the time the second expanded edition of *The World Viewed* is printed in 1979, the videocassette format had been introduced to America, and while Cavell makes no mention of this technology, the threat of television and other emergent technologies hovers over *The World Viewed*. Even in the movie theatres, audiences have changed just as films have, and Cavell fears that he can 'no longer locate or remain together with my companions among them'.[9] There has been a change in viewing practices, so that instead of arriving at 'no matter what point in proceedings' as early cinema-goers were wont to do, film viewers all arrive and leave at once. For contemporary viewers, used to beginning films at the beginning and ending at the end, Cavell's resistance to this change may seem very strange. But

Cavell feels this shift in habit impinges on his sense of anonymity and privacy: now that everyone is watching the same film, from start to finish, it matters more to him now than it has done in the past that the responses of others to the film are not necessarily the same. At the same time, it seems to him as if the old casualness of movie-going has been replaced by a casualness of movie-viewing.[10] As William Rothman and Marian Keane have it, Cavell feels as if audiences no longer have a stake in the films they view and, correspondingly, 'as if they have no stake in their fantasies, as if they really had no fantasies at all'[11]: where once films asked their audiences to acknowledge their desires, now they help them to deny them altogether.

The World Viewed is thus born of Cavell's increasing unease with the experience of film-going and film-viewing. In essence, it asks the question: what is it about the movies that has changed? Beginning from his own experience, Cavell attempts to answer this question over the course of the book, using the practices that he has already engaged in *Must We Mean What We Say?* In 'Austin at Criticism', for example, Cavell explains how, in proceeding from ordinary language, one assumes such a mindset that it seems

> (1) that one can as appropriately or truly be said to be looking at the world as looking at language; (2) that one is necessarily seeking truths 'about' the world (or 'about' language) and therefore cannot be satisfied with anything I, at least, would recognize as a description of how people in fact talk – one might say one is seeking one kind of explanation of *why* people speak as they do; and even (3) that one is not finally interested *at all* in how 'other' people talk, but in determining where and why one wishes, or hesitates, to use a particular expression oneself.[12]

What Cavell is claiming here is that when we say something about language we are saying something about the world. And to say something about the world is in fact to say something about ourselves, about how we see the world. *The World Viewed* is correspondingly, in the words of John Mullarkey, 'an ontology of the filmed ordinariness of the world or, better, a study of the ontology of the world revealed by the ordinariness of film viewing'.[13] This chapter explicates Cavell's discussion of film in *The World Viewed* in light of his interest in ordinary language philosophy. I aim to show how the writing of *The World Viewed* both extends the work that Cavell does within ordinary language philosophy and at the same time reorients Cavell from questions about words to questions about scepticism via questions of modernism. In many ways, the questions that Cavell is posing here are the same as those posed within *Must We Mean What We Say?* and the same as those posed in later works such as *The Claim of Reason* (which, let's not forget, is adapted from Cavell's long-gestating thesis and so was written concurrently with the other two works). In posing and reposing these questions, Cavell comes to understand something new about their import. For it is a key truth about Cavell that often, when he appears to be going broader, he is in fact going deeper.

Cavell's ontology of film

Before Cavell can ask how film – and his relationship to it – has changed, first he must find out what film is, exactly: or perhaps what it *was*. Having set out his stall in the preface to the book, this is the question he tackles in the first part of *The World Viewed*. He approaches it by engaging, firstly, with what other philosophers of film have said about the ontology of film. In particular he turns to Erwin Panofsky and André Bazin, both of whom argued, in varying ways, that what is unique about film as a medium based in photography is that a photograph is *of* reality. In the essay 'Ontology of the Photographic Image', for example, Bazin argues that the essence of cinema is, as document, a record of the world, a recording made possible by the technologies of the film camera and film stock, which allow the world to imprint itself without need of human intervention.[14] Cavell agrees that film is photographic and its subject reality, but his focus is slightly different to that of Bazin and Panofsky. He is interested in the fact that, in the case of films, the photographic image is *shown before an audience*. Film is not merely an impression of reality (not even, as we shall see) but a *projection* of reality, a *screening* of reality. This leads him to ask the question: 'What *happens* to reality when it is projected and screened?'[15]

Cavell uses a very Wittgensteinian method to approach the problem of what separates painting from photography, seeking to determine what a thing *is* by finding out what it *is not*. What does it *mean*, Cavell asks, that photography is not painting? To answer this, he adapts Austin's method of paying attention to 'what we should say when, and so why and what we should mean by it'.[16] To begin with, he writes, photography does not present us with 'likenesses' of things. When we refer to the photographic image of a famous person – Gary Cooper say – we don't say that is a likeness of Gary Cooper; we say that *is* Gary Cooper (up there, on screen). It wouldn't make sense to say that's a very realistic or lifelike version of Gary Cooper, for example. But, of course, it's also not Gary Cooper himself. As Cavell points out, to say that 'photographs present us with things themselves' sounds 'false, paradoxical'.[17] But we can't say it's not Gary Cooper, either! That would be equally paradoxical.

From this knotty tangle of thoughts, Cavell surmises that we don't really know what a photograph is, or at least, we don't know how to think of the *connection* between a photograph and what it is a photograph of. He tries out a variety of words to denote this connection: a replica, a relic, a shadow, an apparition, a recording, a transcription, a reproduction, a sight, sense-data, surfaces, a moulding (a notion borrowed from Bazin's example of the Turin Shroud), an impression and so on. But none of these will do. Lest we are tempted to object at this point that it's all mere wordplay, Cavell assures us otherwise:

> On the contrary, I am precisely describing, or wishing to describe, what it means to say that there is a photograph here. It may be felt that I make too great a mystery of these objects. My feeling is rather that we have forgotten how mysterious these things are, and in general how *different* different things are from one another, as though we had forgotten how to value them. This is in fact something movies teach us.[18]

Very early on in *The World Viewed*, then, Cavell diverges from the position on film taken by Panofsky and Bazin, a divergence that is important precisely because it is often overlooked by readers of Cavell. As both Rothman and Keane and Daniel Morgan point out, the opening two sections are by far the most widely read part of *The World Viewed*, in part because Chapters Two to Five are reprinted in Mast and Cohen's celebrated anthology of theory.[19] Unfortunately, when these chapters are decontextualized in this manner, they seem to position Cavell as a direct inheritor of a line of thinking that emerges from Panofsky and Bazin and continues through Siegfried Kracauer's *Theory of Film*. According to this view, film emerges at the end of the nineteenth century as a technological solution to an increasing demand for realism across the arts.[20] While it is true that Cavell uses Bazin and Panofsky's work as a jumping-off point for an investigation into the particular mystery of movies and their importance to us, it would be a mistake to argue, as Dan Shaw does, for example, that he 'sides' with Andre Bazin 'in contending that the photographic essence of motion pictures explains the unique impression of reality films can give us'.[21] For Cavell, film is precisely *not* an impression of reality. Like Bazin, he senses that the difference between a painting and photograph is an important starting point and attempts to work out what this difference consists of, but his investigation takes him somewhere rather different.

Cavell can't accept the idea of photographs as impressions in part because photographs are not *hand*made. 'They are manufactured. And what is manufactured is the image of the world.'[22] It is this fact of mechanism in the making of images that Bazin sees as satisfying our obsession with realism. He argues that photography opened the way for abstraction in painting precisely through its ability to offer a perfect likeness of reality: once photos exist, there is, for Bazin at least, no imperative towards mimesis in art, and painting is free to investigate other possibilities of representation – impressionism, for example, in the case of Manet, or cubism, for Picasso.[23] Hence his claim that photography 'freed the plastic arts from their obsession with likeness'.[24] But for Cavell, it is misleading to think of photography as a competing solution to the wish for realism. Instead, he argues, 'so far as photography satisfied a wish, it was the human wish, intensifying in the West since the Reformation, to escape subjectivity and isolation'.[25] This is a key claim – perhaps *the* key claim – in *The World Viewed*, and we shall return to it later in this chapter. For now, it is sufficient to say that Cavell is reframing the competition between the two artistic media – painting and photography – not in terms of realism but in terms of reality and our connection to it, not in terms of an impression of the world but *the world itself*. Cavell, like Bazin, points to the borders of the frame to explain how a photograph is 'of the world' (we can always ask of a photo what lies outside the frame), while a painting is a world in itself – complete, with nothing 'beyond' what is there before us. Here is the key ontological difference between photography and painting.

And what of film? How does that differ from photography? If the photographic frame offers an opening onto the world, implying that there is something more beyond its edges, the screen does likewise. In Cavell's words 'the screen is a frame',[26] but now the frame is mobile, it is 'extendible and contractible, limited ... only by ... the state of its technology and ... the span of the world'.[27] Cinema thus allows us to pay 'perfect attention' to the world – a world sprung from reality. And yet that attentiveness comes at a cost. For the moving pictures not only screen the world *for* us, but they also screen it *from* us. The cinematic screen serves as barrier between us and the world on screen.

Cavell's real interest in film has not to do, then, with what happens to things on film but what happens to us when we see them. Cavell moves swiftly on to the question of how we, as film-viewers, relate to that world, as ontological philosophy gives way to an investigation of film spectatorship. Ontology, it seems, is only really interesting to Cavell insofar as it has to do with how we relate to that ontology. Or else there is no ontology of film that does not involve a film-viewer. That his interest in film is at heart an interest in the viewer is not perhaps very surprising – after all, Cavell's book has as its premise his own experience of film. What is surprising though is how rarely Cavell is discussed as a theorist of spectatorship and therefore placed into conversation with other theorists of spectatorship. In fact, his emphasis on film as medium that crucially is screened in a theatre has correspondences with the work of Christian Metz, whose name (like the term 'spectatorship' itself) Cavell never mentions but whose work likewise emphasizes the invisibility of the spectator to the world onscreen. In one of the few books to explicitly make this connection, Thomas Hilgers notes for example the similarities between Cavell's claim that we are not present to the world on screen and Metz's famous description of the spectator as a 'pure onlooker whose participation is inconceivable' and who is 'entirely on the side of the perceiving instance, absent from the screen'.[28] Metz further argues that 'film is not exhibitionist, I watch it, but it doesn't watch me watching it'.[29] Like Cavell, Metz finally claims that there is an essential metaphysical barrier between the world that a film shows and the world that its recipients occupy: 'The space of the diegesis and that of the movie theatre (surrounding the spectator) are incommensurable. Neither includes or influences the other, and everything occurs as if an invisible but airtight partition were keeping them totally isolated from each other.'[30]

Cavell expands on what it means for the spectator to be absent to the world on screen in his addendum to *The World Viewed*, 'More of *The World Viewed*' – a section added to the enlarged edition of the book and conceived in response to criticisms levelled at the book by Alexander Sesonske.[31] He tells us more about the particular mode of presence of the figures on screen and the particular mode of absence from them of their audience by way of a comparison with theatre. Whether viewing a film (we might take the example of *Tom Jones* (Tony Richardson, 1963), in which Albert Finney's eponymous hero addresses his audience directly at several points) or viewing a play (let's say *Othello*, since Cavell is so fond of Shakespeare), the audience is present at a fiction. But for Cavell the theatre audience is present at something happening, whereas the cinema audience is not. Think of the matter of direct address. When Iago tells the audience that 'I'll pour this pestilence into her ear' he is confiding in a real living breathing body of people, there before the actor and character alike. When Albert Finney, however, winks to camera in *Tom Jones*, there is no such audience before him. The wall between an actor on stage and audience is transparent in both directions. The wall between an actor on screen and the audience is different. It separates two totally distinct spaces and blocks all interaction. Cavell writes:

> The actors are *there*, all right, in your world, but to get to them you have to go where they are, and in fact, as things stand, you cannot go there *now*. Their space is not metaphysically different; it is the same human space mine is. And you are not, as in a theater, forbidden to cross the line between actor and incarnation … In a movie theatre, the barrier to the stars is *time*.[32]

Thus he is led to conclude:

> The fact I am invisible and inaudible to the actors, and fixed in position, no longer needs accounting for; it is not part of a convention I have to comply with; the proceedings do not have to make good the fact that I do nothing in the face of tragedy, or that I laugh at the follies of others. In viewing a movie *my helplessness is mechanically assured*.[33]

Automatism, modernism

Like Bazin, Cavell is concerned with the implications of the 'inescapable fact of mechanism or automatism in the making of [cinematic] images' for the spectator.[34] For Cavell, though, automatism is not a mere synonym for non-interference of the human hand in the production of images (of course, in Cavell no word is to be taken at face value!). Rather, automatism is a complex term, the meaning of which shifts over the course of *The World Viewed*, as theorists such as Lisa Trahair have explicated. In her excellent essay 'Being on the Outside: Cinematic Automatism in Stanley Cavell's *The World Viewed*', Trahair details four distinct but interrelated uses of automatism within Cavell's book, which are as follows:

1. Early in the book, automatism is used in a Bazinian sense to describe the process by which the camera captures images of the world.
2. Soon afterwards, he conceives of automatism as the feature of film by which our absence to the world on screen is assured.
3. Later, Cavell broadens the concept so that it no longer merely indicates a fact about film technology but is linked to the idea of convention in art more generally. In this reading the ways in which automatism is deployed within art works tell

us something about their relationship to modernity and the traditional.
4. Finally, in the chapter 'More of *The World Viewed*', he relates automatism to philosophical scepticism.[35]

Understanding what Cavell means at various points in *The World Viewed* by automatism allows us to gain a clearer sense not only of what he has to say about film but also how this thought on film is informed by and informs his wider philosophical thought. At this juncture, it is worth taking some time to peel back these layers of meaning in order to understand how the concept of automatism works as hinge between Cavell's interest in the ordinary and his interest in scepticism.

Cavell initially describes automatism as the photographic basis of film and therefore an essential component of the medium of film. But it is also the means by which the medium extends beyond its photographic basis to the world as such, to human reality and nature. As Trahair explains, this means that automatism affords film the potentialities of two different 'mediums'.[36] The first is celluloid emulsion which, via the automatic nature of the photographic mechanism, allows an image to occur that shows us the world. The second is the world itself: the human reality and nature that the photograph is of. While Cavell at first engages the concept of automatism in relation to the former, that is to Bazin and the removal of human intervention in the conjuring of the world, he later places more emphasis on the latter, the world that gives itself to be viewed.

In Chapter Eleven, after moving through various features and examples of film, Cavell attempts another definition of the medium: film now is 'a *succession of automatic world projections*'. This rather unwieldy phrase allows Cavell to capture the four features of film that he sees as definitive:

'Succession' includes the various degrees of motion in moving pictures: the motion depicted; the current of successive frames in depicting it; the juxtapositions of cutting. 'Automatic' emphasizes the mechanical fact of photography, in particular the absence of the human hand in forming these objects and the absence of its creatures in their screening. 'World' covers the ontological facts of photography and its subjects. 'Projection' points to the phenomenological facts of viewing, and to the continuity of the camera's motion as it ingests the world.[37]

At this point in *The World Viewed*, it would appear that automatism relates, still, to the technological fact of photography and its assurance that humanity is absent from its production and the world that is projected. 'Reproducing the world is the only thing film does automatically,' Cavell writes.[38] And yet in section 14, which is subtitled 'Automatisms', Cavell broadens the term such that it takes on a rather different set of connotations. He begins to write of film's 'traditions of automatism', by which he means the 'media' that make up an art form. We have already seen that Cavell sees celluloid and the world as constitutive media of film, but now he lists others. Cycles, genres, types and stars are amongst the media produced by the camera, for example. He describes how the

> genres and types and individualities that have constituted the media of movies are fixed in the specific collection of human beings with which movies have been made – in their utterly specific rhythms of voice and gesture and posture, and in those particular streets and carriages and chambers against and within which those specific beings had their being.[39]

Film noir is an automatism, as we readily recognize its characters and visual style; so is Humphrey Bogart, who brings a set of tendencies, characteristics and expectations to each of his roles. So, too, are formal devices like shot/reverse-shot constructions – what we might call the syntax of cinema – since their appearance allows us to recognize, without thinking, that we should be oriented around a specific character.

What Cavell is saying sounds today hardly radical, and indeed even at the time similar ideas were circulating (though it's unclear as to whether Cavell was aware of them). By 1971, Bazin had already posited that cinema was a kind of language; by the time of *The World Viewed*'s release, Christian Metz was putting forward the notion of a *grande syntagmatique* aimed at identifying and classifying the elements of film that 'tell the story' on screen, shaping spectators' expectations and comprehension of the images, while Richard Dyer was attempting a theoretical approach to stars by combining sociological and semiological analysis.[40] Still, there are a number of original points being made here.

Firstly, Cavell believes that the way in which we experience these phenomena – types, genres, stars and so forth – is as natural to cinema as the way in which we experience its photographic basis. This is very important – if the photographic basis of the movies is only one of many automatisms then it no longer is necessarily definitive; hence it is possible for film theorists such as David Rodowick to read digital cinema through a Cavellian lens.[41] Unlike Bazin, Cavell's understanding of cinematic ontology is not *intrinsically* bound up with the celluloid technology.[42]

Secondly, Hollywood has developed its own distinct set of types and genres distinct from any other medium, and these types are therefore part of what constitutes or defines the medium of (Hollywood) film. Cavell lists for example:

> the Public Enemy, the Priest, James Cagney, Pat O'Brien, the Confederate Spy, the Army Scout, Randolph Scott, Gary Cooper, Gable, Paul Muni, the Reporter, the Sergeant, the Sheriff, the Deputy, the D.A., the Quack, the Shyster, the Other Woman, the Fallen Woman, the Moll, the Dance Hall Hostess.[43]

He adds that we do not need psychological explanation as to why these types behave as they do; Jimmy Cagney does what he does simply because he's Jimmy Cagney. (That's part of the magic of Hollywood.) But the fact that a type functions as an automatism does not mean that he or she remains fixed, necessarily: filmmakers innovate within a tradition by producing variations on automatisms, playing with the expectations they generate (an idea at the very heart of genre theory). Hence, in Cavell's view, meaning is not controlled by one individual but emerges in the encounter between the film and the viewer.

The question of innovation leads us on to Cavell's third insight. At the time that Cavell writes *The World Viewed*, the types described above are gone or old. 'Hollywood is ended. Its significance is the end of its media, of those arrangements whose significance was unquestioned, conviction in which was immediate.' The 'traditions of automata' are being broken. Remember that Cavell's natural relation to the movies has been broken too, transformed from an 'ordinary' appreciation to a philosophical one, and that the causes for this were both a change in screening and viewing practice and in the films themselves. In the chapter 'End of the Myths' and beyond, he expands upon the nature of the changes to film, arguing, to put it briefly, that film has entered a modernist phase. This modernist turn has precisely to do with its deployment of automata and its breaking of traditions. Cavell claims that certain possibilities of Hollywood cinema are 'drawing to an end'.[44] The cycles, plots and types that he understands as definitive of film are dying out; where they are still in place they are no longer taken as seriously as they once were. Audiences are tired of these forms; they seem dated, irrelevant. Or else they are 'dressed up' with 'fancier cutting and dreamier colour and extremer angles and more explicit dialogue'.[45] Such superficial dressings-up are not new possibilities for film, merely splashy flourishes that add little of substance – in part, it seems to Cavell, because no one really knows what to do with them. Cavell asks: why are directors led to push possibilities to their limits with no apparent agenda? An answer to this question would be part of an investigation of modernism itself. If, as Cavell claims, 'within the last decade film has been moving into the modernist environment inhabited for generations by the other major arts',[46] it behooves us to ask: What is this modernist environment? How has it been inhabited by the other major arts? And why has film only recently moved to occupy this space?

In order to answer these questions, we – after Cavell – must turn back to painting. Historically, painting connects with reality by imposing man's will upon it, by demonstrating man's 'presence to the world' through 'the acknowledgement of the endless presence of the self'.[47] Cavell offers the elegantly phrased example of Wordsworth (a poet rather than a painter) 'writing himself back into the world', but we might just as well think of J.W. Turner or Caspar David Friedrich's 'images of the transitoriness of human life and the premonition of death'.[48] These artists, to Cavell's mind, master their fates 'by creating selfhood no matter what odds', 'sealing the self's fate by theatricalizing it'.[49] Photography, on the other hand, connects with reality in a way undreamed of by painting: by automatically removing the human agent from the task of reproduction. Cavell concludes that painting and photography were never in competition. Instead:

> What happened was that at some point the quest for visual reality ... split apart. To maintain our presentness, painting accepts the recession of the world. Photography maintains the presentness of the world by accepting our absence from it. The reality in a photograph is present to me while I am not present to it; and a world I know, and see, but to which I am nevertheless not present ... is a world past.[50]

From very early on in *The World Viewed*, Cavell argues that photography satisfies a desire not for realism but for the overcoming of subjectivity. At the same time he denies that painting was ever really 'obsessed', as Bazin had it, with likeness; rather painting craved both a 'connection with reality' and a 'conviction in its powers to create meaningful objects' (hence Wordsworth painting himself back into the world).[51] This craving for connection stems from what Cavell refers to as an 'unhinging' of our consciousness from the world, which 'interposed our subjectivity between us and our presentness to the world'. As a result, he writes, 'our subjectivity became what is present to us, individuality became isolation'.[52]

As Rothman and Keane point out, *The World Viewed* 'returns again and again to this idea of the unhinging of our consciousness from the world'.[53] Indeed, we might phrase it otherwise as a loss of 'natural relation'. It is a loss that functions on numerous levels and is quasi-religious in tone, echoing the myth of the Fall in the Garden of Eden.[54] According to Cavell, it has to do with both a particular historical moment (the Protestant Reformation, Shakespearean tragedy, the birth of modern philosophy in Descartes's confrontation with sceptical doubt) and a particular moment in every modern human being's life history, which, once having taken place, is repeated again and again in that individual's life. Rothman and Keane put it thus:

> Picture it as a philosophical and spiritual and psychological and political cataclysm that presents us with a new fact (or is it a new consciousness of an old fact?) We now find ourselves, know ourselves as, isolated by our subjectivity. It is our subjectivity that is present to us, not a world we may objectively apprehend. Nor do we objectively apprehend our own subjectivity: even our subjectivity is only present to us subjectively. Our consciousness has become unhinged from ourselves, too.[55]

Put simply, what Cavell is talking about is a loss of innocence and corresponding entrance into human lives of doubt. This is what is described in the book of Genesis, when Adam and Eve realize that they are naked. It is what occurred in the Enlightenment, when absolute monarchy and church dogma were rejected in favour of Cartesian scepticism and political libertarianism. It is what happens to us as we pass from childhood into adulthood and come to question the wisdom of our parents and other authorities. And it is what happens in art, after the faith of both its producers and consumers in the power of conventional representation has been shaken.

According to Cavell, then, a peculiarly Western existential crisis thus arises in the wake of the decline of religious idealism, 'namely, the wish to nullify the condition of subject hood that inserts itself between ourselves and nature'.[56] After the death of God, the world is now something that we cannot connect to, cannot perhaps even see. This is what modern philosophy – from Kant through Locke to Hume, Hegel to Marx, Kierkegaard and Nietzsche – tells us: that the world is beyond our reach. Martin Shuster is amongst several commentators who have argued that in this respect Cavell's characterization of the modern condition is closest to Martin Heidegger's, with both men describing the modern world as a kind of 'picture'. Shuster points out that Heidegger's claim that our current age is one in which the world is 'conceived and grasped and a picture' finds clear echoes in Cavell's admonition that 'our natural mode of perception is to view, feeling unseen. We do not so much look at our world as look *out at* it, from behind the self'.[57]

And yet, precisely because of this lack, we strive for an unmediated presence, a direct connection to nature. To find it, we look to art. This understanding of the world as 'out there' entails that our only access to it is through representation. Hence Cavell's belief – which he expands upon in the chapter 'Excursus: Some Modernist Painting', with reference to the theorist Michael Fried – that we are no longer present to the world, and neither is it present to us. In painting, expressionism and romanticism both respond to this, expressionism by representing our 'terror of ourselves in isolation' and romanticism by honing in on subjectivity and making it 'the route back to our conviction in reality'.[58]

Elsewhere in *The World Viewed*, Cavell explains that he uses the term 'modernist' to describe 'the work of an artist whose discoveries and declarations of his medium are to be understood as embodying his effort to maintain the continuity of his art with the past of his art, and to invite and bear comparison with the achievements of his past'.[59] In the section entitled 'More of *The World Viewed*', Cavell connects modernist art most clearly to the notion of automatism. In traditional art, the master artist knows how to deploy, or 'activate', the automatisms of the form according to a set of conventions which are mutually accepted by practitioners and consumers of that art. In the modern age of any art form, however, the rules fall away. Success no longer depends on mastering the rules and working out how best to move within them. Rather, the modernist artist is left to forge his or her own rules. In cinema's modernist phase, that is, 'there is no longer a *natural relation* between your work and its results, you are looking for what works'.[60] What this means, as Martin Shuster points out, 'is that whereas someone working in the traditional form might produce a piece of work that simply isn't any good, the modern artist – who is actively trying to produce something without the guide of a fixed tradition – might fail to produce art altogether'.[61] Hence the modern artist is forced to turn inward, to reflect upon itself and the history of its medium, to ascertain the limits and capacities of its medium and to experiment with the conditions that will secure its pertinence.

How does film relate to modernism? In *The World Viewed*, Cavell makes explicit a position hinted at in his discussion of Fellini's *La Strada* in 'A Matter of Meaning It' that film in its early incarnation has avoided the predicament of modernism.[62] The fact that film is the only art to do so is due in part to its relative newness: Cavell suggests that 'the first successful movies – i.e. the first moving pictures accepted as motion pictures – were not applications of a medium that was defined by given possibilities, but the *creation of a medium* by their giving significance to specific possibilities'.[63] In *The Claim of Reason*:

if it is the task of the modernist artist to show that we do not know *a priori* what will count for us as an instance of his art, then this task, or fate, would be incomprehensible, or unexerciseable, apart from the existence of objects which, prior to any new effort, we do count as such instances as a matter of course.[64]

Film elucidates and adds nuance to this claim, as a medium that has had to establish its traditions before it can query them. In the early years of the movies film is still establishing its foundational instances. The automata that film discovers during its first fifty years – Chaplin, noir, the long take, the gangster, the moll – simultaneously create film. These are the media through which film learns to communicate. In Cavell's words, they provide 'particular ways to get through to someone, to make sense: in art, they are forms, like forms of speech'.[65]

For its first fifty years, then, film exists in a pre-modern state. It cannot question its rules as it is still going about the business of making them up. As such, it returns us to an age of innocence. Just so, the mechanical basis of film dispenses with the problem of subjectivity since it promises us a direct relation to reality. That is, in the traditional era film appears to offer us a way out of the trap of subjectivity by dispensing with human artistry altogether. Photography, and by extension film, makes the world present to us directly, without intervention. And this presence is premised precisely on our absence from it. Movies allow us to view the world unseen, granting us 'not a wish for power over creation ... but a wish not to need power, not to have to bear its burdens'.[66] Unlike the other arts, cinema frees us of the weight of responsibility – a responsibility for connection with the world – that the death of God placed on man's shoulders.

Film places the world back within our reach. The world that reveals itself to the camera, and whose candour rests on the fact that nothing it reveals to the presence of the camera is lost, repudiates the teaching of modern philosophers, from Descartes to Heidegger, preoccupied with nature's ability to reveal the truth and to deceive us. To quote Lisa Trahair:

> Just when modern philosophy lost faith in nature's capacity to disclose itself to us … along comes film and, by virtue of its automatism, … gives us the unseen view of the world that Kant, Locke and Hume had thought was beyond our empirical reach and that Hegel, Marx and Kierkegaard thought beyond our metaphysical reach.[67]

Almost as soon as it has established itself as a traditional art, however, film becomes subject to the conditions of modernism. Cavell distinguishes between a past age of cinema, 'where the new medium innocently pursued forms of happiness',[68] and the current age, the time in which he is writing, where cinema is coming to reflect on its own status as artistic form. Where the first nine chapters of the book attempt to account for the traditions and conventions that Hollywood established in its past, the second half, by contrast, considers the cinema of Cavell's present in light of the division that he perceives. Daniel Morgan's short but extremely insightful essay on Cavell and the contingencies of film theory concludes from this that, despite appearances to the contrary, *The World Viewed* is 'essentially a book about cinema under the condition of modernism' and that Cavell is 'a theorist of cinema in crisis and transformation'.[69] In this much, Cavell has a point of commonality with Gilles Deleuze: both men understand film as undergoing a fundamental change after the advent of the Second World War and see the cinema as split in two. In the aftermath of that war, Cavell writes:[70]

> We no longer grant, or take it for granted, that men doing the work of the world together are working for the world's good, or that if they are working for the world's harm they can be stopped. These beliefs flowered last in our films about the imminence and experience of the Second World War, then began withering in its

aftermath – in the knowledge, and refusal of knowledge, that while we had rescued our European allies, we could not preserve them; that our enemies have prospered; that we are obsessed with the ally who prospered and prepared to enter any pact so long as it is against him; that the stain of atomic blood will not wash and that its fallout is nauseating us beyond medicine, aging us very rapidly. It is the knowledge, and refusal to know, that we are ceding to Stalin and Hitler the permanent victories of the war (if one of them lost the old world battle, he shares the spoils of the present war of the worlds), letting them dictate what shall be meant by communism and socialism and totalitarianism, in particular that they are to be equated. We lash ourselves to these ideas with burning coils of containment, massive retaliation, moon races, yellow perils, red conspiracies, in order that in the spasms of our fixed fury we do ourselves no injury, in order not to see the injury we have done, and do. So the mind pulls itself apart trying to pull free.[71]

After the Second World War, 'a general disillusionment with mankind's ability to work towards a common good results in the loss, or bafflement, of any conviction in the movies' originating myths and geniuses'.[72] Film's automatisms, its stories, types and genres, cease to have any hold on our collective imagination. Its innocence, and our innocent belief in its ability to connect us to the world – to make the world present to us – is lost. As a result, the movies are no longer magical. They no longer relieve us of the burden of creation. And so film comes to resemble the other arts that have gone before it in becoming unreliable:

> As with painting, so with film: the 'presentness' of the world of film is not absolute or guaranteed simply by the basic automatism of the camera. It becomes necessary to *achieve* presentness, and so film enters a modernist phase. For even with the camera's automatism, conviction in or 'presentness' to a world can be undermined.[73]

To sum up, the history of the West is figured by Cavell as a loss of authority: religious, political, personal, linguistic and artistic. After the Second World War, film becomes part of this narrative. It too has lost its authority, an authority hitherto mechanically assured: the photographic reproduction of the world is no longer something that can be taken for granted. '[Hollywood films] no longer naturally establish conviction in our presentness to the world.'[74] So film, like the other arts, has to turn inwards and question the basis of its certainty up to now. Its physical basis is as much subject to this process of questioning as its other automata: 'Its awareness and responsibility for the physical basis of its art compel it at once to assert and deny the control of its art by that basis.'[75] But as Martin Shuster points out, it is the screening of the world, more than the mechanical automatism of the camera or the fact of the screen, that film must reflect upon.

> Of utmost importance to the survival and prosperity of film in its modernist phase is ... not the productive automatisms that have emerged and will continue to emerge (say, mechanical automatism of the camera, computer generated imagery, 3D cameras, and so forth), but rather exactly the continued possibility of automatic world projection, with the stress in that phrase, above all, but not solely, on *world*.[76]

Like Rodowick, Shuster thus stresses that Cavell's discussion of film maintains its relevance, power and conviction in the digital age. What is important is not film – or any developments in its technology – but our continued response to it.

The age of scepticism

Film in its traditional age at once reassures us that we can know the world and reminds us that we are always shut out of it. Here is the world, it says to us, mechanically reproduced: the world has presented it itself to you. But we should not forget that the motion picture camera makes a world present to us *from which we are absent*. It causes live human beings and real objects in space to appear to us when they are in fact not there. It makes present a no-longer-existent world. For Cavell, our relation to such an image of the world – to something which presents our sense with nothing less than reality but which is nevertheless nothing more than image – exemplifies what he sees as scepticism's understanding of our relation to the world itself, since for the sceptic, what we take to be the world is but a moving image of it.

Cavellian scepticism distinguishes itself from other antecedent versions of scepticism in various ways. Crucially, scepticism is not, for Cavell, an exercise or a thought experiment, a game played by philosophers as a test of their logical skill. Far from it: our lack of certainty is at the heart of mankind's ongoing existential crisis. Theories that claim to prove the sceptical view that we can never really know the world cannot defeat our ultimate, enduring belief in something out there. But neither can pragmatic appeals to reality, claims that of course we know there's something there, free us from the anxiety that maybe, after all, the world is not as it appears. For Cavell, scepticism – an approach that questions the possibility of certain knowledge – goes hand in hand with the loss of authority that Cavell sees as definitive of recent human history. With no higher authority to have recourse to, we find ourselves in a position akin to that hypothesized by Descartes: that all one can be certain of is one's own subjectivity. This is felt as 'a sense of powerlessness to know the world, or act upon it ... a sense of the precariousness and arbitrariness of existence, the utter contingency in the fact that things are as they are'.[77] The wholly mechanical basis of photography removes human subjectivity from the process of reproducing reality, and thereby it perfects the process – capturing a world which is in every feature indistinguishable from reality. The price to be paid for the world's presentness is the screening of human subjectivity from that world – it is a world from which viewers are helplessly, mechanically absent. In other words, photography's automatism accomplishes the overcoming of human subjectivity that the sceptic deems necessary for our conviction in the presentness of reality, but the world captured is a world which recedes beyond our grasp.

Cavell calls cinema in its traditional form a 'moving image of skepticism' in part because it satisfies our sense of reality even while that reality does not exist. More than this, it satisfies our sense of reality in this way precisely because the reality that is made present does not exist in our current time and space, 'because viewing it is all it takes'.[78]

> By my account, film's presenting of the world by absenting us from it appears as confirmation of something already true of our stage of existence. Its displacement of the world confirms, even explains, our prior estrangement from it. The 'sense of reality' provided on film is the sense of that reality, one from which we already sense a distance. Otherwise the thing it provides a sense would not, for us, count as reality.[79]

This much is true for traditional film. But what of cinema under modernism? Here, the world's presence is no longer assured by our mechanical absence from it for the screen no longer naturally holds a coherent world *from* which we are absent, as Cavell explains in Chapter Seventeen, 'The Camera's Implication'.

> The images keep staying back, as in photographs they will. That we now feel this as a loss of connection, as staying away, underlies the camera's efforts to engulf its subjects – by widening its reach, by staying close enough to them to hold their scent (as a blinded man might), by freezing them in their tracks or slowing them down as if to glimpse them before they vanish. The massiveness of sounds and amplifications of figures in works like *Point Blank* and *The Dirty Dozen* are as if so maddened by the threat of nature's withdrawal that they would in vengeance blot it out on the spot.[80]

Cavell describes this loss of connection, this loss of conviction in film's capacity to carry the world's presence as a new theatricalizing of its images. He launches an attack on a number of films – Stanley Kramer's *Ship of Fools* (1965), Truffaut's *Une Femme Mariée* (1964) and *La Sirène du Mississippi* (1969) – that use film's automata heavy-handedly, tritely, and which tie their mysteries up in too pat a manner. Alfred Hitchcock's *Psycho* (1960) diagnoses this obsession with 'the phony psychological explanations we give ourselves to ward off knowledge', in its 'vulgar', 'penny-ante' ending in which a psychiatrist ties up the film's loose ends and contains its frightening violence.[81] Such triteness leads Cavell to speak of 'film's growing doubt of its ability to allow the world to exhibit itself, and instead taking over the task of exhibition, against its nature'.[82] Put very simply, film has started to tell, rather than to show. Directors work harder to impose their vision of the world upon it, as opposed to allowing the world to present itself. It's no coincidence that the shift from traditional to modern cinema coincides with the growing impact of auteur theory on thinking about film.[83] The cult of the director is symptomatic of film's move into a state of modernism. Indeed, referring to earlier author-directors such as Eisenstein in 'More of the World Viewed', Cavell modifies his conception of modernist film by saying that through the work of such figures we see that 'movies from their beginnings have existed in two states, one modern, one traditional, sometimes running parallel to and at varying distances from one another, sometimes crossing, sometimes interweaving'.[84]

If film in its traditional form offers us a moving image of scepticism, a reinscription of our state of being in the world, film in its modern age undergoes a sceptical crisis, and so it begins to mirror or present itself as a symptom of the sceptical age in a way that is different but no less powerful. I am reminded here of the children's story *We're Going on a Bear Hunt* by Michael Rosen, in which a group of children face a series of obstacles (grass, mud, a river, some sand dunes). They can't go *over* these obstacles, and they can't go *under* them: they've got to go *through*

Figure 4 Alfred Hitchcock's *Psycho* (1960) diagnoses modernity's obsession with 'the phony psychological explanations we give ourselves to ward off knowledge'. *Psycho* (Alfred Hitchcock, 1960).

them. In different ways, traditional film and modernist film show us that we can't pass over scepticism (with claims to knowledge, the imposition of our subjectivity on the world), nor can we fall under it (by simply abandoning all faith in the world). We must pass through it. But how?

For Cavell, the answer lies in the acknowledgement of our limitations even as we remain aware that we are bound by them. Such acknowledgement must come first on the part of the film itself. Movies must acknowledge their own limits, Cavell stipulates: their outsideness to the world and our absence from it. One first step towards this is film's self-reference. Cavell writes in the foreword to the enlarged edition of *The World Viewed* that objects projected on the film screen are inherently reflexive or self-referential, meaning that one is led to wonder about their physical origins in past times and spaces, but also that the quality of their presence indicates their absence. He expands upon this position in the chapter 'Exhibition and Self-Reference', where he writes:

> Movies from their beginning avoided the perplexities of consciousness, its absolute seriousness ... Media based upon successions of automatic world projections do not, for example, have to establish presentness to and of the world; the world is there. They do not have to deny or confront their audiences: they are screened. And they do not have to defeat or declare the artist's presence: the object was always out of his hands.[85]

However, it is not enough to be merely self-referential (self-reference in and of itself is essentially solipsistic, it forgets about the other). Indeed, certain types of self-reference work to impose subjectivity and obscure the world. Cavell gives the example of the documentarian who makes his own presence known within the film. Such an act is in bad faith; 'if the presence of the camera is to be made known, it has to be acknowledged in the work it does'.[86] This kind of self-reference, born of the modernist cinema, places the artist's self-consciousness between himself and his work, forcing him to justify his works even as he performs them. To place the camera or its operator before the lens is to deny the filmmaker's own absence from the world. After all, Cavell insists:

> The camera is outside its subject as I am outside my language. The abyss of ready insincerity is fixed, but that is what makes truthfulness possible – and virtuous. Wittgenstein is known for his emphases upon the publicness of language. But his emphasis falls equally upon the absoluteness of my responsibility for the meaning I attach to my words. Publicness is a shared responsibility.[87]

Conclusion: Towards acknowledgement

In *Must We Mean What We Say?*, Cavell admonishes: 'In the absence of a strict set of rules that tells us how to communicate, we are ourselves responsible for the way in which we mobilize the available resources in order to get our message across.' Just so, in a world where communication is fraught with the possibility of misunderstanding, film-viewing – a communicative act – is as open to failure of meaning as any other act. So if the film must acknowledge something, so too must the viewer. Cavell explains that an acknowledgement (for example, 'I know I [promised; am withdrawn; let you down …]') is an act of the self, and it is not done *apart from an admission of the existence of others*.[88] Both parties must take responsibility – shared responsibility – for what is being communicated.

What Cavell comes to understand about language is structured by what he comes to understand about film. Acknowledgement between film and viewer thus teaches us something about acknowledgement in language. It recognizes that yes, my way of seeing, thinking, feeling and expressing myself might not be the same as yours – in fact, it cannot be the same as yours – and it pledges that, despite this, I will try my best to share my way with you and to understand yours. In Trahair's beautiful words, acknowledgement 'is a means of repairing a relation that is damaged and that has broken or threatens to break the connection between people … a restoration of a connection that nevertheless recognises the separateness of the two parties'.[89]

Cavell offers examples of how particular films – through self-reference or through narrative conceit – think about acknowledgement. Towards the end of the 1971 version of *The World Viewed*, he offers up the example of Buster Keaton's *Sherlock Junior* (1924), an 'extendedly reflexive movie' in which Keaton dreams of himself as the great sleuth. As he dreams, shifting scene placements repeatedly undo him in a sequence that is 'more sublime in execution and effect than is knowable without its experience': 'it's as if every lie ever told by a photographer's backdrop or prop … had suddenly come to life'.[90] Keaton uses film, Cavell tells us, to show us our lack of control over both fantasy and reality. This comedy of self-reference satirizes our efforts to escape the self by viewing it, undermining the possibility that we can ever be sure of knowing – or seeing – the truth.

Figure 5 Buster Keaton's *Sherlock Junior* (1924): 'it's as if every lie ever told by a photographer's backdrop or prop ... had suddenly come to life'. *Sherlock Junior* (Buster Keaton, 1924).

In the next chapter, we will see how Cavell posits acknowledgement as the central theme of a series of romantic comedies made during Hollywood's golden era. Still, as Cavell has it in *Pursuits of Happiness*, 'no event within a film is as significant as the film itself', and perhaps no one film is as significant as the fact of film itself.[91] It is not just individual movies but *all* film – at least in its traditional form – that makes a case of sorts for how to live through scepticism. In mechanically assuring our absence, film reminds us that we *need not be absent* from the world outside the cinema. Life is not a film, and our relationship to the world might feel, at times, like watching a movie, but it is not really like watching a movie. The power of film thus lies in its potential to present us with a 'perfected' version of the modern condition precisely so that we might realize how imperfect the one 'out there' is, that we might 'reawaken from the slumber of our natural existence to arrive at a self-conscious relation to it'.[92] Film cannot solve the problem of scepticism, nothing can. But it can call it to our attention. And it can teach us how to live through it. After that is up to us how we behave in the face of the challenge that film throws down. As Cavell has it, 'We may wish for freedom from responsibility, but the denial of its claim is no route to that freedom.'[93] In this manner, Cavell conceives a moral dimension to seeing and being seen in relation to art and to film in particular, one that will come to have an increasing significance for him over the course of his subsequent writing. *This* is a first answer as to why movies are important.

4

Acknowledgement, Other Minds

But this story begins where others end: a boy and a girl in love, a wedding, a happily ever after.

– Jamie Quatro, *Fire Sermon*

I don't know what a happy ending is. Life isn't about endings, is it? It's a series of moments. If you turn the camera off, it's not an ending, is it? I'm still here. My life's not over. Come back here in ten years, see how I'm doing then.

– Tim, *The Office*

Cavell understands scepticism to be modern humankind's condition. Stripped of the certainties first provided by religion (the belief in God) and then by the state, our consciousness was, and remains, unhinged from the world. We might think of this as the disappearance of a common, objective point from which to understand and feel the world: our newly revealed subjectivity comes between us and our 'presentness' to the world. William Rothman and Marian Keane put it this way: 'The world as it is cannot satisfy the wish for the world, our wish to have this world, to possess it, or at least to be meaningfully connected to it.'[1] As such, scepticism is not, Cavell stresses, a mere philosophical exercise that turns around questions such as 'how can I be sure that I am not being tricked by an evil demon (or manipulated by computer stimulation of my neurons)?' Rather, it expresses a deep-seated anxiety or feeling of untetheredness. The result is that in the last five hundred years mankind has become obsessed with finding some way – any way – of believing in the world. In the words of Karl Marx: 'the criticism of religion is in the main complete' and that 'the task of history, once the world beyond the firth has disappeared, is to establish the truth of this world'.[2]

In *The World Viewed* and in *The Claim of Reason*, Cavell reflects upon this state of affairs and reaches two important conclusions. The first of these is that scepticism has come to define our relation to the world. The second is that we should neither give in to scepticism nor attempt to refute it by searching for certainty:

> It is not quite right to say that we *believe* the world exists (though certainly we should not conclude that we do not believe this, that we fail to believe its existence), and wrong even to say we *know* it exists (while of course it is equally wrong to say we fail to know to this) ... our relation to the world's existence is somehow *closer* than the ideas of believing and knowing are made to convey.[3]

It is silly to talk of believing or not believing in the world, Cavell claims. Even more so to talk of knowing or not knowing of its existence. Where does such talk get us? Cavellian scepticism is an ontological problem, not an epistemological one, and so there is no point thinking about it in epistemological terms. Put otherwise we can't overcome scepticism, but we do have to live with it. So a more useful, and more sensible, way to think about our relationship to the world is not in terms of belief but in terms of action: what one does or says in the face of the state of uncertainty that we're living in.

We are sceptical about not only the existence of the world, though, but also the existence of other minds. As Karen Hanson points out in her essay, 'Being Doubted, Being Assured', if the cogito (I think, I am) offers absolute reassurance of our existence, it intensifies the problem about the existence of others. That is,

> if my essence is thinking, if this is what I know human existence to be, then to know the existence of another human, I must know that

other's thinking. But when I turn to examine the possibility of there being other beings, try to meet a like, another human mind, I see, hear, touch only what might be called human bodies.[4]

Thus the Cartesian certainty of self-existence produces a profound uncertainty about the existence of others. And – ironically – that uncertainty rebounds back on myself. To quote Cavell in *The Claim of Reason*:

> The question about whether there are other minds is exactly as much a question about me as about anyone else. If anyone is an other mind, I am one – i.e. I am an other to the others .... Then the question is: Do others know of my existence?[5]

It is for this reason that Cavell, unlike other contemporary philosophers such as Slavoj Žižek, Jean Baudrillard or Alain Badiou, is relatively uninterested in films such as *The Matrix* (Lana and Lilly Wachowski, 1999), *Fight Club* (David Fincher, 1999) or *Existenz* (David Cronenberg, 1999). Such works stand in a long tradition of films that contrast 'worlds of the everyday with words of the imaginary', in which the visible world is illusory but there is a real, intelligible world out there waiting to be discovered, if only one can unlock the right door or take the right pill.[6] Why worry about what's behind the door when the person sitting in the room with us is already a mystery?

So how *can* we know that other beings exist? And even if they do exist, how could we know that they experience the world – see the world, understand it – as we do? We might return here to Wittgenstein's example of the *word* 'pain' and its relation to the *experience* of pain. How do we know if someone else is in pain? It's insufficient that they demonstrate a set of behaviours that fit our criteria for being in pain (screaming, wincing, saying 'ouch') since they may be only pretending to be in pain. At best, then, we can say that the person is *expressing* pain. In any case when we frame the question of pain in terms of knowledge, Cavell says, we are leaving something out. That something is not the pain itself – how it feels – but our response to the pain. That is, when we are faced with a person showing signs of pain, we are asked for something other than a statement of facts. We are asked for 'comfort, succor, healing; for a response which helps to assuage the pain to or to acknowledge that it is unassuageable here and now'.[7] We are asking not for knowledge but understanding.

> When I say 'He's in pain' (supposing I do, supposing that's what I have to say) my knowledge is expressed (roughly as his is, i.e. *analogously* with his?) by the fact that it is called from me, cried out (though we generally keep our voices down) ... Sometimes my problem will be *not* to cry it out, but to free my response *from* the other. Instead of responding to him from my freedom, I am engulfed by his suffering or anxieties, or by his opinion of me, or his hope for me; as may be. – But all this makes it seem that the philosophical problem of knowledge is something I impose on these matters; that I am the philosophical problem. I am. It is in me that the circuit of communication is cut; I am the stone on which the wheel breaks.[8]

Through film, Cavell is able to develop an idea that he first broaches in 'Knowing and Acknowledging', a late essay in *Must We Mean What We Say?*, and then again in *The Claim of Reason*. Simply put, part of knowing that another is in pain is knowing that the other's pain *demands a response* from me, and this being the case, knowing takes the form of acknowledging. This doesn't mean that the person who is in pain will always get the sympathy he or she may feel is deserved: we might, Mulhall suggests, feel irritated, dismissive, pleased or unmoved. The point is that such responses are failures of acknowledgement, and the applicability of the concept of acknowledgement is evinced as much by its failures as by its successes:

> It is not a description of a given response, but a category in terms of which a given response is evaluated ... A 'failure to know' might

just mean a piece of ignorance, an absence of something, a blank. A 'failure to acknowledge' is the presence of something, a confusion, an indifference, a callousness, an exhaustion, a coldness. Spiritual emptiness is not a blank.[9]

In short, when someone shows signs of pain, we cannot know they are in pain, but we must either acknowledge that pain or choose not to acknowledge it. What matters is not *what* we know but *how* we respond to what is in front of us. Once again it is action, rather than belief, that is important.

To sum up, the sceptic pictures the human being as split between an outside and inside. The outside consists of expressions and behaviour. The sceptic rightly argues that such expressions and behaviour might be deceitful. How, he asks, can we get beyond such outer displays to what we actually want to know – namely the feeling, thought or sensation? His conclusion is that we can never know or we can know only for practical purposes. Against this, Cavell argues that we often do know quite well how others are thinking and feeling. Not always. Not perfectly (which is what the traditional sceptic wants: to know perfectly or to abandon knowledge altogether). But sometimes, I do understand another. At the very least, I understand what he or she wants of me. The question is: what am I going to do about it?

In order to move away from questions of belief and knowledge and towards matters of behaviour, Cavell turns to the notion of acknowledgement, which is not something we know but something we *do*. Acknowledgement is not the opposite of knowledge; rather it acts on knowledge: 'From my acknowledgement that I am late it follows that I know I am late … ; but from my knowing I am late, it does not follow that I acknowledge I am late … One could say: Acknowledgement goes beyond knowledge … in its requirement that I do something or reveal something.'[10] Attempts at acknowledgement reveal us: who we take ourselves to be, how we picture our *relationship* to the other.

In a modern age in thrall to scepticism, the existence of the world and of others in it is 'not a matter to be known, but one to be acknowledged', he writes. More precisely what is to be acknowledged is this existence as 'separate from me'.[11] In the previous chapter we looked at some of the ways in which film might present us with the problem of scepticism about the existence of the world as well as some of the ways in which Cavell suggested film might help us to live through the sceptical crisis. That is, we saw how film might help us to acknowledge that the world exists separately from me, but that I must nonetheless try my best to engage with the world. One of the important discoveries of *The World Viewed* is the way in which film, by its very nature, calls our attention to parts of the world that we might otherwise overlook. Film allows us to look 'as if anew' at what is onscreen, in part by asking what might be unseen. As David MacArthur has it, film can reawaken 'the everyday powers of being fully alive to the expressions of others in word and deed' that we seem to have lost or neglected, 'through habit, familiarity, inattention, and dullness'.[12] This is the invisible that the medium of film is especially suited to render visible.

Let's look again at a passage from Cavell's article 'The Thought of Movies' that we discussed in Chapter 2:

> I understand it to be ... a natural vision of film that every motion and gesture and station, in particular every human posture and gesture, however glancing, has its poetry, or you may say its lucidity ... Any of the arts will be drawn to this knowledge, this perception of the poetry of the ordinary, but film ... democratizes this knowledge ... It says that the perception of poetry is open to all, regardless as it were of birth or talent, as the ability is to hold a camera on a subject, so that a failure to perceive, to persist in missing the subject, is ascribable only to ourselves, to failures of our character; as if to fail to guess the unseen in the seen, to fail to trace the implications of things – that is, to fail the perception

that there is something to be guessed or traced, right or wrong – requires that we persistently coarsen and stupefy ourselves.[13]

We can note here the similarities in the language that Cavell uses to describe the failure to acknowledge something in the example derived from Wittgenstein (pain) and the language he uses here to describe the failure to perceive something (the unseen). In both cases, Cavell asks us to pay attention to what is visible (pain behaviour, the ordinary) and to extrapolate something invisible (an inner life, poetry) by way of a response. The processes of perception and acknowledgement are thus intricately bound up with one another: hence the privileged relationship of film – a medium that foregrounds perception – to the overcoming of scepticism.

But *The World Viewed* also suggests that what scepticism poses a threat to is the *ordinary*: the everyday things, people and situations whose familiarity makes them all but invisible to us. (Wittgenstein famously remarked that 'the aspects of things that are most important for us are hidden because of their simplicity and familiarity. (One is unable to notice something – because it is always before one's eyes)'.)[14] It does this by disconnecting us from the world: firstly through the break in the natural relation and secondly through our attempts to overcome this break, attempts that, paradoxically, push the world further away. Thus, Andrew Klevan points out, Cavell understands the avoidance of acknowledgement, the surrendering to the burden of scepticism, as 'nothing less than a modern tragedy'.[15] It is tragic

> not only because of our vulnerability to knowledge, but also because of the vulnerability *of* knowledge itself, of its inadequacy: we are endlessly dissatisfied with the world as we see it and we wish for something more of it. In wishing to escape our subjectivity, in craving to be present to the world, we transform it into something capable of satisfying this yearning.[16]

But that transformation comes at the expense of seeing the world as it is. Crucially, as Cavell conceives it, we need to float away from everyday life because the ordinary world does not satisfy our hunger. The harder we grasp at the world, the further it slips away from us. This is, for Klevan, the paradoxical tragedy of the sceptic: 'He foregoes the world for just the reason that the world is important [and] finds that it vanishes with the effort to make it present.'[17]

Recovering the world is therefore not a matter of imposing our will upon it but of 'finding a way back to the ordinary, our everyday immersion in and acceptance of the world, and our everyday acknowledgement of others', as David MacArthur has it.[18] *The World Viewed* suggests that film can help us to do that by reanimating our powers of perception. Film shows an affinity for the ordinary as it is described by Emerson, who asks not for the 'great, the remote, the romantic', but 'the familiar, the low [...] The meal in the firkin; the milk in the pan; the ballad in the street; the news of the boat; the glance of the eye; the form and the gait of the body'. Cavell connects Emerson's emphasis on the low to both ordinary language philosophy and to film, suggesting that this list epitomizes a 'physiognomy of the ordinary' that pre-empts the invention of photography. It is film's unique ability to call our attention to the milk in the pan and the glance of the eye, and this ability accounts for its poetry, its sublimity.

Film's special power lies not only with perception but also with exemplification. The use and giving of examples is a key theme of *The Claim of Reason*, Cavell's great study of scepticism; it is also at the heart of his book *Pursuits of Happiness*, published two years later in 1981. Here, Cavell turns to a group of seven films made during the 1930s and 1940s in order to demonstrate what it might look like to live through scepticism by re-engaging with the ordinary. The narratives of these films, which constitute a genre that Cavell calls the 'comedy of remarriage', are derived in part from Shakespearean comedy and revolve around the getting back together of a couple (ostensibly) already married and separated. Within them, marriage, as we will see, is closely linked to the everyday; the threat of divorce, meanwhile, is tied to the threat of scepticism. In the rest of this chapter, then, we will turn to that book in order to examine, with Cavell, how exactly acknowledgement as it is modelled in these films might help us to overcome the threat of scepticism and recover a world once lost to us. In so doing, we will also see how Cavell's consideration of the remarriage comedy allows him to think about scepticism beyond the limits of literature and philosophy, as well as paving the way for a turn, in subsequent work, towards a more explicit engagement with questions of ethics.

From tragedy to comedy

Across a number of works, Cavell draws on Shakespearean tragedy in order to demonstrate that the tragic is – at least within these plays – the result of a failure of acknowledgement. In 'The Avoidance of Love', for example, the last essay in *Must We Mean What We Say?*, he argues that the tragedy of *King Lear* results 'not from the failure of knowledge but from the horror of its success'.[19] Lear's demand of his three daughters that they profess their love for him expresses a desire to know their thoughts and through them the world itself, but it results in Lear pushing away the one child who truly loves him. Thus Cavell describes Lear's actions as the avoidance of love. This avoidance of love might also be expressed from its reverse perspective: as the lengths to which we may go in order to avoid being revealed ourselves 'even to those we love and are loved by … [indeed] to other people it is easy not to be known'.[20] Likewise, Cavell's reading of Othello in *The Claim of Reason* emphasizes the tragic hero's obsession with certainty over his wife Desdemona. For Cavell, it is not Othello's doubt over Desdemona's faithfulness that seals his fate but his obsessive desire to know whether she has or has not been faithful. This desire is in itself the result of an avoidance of a genuine understanding or acknowledgement of Desdemona as a separate being with an inner life of her own. Othello demands being 'the whole world to his wife, as some sort of price for his joining her in wedlock'.[21] Unable to accept a wife over which he has nothing less than absolute control, he kills her and himself and so obliterates at the same any hope for connection with the world – falling under the sceptical impulse.

In order to avoid the tragedy of scepticism, Cavell thus concludes, we must be willing to let go of our desperate desire for knowledge. But how can we learn to do this?

> How do we learn that what we need is not more knowledge by the willingness to forego knowing? For this sounds to us as though we are being asked to abandon reason for irrationality ... or to trade knowledge for superstition ... This is why we think skepticism must mean that we cannot know the world exists and hence that perhaps there isn't one (a conclusion some profess to admire and others to fear). Whereas what skepticism suggests is that since we cannot know the world exists, its presentness to us cannot be a function of knowing. The world is to be accepted; as the presentness of other minds is not to be known, but acknowledged.[22]

The films discussed in *Pursuits of Happiness*, a book that Cavell describes as 'an expression of the relief in completing the study of scepticism and tragedy in *The Claim of Reason*', go some way to answering this question, presenting us with models of acknowledgement and describing the paths that the characters take to reach a point where they will happily abandon the pursuit of knowledge in favour of happiness – the implication being, of course, that the two ends are mutually exclusive.[23]

In this book, Cavell groups together seven films of the 1930s and 1940s: *The Lady Eve* (Sturges, 1941), *It Happened One Night* (Capra,

1934), *Bringing Up Baby* (Hawks, 1938), *The Philadelphia Story* (Cukor, 1940), *His Girl Friday* (Hawks, 1940), *Adam's Rib* (Cukor, 1949) and *The Awful Truth* (McCarey, 1937). *Pursuits of Happiness* proposes that the films it is concerned with are members of a genre, a genre that Cavell labels the 'remarriage comedy'. This is a genre derived from Shakespeare's comedies, and especially what Northrop Frye terms Old Comedy, in which it is the heroine, rather than the hero, who holds the key to the couple's union, and in which this union is not merely a coming together but a coming *back* together.[24] The grouping of these films under this particular moniker is – unsurprisingly, given the importance that Cavell places on words – both important and idiosyncratic. Elsewhere, these films tend to be referred as 'screwball comedies' and placed alongside other works such as *The Palm Beach Story* (Sturges, 1942) and *The Seven Year Itch* (Wilder, 1955).[25] Steve Neale, for example, states that *The Awful Truth* and *Bringing Up Baby* share many of the characteristics associated with screwball films: both emphasize gender equality, feature marriage as a central theme and share an energetic mix of slapstick, wisecracks, intricately plotted farce and the comedy of manners combined with vividly eccentric characterization and an undercurrent of sexual innuendo.[26]

Cavell, however, thinks about both the genre and genre itself somewhat differently from classical film theorists such as Neale. He insists that instances of a genre do not share a set of features that can in principle be completely specified. We may say that they share every feature, so long as we remember that firstly, what counts as a feature is not determinable except by the films themselves, and that any member of the genre may (and here Cavell is loosely in alignment with received genre theory[27]) 'evolve' the genre, losing certain features and compensating with innovations (in *The Awful Truth*, for example, the heroine's father is notably absent; however, her maiden aunt comes to stand in for this part). Cavell prefers to think of a genre's members as versions of a story or a myth: variations on a theme, we might say.

He describes the films under consideration in *Pursuits of Happiness* as inheriting 'certain conditions, procedures, and subjects and goals of composition' described in this myth. But at the same time he argues that the myth does not precede any of the individual films; rather it is something that the films construct and we reconstruct. Furthermore, the genre is not 'saturated' yet – there might be more examples to come – so the myth can only be provisional. Cavell therefore explains that he is not writing the history of the genre so much as proposing its logic.[28]

Since this logic, or myth, is at the very heart of Cavell's analysis of the films in *Pursuits of Happiness*, it is worth reproducing it in detail here.

> A running quarrel is forcing apart a pair who recognize themselves as having known one another for ever, that is from the beginning, not just in the past but in a period before there was a past, before history. This naturally presents itself as their having shared a childhood together, suggesting that they are brother and sister. They have discovered their sexuality together and find themselves required to enter this realm roughly at the same time that they are required to enter the social realm, as if the sexual and the social are to legitimize one another. This is the beginning of history, of an unending quarrel. The joining of the sexual and the social is called marriage. Something evidently internal to the task of marriage causes trouble in paradise – as if marriage, which was to be a ratification, is itself in need of ratification. So marriage has this disappointment ... And the disappointment seeks revenge, a revenge, as it were, for having made one discover one's incompleteness, one's transience, one's homelessness.
>
> ...
>
> the quarrel is going to have to take up questions about who is active and who is passive, and about who is awake, and about what happiness is and whether one can change ... Then the ending clarifies these themes by deepening the mystery of the pair's

connection. It is the man's turn to make the move – the woman had presumably started things with something called an apple, anyway by presenting a temptation; the man must counter by showing that he has survived his yielding and by finding a way to make a counter claim. To make a correct claim, to pass the test of his legitimacy, he must show that he is not attempting to command but that he is able to wish, and consequently make a fool of himself. This enables the woman to awaken her desire again, giving herself rather than the apple, and enables the man to recognize and accept this gift. This changing is the forgoing or forgetting of that past state and its impasse of vengefulness, a forgoing symbolized by the initial loss of virginity.[29]

The first half of this myth – in which a couple, once united, find themselves calling the validity of their relationship into doubt – echoes the structures of both Shakespearean tragedy and the sceptical crisis. An original intimacy is found to be lacking, and that lack produces a potent desire for reparation, a desire so strong that it threatens to destroy intimacy altogether: this is where we leave Othello, his marriage destroyed (to put it mildly!). Cavell claims that the idea of remarriage finds a precedent in Shakespeare's *The Winter's Tale* (a play often thought of as a romance rather than a comedy), in which a husband similarly doubts his wife's loyalty and desires to know the 'truth' (a truth which is not the real truth – that his wife is innocent – but is the truth he wants to hear – that she is guilty) with the result that he appears to destroy his family, but the story *does not* end there. Instead, in a second act, the heroes come to perceive something that they were hitherto blind to about the heroines, and between them the couple forgive the mistakes of the past and recommit to their future together. Mulhall adroitly points out that what is being modelled in this myth is both the acknowledgement of another person (one with their own inner life, subjectivity and 'truth') and the acceptance of the world itself. World-consuming revenge is overcome by acknowledging one's responsibility for it and by forgoing it; one's original intimacy with the world is not quite 'restored' as Mulhall would have it, as that would suggest a return to things as they were, but perhaps renewed, revived by acknowledgement of one's interest in the world, 'by finding a way to make one's claims upon it which is not the imposition of a demand but a wish to be claimed by it'.[30]

This is the narrative at the heart of the myth, but the journey from innocence to doubt to reconciliation, as it is described by Cavell and depicted within these films, has a number of other defining characteristics. Although Cavell accords them differing levels of importance in relation to each of the films he writes about, they nonetheless recur as structuring concerns throughout the seven chapters that make up *Pursuits of Happiness*. We can list them as follows.

1. The setting is domestic: the action takes place mainly in homes and occasionally offices.
2. The couple's relationship is childish, innocent and often somewhat chaste-seeming.
3. Reconciliation comes about by way of conversation – a conversation that is witty, full of *double entendres* and concealed meanings.
4. These are conversations between equals, and yet the question of who is learning what is an important one.
5. The plot begins in a city but gets resolved in a move to a world of nature – in Shakespeare this is called the green world; in four of the seven remarriage comedies it is Connecticut.
6. The atmosphere of these films – as a result, often, of the witty dialogue – is comic, festive.
7. But the films do not close with a grand celebration – a festival – that marks the end of the story. Rather, they place emphasis on continuation and the ongoingness of the conversations that we have witnessed: stressing remarriage as repetition.

Each of these characteristics contributes to the special manner in which the comedies of remarriage exemplify the overcoming of scepticism; in what follows I will briefly elaborate upon them, beginning with the domestic and working to the question of the festive, before moving on to examine how these themes play out in a specific example of one film, *The Awful Truth*.

The domestic

Given Cavell's interest in the ordinary, the significance of these films being set within the domestic sphere should be evident enough. As Cavell writes:

> If some image of human intimacy, call it marriage, or domestication, is [or has become available as] the fictional equivalent of what the philosophers of ordinary language understand as the ordinary, call this the image of the everyday as the domestic; then it stands to reason that the threat to the ordinary that philosophy names skepticism should show up in fiction's favourite threats to marriage, namely in forms of melodrama and tragedy.[31]

Since Cavellian scepticism manifests a threat to the ordinary, it is precisely against the most ordinary of backdrops that these dramas of scepticism and overcoming play out. Of course, these are Hollywood films and not neo-realist works and so 'ordinary' is here a relative term. As Cavell admits, the films under discussion in *Pursuits of Happiness*, often referred to as 'fairy tales for the Depression' (a description Cavell expresses some reservations about in the book's introduction), were films that 'took settings of immense luxury and that depicted people whose actions often concerned the disposition of fantastic sums of money'.[32] Indeed, he adds that a certain level of comfort is essential to these films' examination of what happiness is and what a happy marriage might look like, since these concerns are, in and of themselves, luxuries of a sort. Put simply, since these characters have had their basic needs more than met, they are free to concern themselves with the pursuit of happiness. Thus any economic issues that the films do present (for example, Clark Gable's haggling over his expenses in *It Happened One Night*) are understood by Cavell to be tropes for spiritual issues. (In an extended discussion of the relationship of these films to the Depression in the introduction to *Pursuits of Happiness*, we find hints at Cavell's later concern with moral perfectionism: drawing on Emerson and Thoreau he suggests that it is perhaps as important to concern ourselves with our own spiritual and intellectual development as it is to worry about the problems of the poor.)

So the domestic spheres these films inhabit are admittedly rather extra-ordinary: we might think of *The Philadelphia Story*'s splendid family mansion complete with pool, *The Lady Eve*'s ocean liner, *Adam's Rib*'s modern apartment with matching his and hers bathrooms. But this is not necessarily a problem, Cavell argues: a certain level of comfort is natural, since the films concern themselves rather more with higher concerns to do with happiness and equality than basic concerns about food and shelter. And the films are still concerned with the ordinary insofar as the action takes place within the home, the cradle of marriage, where husbands and wives wake every morning and go to sleep at night (where the workplace features, it is usually because the central romantic partnership is also professional). In the remarriage comedies, husbands do not impose their will on the world by murdering their spouses. Instead, divorce comes to symbolize the threat of scepticism. As such, marriage must symbolize the thing to which scepticism is a threat: the domain of ordinary life and language. In Mulhall's words, these films 'interpret the ordinary as the domestic' ('the life of a household, the domestication of desire in married life').[33] The ordinary – in the form of marriage – is what is at stake here.

Remarkably missing from this domestic setting, however, are children; this despite the fact that the central couples are often in their late twenties and early thirties. What is behind this absence? In a first instance, it simplifies the issue of divorce by removing the messy issue of custody (though in fact in many of these films animals come to stand for children, and *The Awful Truth* takes its central couple to court over the vexed issue of pet ownership). In a second, and related, sense, it simplifies the issue of marriage, which cannot be justified or authenticated by the presence of children. As William Rothman explains, 'the films' criteria for what makes a marriage worth having ... have nothing to do with perpetuating the patriarchal line'[34] – a fairly radical point which seems to be mostly overlooked in writing around Cavell and his responses to the women in these films. But the emphasis which these films place on childless-ness, on there being 'just enough for two' (a phrase repeated in both *The Philadelphia Story* and *The Awful Truth*), suggests that there is something more going on. For Cavell, this something is the fact that the absence of children allows the central couple to become childlike themselves. *The Philadelphia Story*'s central couple were literally once children together, but most of the other couples have also grown up together, however briefly – having gained experience as a result of their mutual interaction.

In *Bringing Up Baby*, the pair have only just met, begging the question of how we might exactly consider this a comedy of remarriage. For Cavell the answer lies in the fact that the majority of the film is given over to what he sees as Hepburn and Grant's attempts to create a past for themselves, inventing a shared childhood to which they can, at the film's end, return. When Grant and Hepburn begin *Bringing Up Baby*, they find each other annoying; it is only after they have created a childhood that they can share that each begins to discover the qualities in the other person that justify their attraction to one another. In a different but related manner, the films under consideration all begin in an atmosphere of cynicism and suspicion. The 'married' couples who populate these films are jaded, tired of one another or simply of life. Think of Barbara Stanwyck in *The Lady Eve*, archly sizing up her rivals for Henry Fonda's affections while spying on them in her pocket mirror. Or Cary Grant scheduling in his marriage (but no honeymoon!) between appointments in *Bringing Up Baby*. Or the mutual distrust that opens *The Awful Truth*, *His Girl Friday* and *The Philadelphia Story*. These couples seek to step back from such cynicism, to recover what Cavell, quoting Freud, describes as 'the mood of childhood, when we were ignorant of the comic, when we were incapable of jokes and when we had no need of humor to make us feel happy in our life'.[35] Often the couples (re)discover each other through playing. They play card games (*The Lady Eve*) and hide-and-seek (*Bringing Up Baby*); they play mother and father (*Bringing Up Baby*) or brother and sister (*The Awful Truth*); they play detective (*His Girl Friday*); they dress up (*Adam's Rib*, *The Awful Truth*) and they tell one another stories (*The Lady Eve, It Happened One Night*).[36] At the bottom of all this is a search for purity. Sophisticated as they are, these films 'do not depend on the physics of virginity but rather the metaphysics of innocence'.[37] Play is one way of engaging such a metaphysics; another, as we shall we see, is conversation.

Before turning to the way in which these characters talk to and with one another though, a note on the political significance of Cavell's emphasis on the heterosexual couple within these films (I will return to the matter of gender towards the end of the chapter). As we will see Cavell has received criticism for a lack of political engagement throughout his career. Such accusations are unfair in light of his work elsewhere on the idea of America and the nation's embrace of democracy. Still it's true, the film books in particular seem to avoid any sustained reflection on politics. Yet for Cavell the general always starts with the specific, and within *Pursuits of Happiness* and, later, *Contesting Tears*, the marriage – the meeting and ongoing involvement of two individuals with one another – is for Cavell both an allegory and a building block for broader societal relationships. This is not a heteronormative or conservative claim that positions the family as the basic unit of society. Rather, each encounter between subjectivities is an encounter between one individual and another, and marriage offers one of the most enduring and embattled examples of such an encounter. The question of gender is a vexed one within Cavell's conception of marriage, as we will see later in this chapter and in the next, but he does offer an example of a same-sex remarriage comedy of sorts in George Cukor's last finished film, *Rich and Famous* (1981), where the principal pair, who after years of comings and goings wind up at midnight in Connecticut with a kiss, is made up of two women, Candice Bergen and Jacqueline Bisset.[38] And in a 2006 essay 'The Incessance and the Absence of the Political', he comments that although the feature of a man and a woman constituting the central pair was not breached by any of the films made at the moment in American history at which the genre was established, 'there is intuitively no reason why the pair should not be realized by two men or by an interracial pair, et cetera'.[39] Cavell draws an analogy between the will to marriage and the will to knowledge (which he conceives of here as the capacity to put one's experience and the world into language). Both, he argues, are subject to limitations imposed by society. Both tell us something not only about the relationship but also about society more broadly: its expectations and horizons, its rules and agreements – a set of parameters that Cavell will link, in *Cities of Words*, to the social contract theory of John Rawls.[40] He gestures towards the repeated motif of the newspaper in the remarriage comedy, from the newspaper room setting of *His Girl Friday* and the very obvious presence of journalist and photographer Mike and Linda at the wedding of Tracey and George/Dexter in *The Philadelphia Story*, to the press coverages surrounding the Bonners's legal battle in *Adam's Rib* and Jerry's romance with heiress Barbara

Vance in *The Awful Truth*. In each of these films, Cavell suggests, the press mediates between 'society' marriages and the broader social community. In Robert Sinnerbrink's words,

> The presence of the press shows how the 'ordinary' can become news, a social ratification of the personal opening out 'beyond the privacy of privilege'; it also serves to ratify the society within which the characters exist as a 'locale in which happiness and liberty can be pursued' – offering, in short, an allegory of the free consent required for democratic community.[41]

Marriage is at the same time an individual achievement – a person moves from narcissism and privacy to objectivity and the acknowledgement of an other – and a social achievement, one that is public and subject to the laws of society.[42] (Which is not to say that privacy can't involve happiness or that publicness can't involve loss, as Cavell will make clear in *Contesting Tears*.) The way in which it bridges the divide is through conversation.

Conversation

We have seen in Chapter 2 that one of the ways in which Cavell took up ordinary language philosophy was by insisting that the meaning of any particular word or action must be determined anew in different circumstances. Speech and actions follow, alter or even make up their rules depending on what they are wanting to say to whom they are wanting to say it. For Cavell, the real breakthrough of ordinary language philosophy, as proposed by Austin, lies in the attention it gives to specific cases of communication without seeking to generalize them. Each instance of communication is not a matter of obeying a preexisting rule but of a negotiation with the prevailing conditions of language and the figuring out of a way to make oneself understood within them.

Understood in these terms, it should be clear that the problems that Cavell was tackling in *Must We Mean What We Say?* were, at least implicitly, bound up with questions of Cavellian scepticism, which would remain a primary philosophical concern throughout the rest of his career, although matters of moral perfectionism would come to play an equally important role later in his work.[43] As Rex Butler explains,

> Successful communication necessarily takes place against a background of potential misunderstanding or confusion: the inability to know or master the conventions that would say what we mean. The speaker cannot be certain that their words have conveyed the meaning that they intended, that they have successfully communicated their message to others. What we must do then is to recognise or, to use Cavell's word, 'acknowledge', those criteria or conventions that would help make us clearer and connect us to others. In the absence of a strict set of rules that tells us how to do this, we are ourselves responsible for the way in which we mobilise the available resources in order to get our message across. And it is that which our listeners respond to: not some unchanging meaning that remains the same in all circumstances, but the ongoing attempt to communicate in the always different circumstances that we, as speakers, and others, as listeners, both inhabit.[44]

As Cavell writes on the experience of hearing another complain of pain, 'Your suffering makes a claim upon me. It is not enough that I know (am certain) that you suffer. I must do or reveal something. In a word, I must acknowledge it.'[45]

The body of work discussed in *Pursuits of Happiness* demands the portrayal of philosophical conversation and hence 'undertakes to portray ... philosophical dispute'.[46] For this reason, Cavell places heavy emphasis on a film's dialogue, on its words. Not for nothing is the title of his introduction to this book 'Words for a Conversation'. It is important to Cavell, too, that each of these films features a long passage in which one or both of the principal characters attempt to articulate what marriage is and what the obstacles to it might be, often in very abstract terms (the concluding conversation of *The Awful Truth*, to which we turn in due course, epitomizes this predilection). When Cavell expresses an interest in a film's words, however, he means not words as they are written on the page of a screenplay (as is the case when he analyses the Marx Brothers' screenplays) but words as they are articulated by the characters on screen by the actors who play them: actors who are able 'to bear up under [an] assault of words, to give as good as you get, where what is good must always, however strong, maintain its good spirits, a test of intellectual as well as spiritual stamina, of what you might call "ear"'.[47] Delivered by Cary Grant, Katherine Hepburn, Barbara Stanwyck and James Stewart, these words 'declare their mimesis of ordinary words, words in daily conversation'.[48] That is, these films show us ordinary language in action. More than that, they show us how the use of ordinary language – through the trope of talking together – models a form of acknowledgement.

Comedy

Cavell explains that in these films 'talking together is fully and plainly being together, a mode of association, a form of life, and I would like to say in these films the central pair are learning to speak the same language'.[49] The ongoing attempt at communication lies at the heart of the comedies of remarriage. If married life is characterized by a sharing of a space (the home) and a life (through the promise of marriage), that sharing can only take place via a shared language. The tone of that conversation is, however, as important as the content. Conversation within these films is a source of pleasure, for both the audience and the central couple alike. Cavell refers to, after John

Milton, 'a meet and happy conversation'. In Milton's time, 'meet', used as an adjective, was synonymous with 'suitable', 'fitting', 'proper'. 'Happy' meanwhile evokes contentment, joy, smiles – possibly even laughs – and therefore ushers in the possibility for comedy and, beyond this, 'the tracking of the comedic to its roots in the everyday'.[50]

The remarriage comedies are comedies. But they are distinctive in their deployment of their comic elements. Cavell accounts for several features of the genre that differentiate it from other comic forms. The first of these is the lack of a traditional 'happy ending' to these films. Cavell repeatedly points to the absence of a concluding festival that marks the ending of these films and ties their loose ends together. Typically, that festival would be a wedding. The reason for this absence is embedded within the logic of the genre itself – these are not films about marriage, about getting married, about the wedding as an endpoint but rather about remarriage, about marriage as an event that is repeated every day in the everyday. These films end inconclusively. Cavell refers to their conclusions as 'aphoristic'.[51] They do not reward a good relationship with a happy ending but rather ask the couples at their centres to go on forging that good relationship, finding happiness 'alone, unsponsored, in one another, out of their capacities for forging a world, beyond ceremony'.[52] (Since no film 'fits' the model exactly, *The Philadelphia Story* does in fact culminate with a wedding; it is a wedding however that is absorbed into the everyday by being framed as a feature within a daily newspaper.)

Put otherwise, 'all of our life should be festival'.[53] The couples in these films are not only able to talk together but to laugh together. 'Not one laugh at life – that would be a laugh of cynicism. But a run of laughs, within life; finding occasions in the way [these couples] are together.'[54] And yet in the essay on *It Happened One Night* where Cavell references Milton, he comments that the form of discourse most readily associated by these films with marriage is bickering. He gives the example of *It Happened One Night*, in which Claudette

Colbert and Clark Gable pretend to be a married couple by 'bickering and screaming' at one another in a manner that is only slightly different from the bickering they have engaged in throughout the rest of the film.[55] Perhaps, Cavell speculates, bickering in this context is a sign of caring.

The centrality of bickering may also relate to a further feature that distinguishes these comedies from other comedy, which is that the obstacles that these characters face are not external to the relationship and the individuals within it, but internal. That is, the central 'problem' that these films work through is precisely how to talk and laugh together, and the only way for the characters to resolve it is to tussle with language, with values, and to learn to communicate better. Bickering is a step on this journey. So what is being corrected then is not an error but an experience or a perspective on an experience.

Repetition

The comedies of remarriage conclude not in an ever after but in a present continuity of before and after; they transform festival into festivity; they correct not error but experience. These three features lead Cavell to describe the remarriage comedies as 'diurnal comedies' or comedies of dailyness. He notes that reconciliation often occurs after a visit to what Nobert Frye refers to in Shakespeare as the 'green world' – a location away from the usual domestic setting, which in these films is in Connecticut – but adds that it is imperative that the couple return from the green world – that is, from their holiday in Connecticut – since in a sense the green world functions a little like Wittgenstein's frictionless ice. Put it this way: it's one thing to coexist peaceably in a world apart from the everyday stresses and pressures of the wider world – family, work, society and its expectations – it's another entirely to put one's relationship to the test in the ordinary world: a world that is banal, messy and ongoing. Hence marriage is conceived of by Cavell as remarriage: the decision to wake up each morning and commit oneself anew to the other person. There is no happy ending; there is only the beginning of a new day. This is why Cavell and the films that he considers within *Pursuits of Happiness* are diurnal: they stress what Stephen Mulhall calls the 'the unending succession of days that makes up the everyday'.[56]

In *Pursuits of Happiness*, marriage is not understood as a ceremony but as a mode of repetition. Cavell explains that

> the validity of marriage takes a willingness for repetition, the willingness for remarriage. The task of the conclusion is to get the pair back into a particular moment of their past lives together. No new vow is required, merely the picking up of an action which has been, as it were, interrupted; not starting over, but starting again, finding and picking up the thread. Put a bit more metaphysically: only those can genuinely marry who are already married. It is as though you know you are married when you come to see that you cannot divorce, that is, when you find that your lives simply will not disentangle. If your love is lucky, this knowledge will be greeted by laughter.[57]

That is, marriage involves repetition in that it asks those who would be married to repeat themselves, to repeatedly commit to the marriage. But it also asks them to be willing to accept the repetitiveness of the everyday: to put up with the boring, humdrum and banal. This itself brings us back to the question of scepticism, since to overcome scepticism is to accept the world as it is, rather than to seek to transform it. Andrew Klevan puts it well: 'To acknowledge and live with skepticism means not craving for something out of this world to satisfy our sense of the world, our touch with the world; instead, we must seek what is not out of the ordinary. This is how Cavell defines the everyday – as against the human yearning for things out of the ordinary'.[58] Klevan explains that quelling this yearning is crucial to overcoming scepticism: 'We must embark on a quest to find fascination in the parts of the world we share (not parts we create privately), even though it is exactly those shared things that might appear boring because of their obviousness and repetition.'[59] For Cavell, our problem 'will not be to find the thing we have always cared about, but to discover whether we have it in us always to care about something.'[60]

The Awful Truth

Let's turn now to one of Cavell's examples, to see how these themes play out within it. Cavell writes that *The Awful Truth* is 'the best, or the deepest of the comedies of remarriage': 'the only member of the genre in which the topic of divorce and the location in Connecticut are undisplaced'.[61] Certainly, *The Awful Truth* seems to exemplify Cavell's foundational myth very well. At the beginning of the film, Lucy (Irene Dunne) and Jerry Warriner (Cary Grant) are married, but in the film's second scene a disagreement sees them decide to separate. Jerry returns from a trip away (supposedly to Florida, but in the opening scene we learn that he has in fact been elsewhere) to discover that Lucy has spent the night with her music teacher, Armand. Lucy claims the night was chaste, a result of a broken-down car. Jerry is embarrassed in front of their mutual friends and refuses to believe her. Following this loss of faith, Lucy phones a lawyer to arrange a divorce. Despite the lawyer's protestations that marriage is a beautiful thing, their phone call is repeatedly interrupted by his nagging wife. The divorce is granted and Lucy and Jerry both take up with new potential partners: she with naïve Southerner Dan Leeson, he firstly with nightclub singer Dixie Belle Lee and then 'madcap heiress' Barbara Vance. Still, the pair continue to hanker after one another, though a series of misunderstandings between them prevent a reconciliation. The night before the final divorce decree, Lucy sabotages Jerry's relationship with Barbara by posing as his sister, imitating Dixie Belle's nightclub performance and once more embarrassing him in public. As the pair drive home from the party, Lucy deliberately wrecks the car, leaving them stranded in the vicinity of her aunt's cabin, where they decide to stay for the night. Jerry admits to having been a fool, and the pair are reconciled just before the clock strikes midnight.

The film opens in an atmosphere of doubt and suspicion. Following his opening admission that 'what wives don't know, won't hurt them', we, the audience, are already dubious about Jerry. When Lucy arrives home with Armand, Jerry, in turn, becomes suspicious (that this incident takes place before their friends foregrounds the social element of marriage). And when he tosses Lucy an orange marked not Florida but California, she, too, has reasons to believe he may not have been entirely honest with her. Since the film ends at the point of reconciliation but does not show us the morning after – that is, we precisely do not see in this film a return from the green country – we never see the Warriners happily married. Yet as David Macarthur writes, 'the task of the film is to make it, or its possibility, visible to us'.[62] Thus what we *are* shown is a divorcing couple who, through a more or less undramatic accumulation of comic scenes, we see to be as if made for each other: the 'awful truth' of the title. Throughout the film, Lucy and Jerry trade witty insults, and it is clear to the audience that they share a worldview that Dan and Barbara do not (although Dixie Lee is perhaps another story). They share some 'grand laughs' together, many of which could be described as in-jokes: references that the pair share that exclude others from their private universe. Often these jokes are at the other's expense: Jerry forces Lucy into an embarrassing spectacle of a dance with Dan; she embarrasses him by giving his wealthy would-be in-laws to understand that he's from an impoverished, lower-class background; he humiliates himself by barging in on a recital after mistaking it for a tryst. It's notable that the pair share a secret smile at these jokes, even as they express exasperation. It's important, too, that they perform these acts publicly, suggesting that although the publicness of marriage is important to this film, so too is what we might call a shared privacy. Cavell does not say it in so many words, but the film flirts with the border between 'me', 'you' and 'we' – 'us' and 'them' in a complex and fascinating manner.

It is the film's final scene, however, that receives the most extensive consideration from Cavell, and that has – as we will see – provoked the most discussion amongst Cavell's critics and admirers. Lucy and Jerry are in Connecticut, in her aunt's cabin. They have gone upstairs to sleep in adjacent rooms. Both are dressed in ill-fitting night garments, which Cavell says make them look like children. It is a blustery night, and the door that separates their room is faulty: it keeps blowing open. Jerry comes into Lucy's room, and the following dialogue takes place:

LUCY: It's funny that everything's the way it is on account of how you feel ... Well, I mean, if you didn't feel the way you do things wouldn't be the way they are, would they?
JERRY: But things are the way you made them.
LUCY: Oh, no. No. Things are the way you think I made them. I didn't make them that way at all. Things are just the same as they always were, only you're the same as you were too, so I guess things will never be the same again ...

Jerry retreats but a little while later returns to Lucy's room:

LUCY: You're all confused, aren't you?
JERRY: Uh-huh. Aren't you?
LUCY: No.
JERRY: Well, you should be, because you're wrong about things being different because they're not the same. Thing are different, except in a different way. You're still the same, only I've been a fool. But, I'm not now. So, as long as I'm different, don't you think that, well, maybe things could be the same again? Only a little different, huh?

This scene is perhaps the quintessential scene of remarriage. It is premised on repetition – we see Jerry return to Lucy's room three times, building into the scene an 'acceptance of repetition' that entails the 'acceptance of human relatedness'.[63] These returns imply Jerry's willingness for remarriage is a willingness for repetition: it shows communication as a series of attempts to find common ground. The pair seal the deal not with a marriage ceremony or even a clinch; instead a cut to a cuckoo clock, which has been steadily marking the minutes until the couple's divorce is finalized, shows a little male figure following his female counterpart into the tiny Swiss cottage. The pair literally move into the clock, the constantly rotating hands of which mark the ongoing sweep of time. Instead of the festival of marriage – or sex – then, what we are left with is the festivity of this closing scene, a festivity which, it is implied, will play out over the days and nights to come. Even more crucially for Cavell, the scene – and the film as a whole – perfectly exemplifies remarriage as the overcoming of scepticism because *it is not that funny*! That is, it lacks a 'knockout climax', which would mark the end of the farce. Instead, as Stephen Mulhall says, the film offers a 'contesting [of] the irregular outbreak of extraordinary comic events with a continuous line of unbroken comedic development, in order to suggest that the rhythmic recurrences of ordinary diurnal life provide fun and interest enough to inspire life and a commitment to its continuation'.[64] Andrew Klevan adds that the film's penultimate shot shows Jerry looking bemused, while Lucy giggles gently: implying that 'any commitment to married life will be without certainty' but will be made in the spirit not of the last laugh but of a continued commitment to laughter.[65]

A question lingers, however, over who is learning what from whom here. Certainly, the pair *as a pair* are learning to imbue their language with shared meaning, that is, to speak the same language. But it seems that rather than the woman being educated, or 'created', to use Cavell's term, by the man, it is Jerry who is finally coming to understand to

Figure 6 In the finale of *The Awful Truth*, Jerry returns to Lucy's room three times, building into the scene an 'acceptance of repetition' that entails the 'acceptance of human relatedness'. *The Awful Truth* (Leo McCarey, 1937).

Figure 7 Instead of the festival of marriage *The Awful Truth* closes with a shot of a cuckoo clock, which implies that the festivity of marriage will play out over the days and nights to come. *The Awful Truth* (Leo McCarey, 1937).

that, if he and Lucy are to stay together for ever – for *every day* that is to come – then he must scrutinize himself and his relationship to Lucy. We can compare this scene to the closing moments of *Adam's Rib* in which Amanda (Katherine Hepburn) and Adam Bonner (Spencer Tracy) discuss Adam's ability to cry on cue. Like that of the Warriners, their dialogue turns around the finding of shared meanings. ('Those were real tears', Amanda says of an earlier incidence of Adam crying, to which he replies, 'Of course they were, but I can turn them on at will', suggesting that real can mean both actual and authentic.) It culminates with a discussion of sameness and difference:

AMANDA: Alright. But what does that show? What have you proved?
ADAM: It shows the score.
AMANDA: It shows that what I said was true, there's no difference between the sexes: men, women ... the same.
ADAM: They are, huh?
AMANDA: Well, maybe there is a difference, but it's a little difference.
ADAM: Well, you know, as the French say ...
AMANDA: What do they say?
ADAM: *Vive le différence.*
AMANDA: Which means?
ADAM: Which means hurray for that little difference.

Adam and Amanda settle on the meaning of real and come to see, like Jerry and Lucy, that things – people – can be the same *and* different. Sharing a language does not require saying the same things. Quite the opposite, in fact: it is vital that we acknowledge our partner's separateness from us (this is precisely what Othello is unable to do). But in *Adam's Rib*, it is quite clearly Adam who has a lesson to teach Amanda: in this closing dialogue we see that it is she who asks questions and he who provides answers.

Figure 8 *Adam's Rib*: 'Vive le difference!' *Adam's Rib* (George Cukor, 1949).

Gender

In this much, *Adam's Rib* is true to Cavell's conception of the genre of the remarriage comedy as being about 'the creation of a new woman'.[66] Cavell also phrases this as 'the new creation of a woman' and 'a new creation of the human'.[67] He argues:

> Comic resolutions depend upon an acquisition in time of self-knowledge; say this is a matter of learning who you are. In classical romance this may be accomplished by learning the true story of your birth, where you come from, which amounts to learning the identity of your parents. In comedies of remarriage it requires learning, or accepting your sexual identity, the acknowledgement of desire. Both forms of discovery are in service of the authorisation or authentication of what is called marriage.[68]

For Cavell, the genre is partly defined by the fact that it is the woman who comes to accept her sexual identity, acknowledge her desire. He writes:

> The man's lecturing indicates that an essential goal of the narrative is the education of the woman, where her education turns out to mean her acknowledgement of her desire, and this in turn will be conceived of as her creation, her emergence, at any rate as an autonomous human being.[69]

The women of these films listen to their lectures, 'because they know they need to learn something further, about themselves, or rather to undergo some change, or creation, even if no one knows how the knowledge and change are to arrive'.[70]

So a woman wants to bring about a change in herself; she wants to be 'created'. And in order to do that she turns to a man, one is able to educate her. Within these films it can only be a man who educates her: she has no mother, no female friends. There is the odd spinster aunt, but Cavell has little to say about these figures. The creation of woman seems a sensible enough way of framing *The Philadelphia Story* (a film which has more in common with *The Taming of the Shrew* than *The Winter's Tale*). Perhaps it holds for *Adam's Rib*. But it works less well for *It Happened One Night*, *Bringing Up Baby* and *His Girl Friday*. Still less for *The Lady Eve*. Not least because, as Kathrina Glitre points out, within the narratives of these films, the male's lecturing is usually mocked or proven unsound.[71]

> Cavell cites Peter's lectures in *It Happened One Night* as key evidence: the equation of correctly dunking doughnuts with becoming autonomous is baffling; but ignoring the fact that it is Ellie who succeeds when Peter's hitch-hiking demonstration fails is inexcusable. Elsewhere 'lectures' are given by: Walter Burns/Cary Grant (*His Girl Friday*) – a proven liar, cheat and manipulator; David Huxley/Cary Grant (*Bringing Up Baby*) – who is constantly ignored; and Charles 'Hopsie' Pike/Henry Fonda (*The Lady Eve*) – who even Cavell acknowledged is 'treated to [a relentless] exposure of pompous self-ignorance.'[72]

One doesn't need to look too hard to see the paradox at the heart of the creation of 'the woman of equality' by the man.[73] How is it possible, exactly, that a marriage of equals is premised on the man's education of the woman? And what does it mean that *The Awful Truth* seems to avoid this paradox (and yet that Cavell fails to acknowledge this particular difference?). In separate articles, Glitre and Catherine Constable criticize Cavell's inability to grant Lucy the same autonomy that the film grants her. Constable flags up an important mistake that Cavell makes, in misattributing a key speech to Jerry. The lines 'Don't you see that there can't be any doubt in marriage? The whole thing's built on faith and if you've lost that, well, you've lost everything' are, in fact, spoken early in the film by Lucy and are, to Constable's mind, indicative of a remarkable consistency in her conception of marriage.[74] Constable argues that it is Lucy who teaches Jerry how to change in *The Awful Truth*, while she herself remains unchanged. Constable agrees with Cavell that Lucy's performance of Dixie Belle's routine teaches Jerry to see something but argues that what Lucy adds to the routine – the difference in the repetition – is an element of comedy that springs precisely from the fact that beneath the performance lies 'the real Lucy', the one who is as she always was. As such, she demonstrates to Jerry that what distinguishes her from other women is, firstly, her un-sexiness (she is not available to other men), secondly, her humorousness (she is funny, but only to Jerry) and finally, her constancy (she is the same old Lucy). Cavell understands Lucy's differential repetition as a willingness to change, one that requires a reciprocal response from Jerry. Constable understands it as a declaration that she has not changed, that Lucy is faithful and always was faithful. It is Jerry's perspective that has to change. It is, she points out, Jerry who enters Lucy's room to bring about the reconciliation at the film's end, just as it is the male figure that has to follow the female figure into the Swiss clock.

In the same vein, Katharina Glitre argues that *The Awful Truth* revolves around not Lucy's but Jerry's re-education – his coming to fully appreciate the nature of marriage within Lucy's terms.[75] She criticizes Cavell for assuming that remarriage comedies revolve around man's re-education of the woman, thereby failing to appreciate the films of the genre that challenge and reverse this gendered dynamic. In this particular case, she argues that the rupture between the couple is caused not by Jerry's doubt over Lucy's faithfulness but by his discovery that Lucy has a life of her own. It is the shock of discovering her autonomy that proves too hard to bear. The task for Lucy is then to teach Jerry to acknowledge that autonomy and live with it. Cavell's repeated characterization of Lucy's desirability in terms of passivity results in her ultimate subordination to Jerry's desires: 'she gives rise to herself, recreates herself ... *in his image*, though it is an image he did not know he had or know was possible in this form'.[76] Constable and Glitre point out that in constructing female desirability as conformity to a male defined image, Cavell overlooks the ways in which Lucy teaches Jerry to see her *as she wants to be seen*.[77] When Jerry repeats Lucy's words about faith in marriage to Barbara towards the film's end, adding 'I think I read it in a book or something', he is unconsciously revealing he has learned a lesson from Lucy.

Glitre concludes that Cavell's writing on the remarriage comedy is underpinned by 'a level of patriarchal assumption', the effect of which is to overemphasize the education of the female at the expense of the male, leading to an unbalanced view of the cycle's conflicts and resolutions. Glitre is not the only critic to find such a problem in Cavell's work. We will return to the question of gender, which poses itself more urgently in relationship to Cavell's writing on the melodrama of the Unknown Woman, in the next chapter. We shall also see, in Chapter 5, how Cavell's reframing of these films through the lens of moral perfectionism allows him to find a mutuality in these relationships that an approach centred around scepticism and its overcoming perhaps does not. For now, let us say that Cavell is not unaware of how thorny the question of gender is in relationship to these films, and indeed he sees the fitness of the man for his educative task as a central question of comedies. The women *choose* these men to educate them, Cavell argues. It is part of the film's business to demonstrate what 'authorizes' this choice. So there is something very complex happening within these films regarding the question of who educates whom, who recognizes the potential in another and who is able to bring that potential to light.

We can clarify something about gender and Cavellian scepticism by turning to the myth of the Fall – which, as we know, Cavell sees as being in a sense the foundational myth of scepticism. Cavell's work is scattered with references to the Fall. He claims that the remarriage comedies pose the question of 'whether the pair of a romantic marriage whose ambitions of intimacy are apt, *outside Eden*, to trail a history of pain and misunderstanding … can become and stay friends'[78] and summarizes the myth of the remarriage comedies along the lines of the Genesis story. Let's look again at part of Cavell's description of the founding myth of the comedy of remarriage:

> It is the man's turn to make the move – the woman had presumably started things with something called an apple – anyway by presenting a temptation. The man must counter by showing that he has survived his yielding and by finding a way to enter a claim. To make a correct claim, to pass the test of his legitimacy, he must show that he is not attempting to command but that he is able to wish, and consequently to make a fool of himself. This enables the woman to awaken her desire again, giving herself rather than the apple, and enables the man to recognize and accept this gift. This changing is the forgoing or forgetting of that past state and its impasse of vengefulness.[79]

The man eats the apple and gains knowledge – this is the Fall. But part of this knowledge is that she knows something and he does not. So the Fall consists of the woman realizing that her view of the world is subjective ('I know a taste that you do not know'); she gets there first, that is. The remarriage comedies seem aware of this origin story – *The*

Awful Truth begins with an orange being tossed from Lucy to Jerry (presumably, Cavell supposes, an apple would have been too obvious); *The Lady Eve* (note that title) opens with a snake in a garden and shortly later Jean clonks Charles on the head with an apple; *Adam's Rib* spends its duration mulling on whether women are indeed made for men – or whether men and women might instead be made for one another. In the comedies, the man's ignorance is played for laughs; his surpassing of vengefulness is expressed in his willingness to be silly, to sacrifice authority over the world.

The sexes take different paths to overcome scepticism. They have to, since their difference is embedded in the foundational myth of scepticism, at least as Cavell sees it. But to be different does not necessarily mean unequal. On the contrary, as opponents and friends they are loosely matched. And what the films model is not only the myth of the Fall but also its overcoming. The remarriage comedies show us that acknowledgement of another person goes hand in hand

Figure 9 The myth of the Fall: in *The Awful Truth* Lucy handles an orange – a substitute for the apple Eve hands Adam. *The Awful Truth* (Leo McCarey, 1937).

with acceptance of the world. World-consuming revenge is overcome by acknowledging one's responsibility for it; one's original intimacy with the world is recovered by acknowledging one's real interest in it, its capacity to elicit and satisfy one's desires, and crucially, 'by finding a way to make one's claim upon it which is not the imposition of a demand but the expression of a wish to be claimed by it'.[80] Hence William Rothman's claim that 'the genre that *Pursuits of Happiness* studies is committed to is a philosophical way of thinking that confirms the possibility, and necessity, of radical change' refers to a change not only in ourselves and our relationship to one another but a change in the way we view the world.[81]

Conclusion: A meet and happy conversation

There is no such thing as a perfect marriage in the comedies of remarriage. The couples who populate the films that Cavell discusses here are forever in *pursuit* of happiness, not in possession of it. This pursuit is visualized by the repetitive coming togethers of *The Awful Truth*; the celebration of difference in *Adam's Rib*; the shot in *It Happened One Night* in which Clark Gable and Claudette Colbert walk away from us into the horizon, mostly silent, side by side. What is happening in this latter scene? In Cavell's words, it is the end of something and the beginning of something.[82] A kinship has perhaps been recognized; an affinity established. The couple are embarking upon an endless journey towards something better and something endlessly out of reach. How they get there matters little to Cavell; what is important is that they do whatever it is together, 'even that they would rather waste time together than do anything else – except that no time they are together could be wasted'.[83]

The sentiment behind this statement – that the relationship matters more than the actions that make up that relationship – finds

Acknowledgement, Other Minds 133

Figure 10 *It Happened One Night*: The couple are embarking upon an endless journey towards something better and something endlessly out of reach. *It Happened One Night* (Frank Capra, 1934).

an echo of sorts in Cavell's assertion, itself an echo of line of thinking in *The World Viewed*, that 'no event within a film (say, no gesture of framing or editing) is as significant (as "cinematic")' as the event of film itself.[84] What Cavell means by this is that any shot, object, performance or other media is only important insofar as it occurs in a film that *matters to us*. 'To express their appearances, and define those significances, and articulate the nature of this mattering, are acts that help to constitute what we call film criticism.'[85] Cavell is drawing a tacit link here between the marriage and philosophical criticism. In both cases, what is at stake is a matter of care. Time and again in *Pursuits of Happiness*, Cavell describes the films under discussion as things that he cares about. He describes himself as 'attached' to them.[86] He compares his relationship to *Bringing Up Baby* with that of David, the film's hero, to Susan, his would-be wife. Like David, Cavell is prompted to ask: 'What am I doing here, that is, how have I got into this relation and why do I stay in it?'[87] The answer, he discovers, must come at least in part from the film itself.

Cavell thus conceives of the relationship between critic and film as a kind of meeting of subjectivities. If we care about these films, Cavell tells us in his discussion of *It Happened One Night*, then we should be attentive to them, we should attempt to understand their gestures and symbols, to hear what it is they are trying to tell us: that is, to speak their language. Recall Cavell's claim in *The World Viewed* that film – all film – exists in a state of philosophy. It is inherently self-reflexive and takes itself as an inevitable part of its craving for speculation. The films under consideration in *Pursuits of Happiness* offer ample evidence for this claim. They should therefore be acknowledged; we should let them teach us how to think about them and our relationships to them. Like the couples at their centre, 'we have neither to know them nor to fail to know them, neither to objectivize nor to subjectivize them'.[88] Acceptance, acknowledgement and overcoming are all, ultimately, about relinquishing (attempts at) control. 'There is nothing and we know there is nothing we can do.'[89]

Correspondingly, we, as critics, must learn to have authority over our experience of the films, to trust in our experience of them. Cavell takes pains to establish that each reading in *Pursuits of Happiness* is at once an interpretation of a film and an account of Cavell's *experience* of a film, at once criticism and philosophy, at once an experiential commitment to being 'guided by our own experience but not dictated to by it', to letting 'the object or the work of your interest teach you how to consider it', to subjecting a given experience and its object 'to the test of one another', and to educating 'your experience sufficiently so that it is worthy of trust'.

> One learns that without this trust in one's experience, expressed as a willingness to find words for it, without thus taking an interest in it, one is without authority in one's own experience …. I think of

this authority as the right to take an interest in your own experience .... Think of it as learning neither to impose your experience on the world nor to have it imposed upon by the world.⁹⁰

Cavell does not yet connect this joint striving – between film and viewer – towards an endlessly deferred ideal to the idea of moral perfectionism, which is the central concern of his subsequent work on film and indeed of his philosophy more broadly. And yet it is, to borrow a phrase from William Rothman, 'curiously submerged' within *Pursuits of Happiness*.⁹¹ After working out, in *Contesting Tears*, the significance of Emerson's work to thinking about both scepticism and ethics, perfectionism surfaces fully formed in *Cities of Words*, where Cavell reframes certain members of the remarriage genre in terms of perfectionism. Of course, it is natural Cavell should return to these films, since repetition and rediscovery is at the heart of acknowledgement. In his own, beautiful words, 'A work one cares about is not so much something one has read as something one is a reader of; connection with it goes on, as with any relation one cares about.'⁹²

5

Self-Reliance

When a few years ago I was asked to say how as a philosopher I had become interested in film, I replied by saying, roughly, that the inflection more pertinent to my experience was how a lost young musician had come to recognize his interests as philosophical, one whose education (in narrative, in poetry, in song, in dance) had been more formed by going to the movies than reading books. I might have included listening to the radio along with going to the movies, since, interweaved with many other matters, broadcasts were the primary attestation I had growing up of high culture as a shared world, of ours as a reformable world, not merely endurable.
–Cavell, *A Pitch of Philosophy*

To become a mother, I feared, was to relinquish your status as the protagonist of your own life
–Ariel Levy, *The Rules Do Not Apply*

In an essay on King Vidor's 1942 melodrama *Now, Voyager*, Cavell explains his motivation for writing about the film as his *caring* for the film. Because he cares about the film, he writes, he is driven 'to find words for it that seem to capture its power of feeling and intelligence, in such a way as to understand why we who have caused it (for who it is made) have also rejected it, why we wish it both into and out of existence'.[1]

Now, Voyager is one of four films that Cavell discusses in *Contesting Tears* under the banner of the 'melodrama of the unknown woman':

a group of films that have to his mind suffered critical neglect and are in many ways as misunderstood as the heroines that populate them. This genre is derived from the comedy of remarriage, and it reiterates many of the earlier genre's themes and concerns. And yet its fate has been altogether different. Part of Cavell's project in *Contesting Tears* is to understand why these melodramas have been so often overlooked by scholars and critics and what it is that they do that the comedies don't. At the same time by turning away from the comedies towards this cognate genre, Cavell is able to understand something about the comedies that remained unarticulated in *Pursuits of Happiness*. This something has to do with their relationship to what Cavell calls 'moral perfectionism'.

Morality – and in particular its connection to scepticism – has long been a theme of Cavell's work. *The Claim of Reason*, for example, has a whole section devoted to 'Knowledge and Morality', while it is a central argument of *The World Viewed* that there is a 'serious moral philosophy internal to the stories that movies are forever telling'.[2] Cavell does not use the term 'perfectionism' in *Pursuits of Happiness*, but it is an implicit theme, one that surfaces briefly in Cavell's invocation of Matthew Arnold's idea of the 'best self' existing in every one of us, claiming that 'more natures are curious about their best self than one might imagine, and this curiosity Arnold calls the pursuit of perfection'.[3] It will become an explicit concern in *Cities of Words*. Sitting between these two books, *Contesting Tears* is commonly held to be the work in which Cavell finally realizes the significance of film and perfectionism to one another, following as it does *Conditions Handsome and Unhandsome*, in which perfectionism is Cavell's central topic. And yet Cavell only makes two mentions of perfectionism within the whole book, one in the chapter devoted to *Now, Voyager* and one in the book's introduction. Both are made in reference to the films discussed in *Pursuits*. So perfectionism still does not emerge as a central theme in *Contesting Tears*.

What *is* front and centre within *Contesting Tears* is the work of Ralph Waldo Emerson, from whom Cavell develops the notion of perfectionism as 'a dimension or tradition of the moral life'.[4] Cavell explains in *Conditions Handsome and Unhandsome* that 'there is no closed list of features that constitute perfectionism' since he conceives of it as 'embodied in a set of texts spanning the range of Western culture'.[5] The list of these texts that 'may not otherwise be thought of together' takes up a whole page of *Conditions Handsome and Unhandsome* and includes Plato's *Republic*, the Gospel according to St Matthew, Shakespeare's *Hamlet*, John Stuart Mill's *On the Subjection of Women*, Matthew Arnold's *Culture and Anarchy*, Sigmund Freud's *The Interpretation of Dreams*, Thorstein Veblen's *Theory of the Leisure Class*, Henrik Ibsen's *A Doll's House* and (and notably Cavell adds here in parentheses 'the films') *The Philadelphia Story* and *Now, Voyager*.[6]

Since, as Cavell tells us, there is no such thing as perfectionism except as it arises from these texts, then it is no exaggeration that *Now, Voyager*, along with the other films considered in *Contesting Tears*, forms the idea of perfectionism for Cavell. It will be part of my argument in this chapter that, alongside *Conditions Handsome and Unhandsome*, *Contesting Tears* marks a turn away from scepticism as Cavell's first concern and towards the explicit moral philosophy that will shape Cavell's work to come. This is a simplification, since scepticism and its overcoming remain a structuring theme in Cavell's later work. We might say these themes find a counterpart in – or marriage with – Emerson's ideas of conformity and self-reliance. But it is nonetheless the case, as we will see, that *Contesting Tears* serves as a hinge between epistemology and ethics and that the book itself turns upon a notion of self-reliance developed from Emerson. Cavell is not yet framing his engagement of film with Emerson in terms of perfectionism – it won't be until *Cities of Words* that ethics becomes an explicit topic within Cavell's film writing. But it is in this book – the writing of which reveals to Cavell a latent interest in gender, one that he will put into contact with psychoanalysis – that Cavell seems not only to lay the foundations for his work on perfectionism but also to discover what these are. Let us begin this chapter in earnest, then, with an overview of Emerson's thought and how it is taken up by Cavell.

Emerson

Emerson first appears in Cavell's work (alongside Thoreau) as the answer to a question that ordinary language philosophy posed for Cavell but could not answer. In *The Senses of Walden* and again in *The Claim of Reason*, Cavell had drawn a connection between Austin, Wittgenstein, the ordinary and sceptic, a connection that is reflected by film, as we see in *The World Viewed*. The ordinary language philosopher, Cavell argues, feels that our relationship to the world's existence is somehow closer than the ideas of believing and knowing are able to convey. That is, we lack the language to account for our relationship to the world: 'What still wants expression is a sense that my relation to the existence of the world is not given in words but in silence.'[7] Ordinary language philosophy thus reveals the problem with existing accounts of our relation to the world but does not offer an alternative account or way of speaking that could better capture that relation.[8] How might we describe our existence in the world? What words can we use? Attempting an answer, Cavell turns first to Thoreau (in the original version of *The Senses of Walden*) and then, later, Emerson (in the expanded edition of that book and subsequent work, notably *Conditions Handsome and Unhandsome*, which is the edited text of three lectures delivered to the American Philosophical Association's Pacific Division in 1988).

Emerson and Thoreau are the apotheosis of another ongoing interest of Cavell's, romanticism. Fragments of a romantic theme can be found in both *The Claim of Reason* (the progress of which 'kept being deflected by outbreaks of romantic texts'[9]) and *The World Viewed*. The theme is given its fullest treatment, however, in *In Quest of the Ordinary*, in which Cavell, citing William Wordsworth, investigates the manner in which romantic writing makes 'the incidents of common life interesting'.[10] Cavell considers Emerson and Thoreau America's belated romantics, whose work foreshadows the occupations central to ordinary language philosophy. He writes that 'the sense of the ordinary that my work derives from the practices of the later Wittgenstein and from J.L. Austin, in their attention to the language of ordinary or everyday life, is underwritten by Emerson and Thoreau in their devotion to the thing they call the common, the familiar, the near, the low'.[11]

Both Thoreau and Emerson, in different ways, diagnose the state of sceptical despair that characterizes modernity. Thoreau famously claims, for example, that the majority lead lives of 'quiet desperation', while Emerson points to his fellow man's tendency towards conformity and resignation. Both, too, hope for renewal, for the overcoming of sceptical despair. The way in which they do this is to write: to use language to convey the sense of intimacy with existence that Cavell describes. Thoreau captures this intimacy through his claim that we neighbour the world, that we are next to the laws of nature, that we are somehow *beside ourselves* (in a sane sense)[12]; Emerson through his idea of the near, or the low, and its marriage to the concept of self-reliance.

Emerson's writing, with its perception of the sublime in the everyday, has long seemed to Cavell a sort of premonition of film. Yet it seems that during the period he was writing *The World Viewed*, it had not yet fully dawned on Cavell to make the connection between the unique combination of the popularity and artistic seriousness of American movies, especially of the 1930s and 1940s, and the concerns of American transcendentalism. Emerson, as the philosophical forefather of Thoreau, is a sort of shadowy presence in *Pursuits of Happiness*, there most pressingly in his elevation of the ordinary and domestic ('the meal in the firkin; the milk in the pan').[13] One can gain a sense of the affinity that Cavell feels for Emerson in the following passage:

> By 'embracing the common', by 'sitting at the feet of the low', Emerson surely takes his stand on the side of what philosophers such as Berkeley and Hume would have called the vulgar. Unlike a certain line of thinkers from Plato through Nietzsche to Heidegger, for whom real thinking requires spiritual aristocracy, those English writers will not depart from and disdain the vulgar altogether. It is internal to their philosophical ambitions to reconcile their philosophical discoveries with views of the vulgar, as Berkeley does when, for example, he says that his denial of the real existence of bodies, or corporeal substance, does not deny the existence and reality of timber, stone, mountains, rivers, when taken in the vulgar sense or in the vulgar acceptation … His direct opponent is … the reputedly sophisticated philosopher. Like Descartes they appeal to uncorrupted human understanding over the head of established philosophy.[14]

Here Emerson is positioned as a champion of the everyman: an underdog hero willing to take on the high-flown sophisticates of established philosophy. We might think of him as Mr Deeds, socking it to the snobbish members of the Algonquin circle. He goes beyond even Hume and Berkeley, according to Cavell, in embracing 'the literature of the poor, the feelings of the child, the philosophy of the street, the meaning of household life'.[15]

In the face of the sceptical crisis, Romantics, as we discussed in Chapter 3, homed in on subjectivity and made it the route back to our conviction in reality. In a 1989 essay entitled 'Being Odd, Getting Even', Cavell explicitly links the self-consciousness demanded in Descartes's *cogito* to the work of Emerson and in particular to his idea of self-reliance. Emerson's basic philosophical faith, as expressed in his essay 'Self-Reliance', is that the ultimate source of truth is within ourselves. Any truth beyond ourselves is secondary, dim: we do not learn it; rather we recognize it (having already known it, somehow). For this reason, Emerson exhorts his reader 'trust thyself'; 'insist on yourself, never imitate', for 'what I must do is what concerns me, not what the people think', 'nothing can bring you peace but yourself'. Individuals, rather than institutions, wield authority, and the community is often a distraction to self-growth, in part because its demands take up time better spent on self-improvement and in part because it encourages conformity: doing what others think is right rather than what the individual thinks.

In 'Being Odd, Getting Even', Cavell argues that Emerson's 'Self-Reliance' proposes a new proof of human existence, one that expresses itself in the form of melodrama.[16] At the centre of the essay is a paragraph that begins 'Man is timid and apologetic; he is no longer upright; he dares not say "I think", "I am", but quotes some saint or sage. He is ashamed before the blade of grass or the blowing rose … they are for what they are; they exist with God today.' Cavell points out that the formulation 'I think, I am' is a reference to Descartes's Second Meditation, where the cogito is expressed in the following way: '*I am, I exist*, is necessarily true every time I pronounce it or conceive it in my mind.'[17] Emerson agrees that we exist only if we think, but he denies, effectively, that we do think. Since so many people are incapable of thinking for themselves, they are incapable of really existing: at best, they haunt the world. This haunting is the life of sceptic or, as Emerson calls it, 'conformity'. The reference to the rose and the grass connects this life to the Fall, implying that we are removed from nature as we are removed from our own natures. We are 'shamed' by our inability to claim our own lives. Emerson thus adds his own answer or argument to Descartes's: I am a being who, to exist, must not only say I exist, but acknowledge it – claim it, stake it, enact it. If romanticism can bring us back to the ordinary, it is only by a process of examining and consulting our own experiences by means of 'a momentarily stopping, turning yourself away from whatever your preoccupation and turning your experience away from its expected, habitual track, to find itself, its own track: coming to attention'.[18] Cavell interprets this consulting of one's own experience as 'authoring oneself'.

From comedy to melodrama

It is just such self-authorship that is at stake within the films discussed in *Contesting Tears*. Already, in 'Being Odd, Getting Even', Cavell had suggested that

> if some image of human intimacy, call it marriage, or domestication, is […] the fictional equivalent of what the philosophers of ordinary language understand as the ordinary, call this the image of the everyday as the domestic, then it stands to reason that the threat of the ordinary that philosophy names skepticism should show up in fiction's favourite threats to marriage, namely in forms of melodrama and tragedy.[19]

And we have seen that it is a lack of acknowledgement that constitutes the devastating outcome of Shakespeare's tragedies, including *Othello*. In the melodramas of the unknown woman, acknowledgement is once more wanting, but here tragedy is (mostly) avoided as a result of the woman's decision to take her fate into her own hands. That is, these films present us – arguably for the first time in any of Cavell's work – with the possibility of overcoming scepticism outside of marriage.

More than this, it is film's privilege to offer us this possibility of overcoming scepticism outside the couple. The remarriage comedies, as we saw, inherited (and perhaps updated) a conceit already familiar from theatrical comedy, notably Shakespearean comedy. Films such as *The Awful Truth* are therefore a variant on a theme: via different means/media, they reach the same end as other art forms. The melodramas likewise have a relationship to older art forms – tragedy, drama, romantic literature and also opera (to which we turn at the end of this chapter). But what they do with the concerns they inherit is uniquely cinematic: relying upon their deployment of genre convention and stars, as well as film form. In what follows, I will examine how, in *Contesting Tears*, the melodramas of the unknown women do not merely reflect Cavell's thinking on Emersonian themes, but they advance it. Effectively, the women who populate these films give birth to Cavell's version of perfectionism.

Cavell describes both the remarriage comedies and the melodramas of unknownness as 'working out the problematic of self-reliance and conformity as established in the founding American thinking of Emerson and of Thoreau'.[20] This working out is most evident in *Pursuits of Happiness* in Cavell's discussion of *It Happened One Night*.[21] Here, he argues that the heroine of that film is on a spiritual quest, like Emerson in his journals or Thoreau in *Walden*. A non-American example of a woman on similar quest that Cavell cites is Nora in Ibsen's *A Doll's House*. He explains:

> The Emersonianism of the films I have written about as genres depict human beings as on a kind of journey ... from what he means by conformity to what he means by self-reliance; which comes to saying (so I have claimed) a journey, or path, or step, from haunting the world to existing in it; which may be expressed as the asserting of one's own cogito ergo sum ... call it the power to think for oneself, to judge the world, to acquire – as Nora puts it at the end of *A Doll's House* – one's own experience of the world.[22]

At the end of Ibsen's play, Nora leaves her husband Thorwald in search of what she calls an education, but which might just as easily be called a transformation or metamorphosis – an entry into 'a new mode of existence'.²³

> NORA: I believe that before all else I am a human being, just as much as you are – or, at all events, that I must try to become one. I know quite well …. That most people would think you right, and that views of that kind [i.e. about how a woman's most sacred duty are to her husband and children] are to be found in books; but I can no longer content myself with what most people say, or what is found in books. *I must think things over for myself and try to get to understand them.*²⁴

Nora tells Thorwald that he is not the man to provide her with the education she needs, implying both that the education she requires is in the hands of men and that only a man capable of providing such an education could count for her as a husband.

Pursuits of Happiness poses the question of whether the pair of a romantic marriage 'whose ambitions of intimacy are apt … to trail a history of pain of misunderstanding' can become and stay friends.²⁵ Crucially, for Cavell, it is the woman who first considers this question and who must judge whether her male counterpart is capable of providing her with the education she needs. The book studies a set of films whose answer to this question is a 'Yes', albeit a conditional one. The melodramas studied in *Contesting Tears* each begin from the same premise: a woman asks herself whether the man in whom she is romantically interested will be able to educate her in the manner that she requires. In these films, however, the woman's answer to the same question is an unreserved 'No'.

The melodramas therefore bear an 'internal relation' to the remarriage comedies, one that has to do with the principal woman's demand for equality, mutual education, playfulness and transfiguration in marriage.²⁶ Like the heroines of the comedies, the heroines of the melodramas pose this demand to a man. Unlike their comedic counterparts however, the male characters in the melodramas do not rise to the challenge. Cavell explains that the underlying myth of the melodramas may thus be formulated in the following way: a woman achieves existence (or fails to) or establishes her right to existence in the form of a metamorphosis (or fails to), apart from or beyond satisfaction by marriage.[27] What both genres make clear is that while a good marriage is a thing to be desired, 'a marriage of irritation, silent condescension, and questionlessness' is not.[28] Indeed, it is better to remain in solitude, unknown: to take one's education out of the hands of men. It is as if the women of the melodramas are saying to their sisters in the comedies, 'You may call yourself lucky to have found a man with whom you can overcome the humiliation of marriage by marriage itself. For us, with our talents and tastes, there is no further or happy education to be found there; our integrity and metamorphosis happens elsewhere, in the abandoning of that shared with and exclusive appreciation.'[29]

Both the remarriage comedies and the melodramas emerge out of Shakespeare and Ibsen, Cavell tells us. But the latter is derived 'by negation' from the former.[30] That is, every feature that made up the foundational myth of remarriage comedy finds its opposite in the melodramas.

> For example, in the melodrama of unknownness the woman's father, or another older man (it may be her husband), is not on the side of her desire but on the side of law, and her mother is always present (or her search for or loss of or competition with a mother is always present), and she is always shown as a mother (or her relation to a child is explicit). With these differences in the presence or absence of parents and children goes a difference in the role of past and memory: in the comedies the past is open, shared, a recurring topic of fun; but in the melodramas the past is frozen, mysterious, with topics forbidden and isolating. Again, whereas in in remarriage comedy the action of the narration moves, as said,

from a setting in a big city to conclude in a place outside the city, a place of perspective, in melodramas of unknownness the action returns to and concludes in the place from which it began or in which it has climaxed, a place of abandonment or transcendence.

[...]

The chief negation of these comedies by these melodramas is the negation of marriage itself – marriage in them is not necessarily reconceived and therewith provisionally affirmed, as in remarriage comedy, but rather marriage as a route to creation, to a new or an original integrity, is transcended and perhaps reconceived.[31]

Much as was the case with the remarriage comedies, Cavell's conception of genre both draws upon and departs from more classical understandings of melodrama. Peter Brooks, for example, famously writes of melodrama as a 'mode of excess', in which the intense desires, hyperbolic emotions and Manichean struggles of characters exceed conventional representational frameworks. Unable to find expression through narrated speech or dramatic resolution, these emotional states 'spill out' through the mise en scène, music, cinematography or performance of the actors.[32] As a genre, it lends itself to psychoanalytic and ideological readings precisely because of this repressive process, whereby the psychological or social life of the characters is suppressed but 'returns' in the form of aesthetic or dramatic excess. And indeed, *Contesting Tears* sees psychoanalysis enter Cavell's purview in a manner hitherto unseen.

Up until this point in his work, Cavell's debt to Freud had, by his own admission, been fairly implicit.[33] In *Contesting Tears*, Freudian psychoanalysis becomes more central to Cavell's work. Of course, true to form, Cavell does not deploy psychoanalysis in line with other film theorists. Prior to *Contesting Tears*, film theory had drawn on Freudian psychoanalytic theory to explore both the 'unconscious' of the film text (analysing it for repressed contents, perverse utterances and evidence of the workings of desire) and aspects of the 'gaze', whether in terms of the viewer's identification with the camera's vision (as in the work of Christian Metz and Jean-Louis Baudry) or in terms of gendered looking (as in the work of Laura Mulvey, Tania Modleski and Mary Ann Doane).[34] Cavell does not directly engage these theories – although Modleski will engage him, in a crucial conversation which we will consider shortly. Rather he asks two questions that link film and psychoanalysis. Firstly, why it is that psychic reality first presents itself to psychoanalysis through the suffering of women? And secondly why, at the same time, is film more interested in the study of individual women than of individual men?[35]

Both of these questions are tied to his interest in scepticism. In short, Cavell concludes that there is a difference between what women know and what men know and that film is somehow aware of and interested in this difference. What's more, this difference is itself linked to the role of the human body in the sceptical problem of other minds, as well as to questions of voice and voicelessness.[36] Thus psychoanalysis raises once more the question of gender, to which we will now turn.

Gender revisited

In his introduction to *Images in Our Souls*, a collection of essays on the topic of Cavell, psychoanalysis and cinema, Joseph H. Smith writes that one of the ways Cavell links philosophy and psychoanalysis is by virtue of their shared (male) scepticism, and one of the ways in which he links psychoanalysis and film is by virtue of their both beginning with the overt suffering and covert wisdom of women.[37] What Smith realizes, perhaps even before Cavell himself does, is that Cavell's work on film genres is bound as much with the intersections between cinema and philosophical scepticism, and between tragedy and melodrama, as it is between scepticism and gender.[38]

The fitness of the man for his educative task is a central question for the comedies. What motivates the woman's choice of him to provide or authorize her education is open to investigation and criticism and never taken for granted. Cavell refers to a 'taint of male villainy' that attaches itself to these men, one which is most explicit in Peter Warne's assertion that what Ellie Andrews needs is 'a guy that'd take a sock at her, once a day, whether she deserves it or not', or in Adam Bonner's brandishing of a pistol at and dispatch of a slap to his wife.

Adam is redeemed by his ability to tread the line between a real pistol and a liquorice one, a slap and a slug. But the men of the melodramas are not equally able to recognize that expressions even of villainous antagonism shouldn't violate certain distinctions. There is an antagonism in the melodramas that displaces the 'battle of the sexes' play-fighting that runs through the comedies. Cavell gives names to the specific forms of villainy or inadequacy that these films show us: 'virtuosic self-absorption and compulsive seductiveness' (*Letter*), 'courteous but advancing irrelevance' (*Now, Voyager*), 'perceptual incompetence' (*Stella Dallas*), 'old-fashioned, fixated menace' (*Gaslight*). We will come back to some of these later in the chapter. While the amatory wars of the comedies were part of a struggle for acknowledgement, in the melodrama the players are not so evenly matched, and the struggle is renounced or avoided as a result of fear, ignorance or condescension. The woman's effort to understand why recognition by the man has not happened or has been denied is thus characterized by Cavell as a struggle over her gender.[39]

The suffering of women (or at least, the suffering of the women in these films) is of a different register to scepticism, nihilism or the doubts of men, Cavell writes in 'Psychoanalysis and Cinema: The Melodrama of the Unknown Woman', published in *Images in Our Souls*. What do women know?, he asks. Do they escape doubt? This might sound like a strange question, but it becomes clearer what Cavell is driving at when he returns to the example of *The Winter's*

Tale. In that play, the conflict between the central male (Leontes) and the central female character (Hermione) turns on the question not merely of her fidelity (as in *Othello* or *The Awful Truth*) but of whether he is indeed the father of the child that she says is his. From this, Cavell makes a somewhat confusing leap: connecting man's doubt as to whether his children are his to the problem of scepticism more widely and in the process suggesting that philosophical scepticism is 'a male business', to borrow a phrase from Smith and Kerrigan.[40] However, he swiftly caveats this suggestion, writing that this is not to say that women do not 'get in the way of skepticism', that is, suffer a crisis of doubt, but rather that the object of this doubt is different. Women might not doubt that their children are their own, but they may well doubt the suitability of the children's father. So Cavellian scepticism, in *Contesting Tears*, is once more a matter of asymmetry between the genders. Scepticism is not the same for a woman as it is for a man. There are certain certainties that women may have available to them that men do not. And men want to know what these certainties are – hence Othello's obsession with Desdemona's knowledge.

Cavell does not provide an immediate answer to the question of what the woman's privileged knowledge is. Instead, he makes a detour via the matter of the body's role in the sceptical problematic. 'To counter the skeptical emphasis on knowing what the other doubts and knows, I have formulated my intuition that the philosophical recovery of the other depends on determining the sense that the human body is expressive of mind', he writes, 'for *this* seems to be what the skeptic of other minds directly denies.'[41] He is guided in this intuition by, on the one hand, Wittgenstein's emphasis on the expressiveness of the human body, articulated in his famous remark that 'the human body is the best picture of the human soul',[42] and on the other by Emerson's remarks, in his essay 'Behaviour', that 'nature tells every secret once … but in man she tells it all the time, by form, attitude, gesture, mien, face and parts of the face'.[43] These philosophical expressions dovetail with Freud's belief that our bodies betray us: the theory that physical symptoms have their roots in psychological or emotional states known as conversion hysteria.

In Chapters 2 and 3, we discussed how film's capacity to record the human body makes it particularly well placed to reveal or draw our attention to the world, its objects and its inhabitants. It is part of the power of moving pictures to find interest in the most insignificant repetitions, turnings, pauses and yieldings of human beings.[44]

> Think of this interest or power as the camera's knowledge of the metaphysical restless of the live body at rest [...] Under examination by the camera, a human body becomes for its inhabitant a field of betrayal more than a ground of communication, and the camera's further power is manifested as it documents the individual's self-conscious efforts to control the body each time it is conscious of the camera's attention to it.[45]

In *Mr Deeds Goes to Town*, the climactic scene of which turns on the body's betrayal of itself, Deeds/Gary Cooper enters into a kind of contract with the camera whereby he offers himself up for scrutiny, and in return the camera, an emblem of perpetual visibility, affirms his existence. The price he pays for this is a perpetual embarrassment or self-consciousness. But it is important to note the terms in which Cavell expresses this self-consciousness: 'Psychologically, submission to [the camera] demands passiveness, you may say demands the *visibility of the feminine side of one's character*.'[46] In the crucial shot of Deeds playing the tuba, in which he reveals himself as thinking, he is posed, Cavell argues, 'as in a glamour shot of a *female* star.'[47] Let's not forget that this is a character who throughout the film is associated with the image of a fairy-tale princess, nicknamed by the newspapers the 'Cinderella man', and whose happy ending is achieved through 'his willingness to reverse roles with the woman', presenting himself as a damsel in distress in need of rescuing.[48]

We need to proceed with a little caution here, for if it seems as if Cavell is associating passivity with the female of the species, that is not necessarily the case. Rather, as Stephen Mulhall carefully phrases it, we are dealing with essentially passive forms of activity, which can be thought of as related to the feminine side of human character and can be said to constitute a proof of psychic reality that Cavell associates with the feminine side of the reality of human existence.[49] Still, it is telling that Cooper is one of the few male stars who Cavell believes can hold the camera's attention as an individual male (and here he is assuming, to some extent, the role of damsel in distress). Film's capacity to capture the human body comes more usually in the service of its fascination with the study of individual women, with the result that it is female stars who are best able to show us what it is to think on screen. The actresses that star in the melodramas of the unknown women all demonstrate this ability, but the actress who has raised it to its highest art is Greta Garbo.

Stardom and unknownness

Garbo is

> the greatest, or the most fascinating, cinematic image on film of the unknown woman. It is as if she has generalized this aptitude beyond human doubting – call this aptitude a talent for, and will to, communicate – generalized it to the point of absolute expressiveness, so that the sense of failure to know her, of being beyond us (say, visibly absent) is itself the proof of her existence .... Such in my philosophy is the proof of human existence that, on its feminine side, as conceived in the appearance of psychoanalysis, it is the perfection of the motion picture to provide.[50]

As Karen Hanson explains in her illuminating article 'Being Doubted, Being Assured' (which also features in *Images in Our Souls*),

Figure 11 Garbo, according to Cavell: 'the greatest, or the most fascinating, cinematic image on film of the unknown woman'. *Queen Christina* (1933, dir. Rouben Mamoulian).

Garbo's knowledge is internally linked to her absence.[51] Her screened unknownness is proof of her existence, both to us and to herself. In *The World Viewed*, Cavell describes how the film audience's absence from the world presented in film is something that we desire: our absence mechanically assured and not a function of our subjectivity. Garbo's absence, on the other hand, is a function of her subjectivity. Cavell finds her 'within a private theatre, not dissociating herself from the present moment, but knowing it forever, in its transience, as finite, from her finitude, or separateness, as from the perspective of her death'.[52] What she projects is her *knowledge* of her separation, her acceptance of her distinction. The image of Garbo thus teaches us the same lesson as Shakespearean tragedy and the comedy of remarriage, albeit through very different means. *We cannot know her*. This is what she tells us through her very being, and *this* is what we should acknowledge. It is a mistake to believe that we can ever know what another knows; humans are always separate from one another. It is only through acknowledging that separateness that doubt about another's existence can ever be overcome. Precisely what distinguishes acknowledgement from knowledge is that it can only ever take us so far.

While Garbo is the epitome of the unknown woman's capacity for private theatre, the women of the melodramas that Cavell discusses all share this ability to theatricalize the self. As characters, Paula, Lisa, Stella and Charlotte are unknown to their male counterparts (and others, too) in the sense that they are unacknowledged. As Charlotte Vale in *Now, Voyager*, for example, Bette Davis

> taps a genius for that expressiveness ... in which Breuer and Freud, in their *Studies in Hysteria*, first encountered the reality of the unconscious, the reality of the human mind as what is unconscious to itself, and encountered first in the suffering of women; a reality whose expression they determined as essentially theatrical, a theatricality of the body as such.[53]

But these women are also deliberately, *willingly* unknown. They make a display of their unknownness. This reminds others that they are beyond their knowledge. But importantly, this enacted unknownness also functions as a proof to themselves of their own existence: paralleling the cogito in much the same way as Emersonian self-reliance can be seen to do.

The visual evidence of this self-reliant proof takes the form of metamorphosis or transformation. Nowhere is this more in evidence than in *Now, Voyager*, in which Charlotte famously transforms herself from an ugly duckling into, if not a swan, then a kind of butterfly, via various incarnations (indeed the image on the cover of *Contesting Tears* shows Davis mid-transformation). Charlotte assumes various names and descriptions throughout her journey. She is, variously, Charlotte Vale, her mother's 'late baby' and 'ugly duckling' who refers to herself as 'my mother's companion' and 'servant'; 'the fat lady with the heavy brows and all the hair'; 'Aunt Charlotte'; 'Camille Beauchamp'; 'Miss Vale', and through it all, 'Charlotte' and 'Bette Davis' simultaneously. This rather heavy-handed symbolism points to what Cavell describes as a 'doubling' within the self, by which the original self brings about a new state of the self, (re)-creating herself. In the words of Stephen Mulhall, 'condemned by the world of her film to a mode of existence in which she at best haunts the world, [Charlotte, like the other women in the genre] stakes her life on her capacity to envision a further state of her self which it is within her power to realize or enact'.[54] The casting of Bette Davis – an actress who may not be beautiful yet is undeniably distinctive and whose performance style is deliberately, provocatively stylized (sometimes to the point of campiness) – redoubles the effect. Davis, like Garbo, exists beyond our knowledge. But she is also – again like Garbo – rarely pitiable, even in her most tragic roles. In her demeanour is a refusal to accept a world that is second-rate. Both she and Charlotte stand above the fray.

Figure 12 Bette Davis: in her demeanour is a refusal to accept a world that is second-rate. *Now, Voyager* (1942, dir. Irving Rapper).

In *Pursuits of Happiness*, the couple's remarriage opened out onto the social, as the central pair were held to exemplify the possibilities of society at large. We might ask, then: since these unknown women turn their backs on marriage, do they also turn their backs on society? If their attention is directed towards the self, where does that leave others? How are we to understand the politics of such self-reliance? Mulhall wisely suggests that both Charlotte and Davis, declaring their distinctness and freedom from the present state of the world, serve as a rebuke to the world as it is, the people who make it and maintain it, people whose existence takes the form of conformity to that world. Davis/Charlotte serves as a model of what self-reliance might look like, just as the couples in the remarriage comedies offer a vision of what mutual acknowledgement might look like.[55] It is telling in this regard that while the couples of the remarriage comedy must always return home from the green world to live out their marriage amongst the fray – putting their marriage to the test amidst a network of wider relations, coming back to where they started, as it were – Charlotte ends *Now, Voyager* in a transformed version of the home that she grew up in, making plans to improve the medical facility where she was treated. She may be self-reliant, but she is not self-absorbed. The difference is everything. As Cavell explains,

> the legitimacy of the social order in which she is to participate is determined (to the extent that it can be determined) by her consent, by whether she, in her state of freedom, finds that she wants the balance of renunciation and security the present constitution of society affords her … That Charlotte consents in the moments we conclude with – and for her own reasons – is clear enough. That she would consent under altered conditions is unknowable. A good enough or just enough society – one that recognizes her say in it – will recognise this fact of, this threat in, or measure by, the woman's unknownness.[56]

Stella Dallas

The earliest draft of Cavell's chapter on *Gaslight* was presented in 1986. Cavell's pair of essays on *Now, Voyager*, 'Ugly Duckling, Funny Butterfly: Bette Davis and *Now, Voyager*' and 'Postscript (1989): To Whom It May Concern', were first published in the journal *Critical Inquiry* in Winter 1990. The immediate response was not positive. The subsequent issue of *Critical Inquiry* features a letter from Tania Modleski, denouncing the essays and rebuking Cavell not only for his treatment of his female subjects – Charlotte Vale and Bette Davis – but also his failure to engage in a thorough manner with feminist writing on the film. Modleski takes particular umbrage with Cavell's claim that he is saving *Now, Voyager* (and the other melodramas in *Contesting Tears*) from 'feminist condescension', when, in fact, 'much feminist discussion of the so-called weepies has aimed to rescue the genre from the contempt of male critics'.

> Inasmuch as Cavell, despite this specific charge against feminists, fails to cite any of the women working in his area, fails to name them (Doane, Jacobs, LaPlace, and others have written powerful critiques of *Now, Voyager* and other Bette Davis films), and inasmuch as *Critical Inquiry* exempts Cavell from the minimal requirements of scholarship, both parties perpetuate the very condition being analyzed: they participate in a system in which women go unrecognized, their voices unheard, their identities 'unknown.' Thus Woman can be maintained as enigma – the dark continent which men explore, colonize, and 'defend,' claiming exclusive rights to territory they need to see as virgin.[57]

Cavell produced a lengthy response to Modleski's letter, and the two were printed one after the other in the same issue. By way of rebuttal, he argues that feminist critics have often understood Hollywood cinema as glamourising and repressing women and that this a problematic assumption since it views Hollywood film as a not only ideologically conservative but also homogenous. Part of Cavell's project in both *Pursuits of Happiness* and *Contesting Tears* is to show that Hollywood is not quite as simple or straightforward as some critics would have it. It is a mistake, he chides, to assume that Hollywood is incapable of producing films whose artistic and philosophical intelligence were consciously and centrally involved in countering Hollywood's characteristic repression of women and whose intelligence (hence) could not match the superior intelligence of the advanced critics now addressing them. Put simply, Cavell believes that feminist critics such as Modleski and those she mentions in her letter deny the work a voice in its own interpretation. Of course, not all weepies think carefully about their construction or about the construction of womanhood within them; this is precisely why Cavell distinguishes the 'unknown women melodramas' from the wider genre as a whole.

While Cavell is quick to mount a defence in the pages of *Critical Inquiry*, however, Modleski's criticisms have a lasting effect on his work. The letter and response prompted an ongoing exchange of ideas that feeds into Cavell's essay on *Stella Dallas*, a version of which was made available by the Cultural Studies Project at MIT in 1991; Modleski's introduction to *Feminism without Women*,[58] published later that same year; and Cavell's introduction to *Contesting Tears*, which was finally published in 1995.

For over half the time that Cavell was thinking about the question of the unknown woman's voice, then, Modleski's commentary on his work was ringing in his ears. We might put it that Modleski has a say in the final version of the essays in *Contesting Tears*. Her criticisms have a profound effect on Cavell, not least insofar as they present to Cavell the possibility that he may be (perceived as) rejecting an offer of conversation and hence failing, in his own way, to acknowledge the existence of others.

> Since philosophy, as I have variously characterized it, is a process, and a process that necessarily distrusts the process, of reading; call it a craving for education that attacks one's education as it stands; and since this takes place as conversation (oneself perhaps taking on different voices); to deny conversation genuinely offered is a denial of philosophy. It is a standing possibility. It is sometimes necessary. Is it true of what I have written? Have I treated an offer of conversation in this way? If my particular history of avoidances, disappointments, rumors, desires, responsibilities, has allowed paranoia to get the better of me here, so that I have from a sense of slight dealt slight, I regret it; I mean to do better.[59]

Cavell means to do better, despite his reservations about certain aspects of feminist film theory. So it is that he broaches the subject of Modleski's criticisms in the introduction to *Contesting Tears* and engages with feminist film theory in a more overt manner in the chapter on *Stella Dallas*, in which he argues that the film overturns archetypal stories of self-sacrifice, revealing Stella's story as one of self-liberation and self-empowerment.

As with his analysis of *The Awful Truth*, Cavell's essay on *Stella Dallas* has prompted a great deal of argument and counterargument. At stake is one central question: should we read *Stella Dallas* as a story of maternal self-sacrifice, or as a woman's decision to shed her familial encumbrances in order to begin her life anew, on her own terms? In Robert Sinnerbrink's words, it is a question of

> whether we understand the film to be an eradication of Stella as a woman and mother, typical of the ideological operations of Hollywood melodrama, or as a vindication of her struggle to find a non-conformist feminine identity – one mediated by cinema's transformative powers – beyond the constraints of a domestic, conservative world in which marriage may be neither possible nor desirable.[60]

It is only in this final chapter that Cavell explicitly joins issue with feminism, in the shape of articles by Tania Modleski, Ann Kaplan, Mary Ann Doane and Linda Williams, whose article 'Something Else Besides a Woman: *Stella Dallas* and the Maternal Melodrama' Cavell engages in some detail in his chapter, 'Stella's Taste: Reading *Stella Dallas*'.[61] Inspired by a review article written by William Rothman,[62] Cavell sets out in the piece to contest the apparently uncontested opinion – established through the work of Williams and others – that Stella, in her concluding, isolating departure from the viewing of her daughter's wedding, is vacating her existence in favour of her daughter's.

The film has been building up to this moment. We first meet Stella (Barbara Stanwyck) as a young woman, hungry for something beyond the small town life she lives, sharing a small cottage with her brother, mother and father. She escapes through marriage to Stephen Dallas, a mill executive. Stephen is from a prominent Midwestern family and has come to Stella's New England mill town after breaking off his engagement in the wake of his father's bankruptcy and suicide. Stella is somewhat coy in her pursuit of him but honest about her desire that he educate her so that she can talk like him and his friends and like the people in the movie they go to watch together. After the pair have a daughter, however, a distance grows between them, for reasons that seem to do partly with Stella's transference of her ambition and affections to the child, Laurel, and partly with Stephen's disappointment that Stella does not come to fit the mould of a demure society wife. Eventually he moves to New York, leaving Stella and Laurel behind. He re-encounters his former fiancée Helen, now a widow, and the pair resume their relationship. He asks Stella for a divorce, which she accepts on condition that she receive a payment sufficient to keep Laurel in the lifestyle that Stephen has been living all these years.

Stella's unconventional behaviour and friendship with drunken bon vivant Ed Munn have hampered Laurel's entrance into the right social circles growing up. Events reach a head when, at a fancy resort, Stella, dolled up with flamboyant inappropriateness, embarrasses Laurel in front of her new beau in what Cavell describes as 'one of the great melodramatic fiascos in the history of classical film narrative'.[63] On the way home from the resort, Stella hears two young girls gossiping about her appearance in connection with Laurel. Soon afterward, she asks Helen if Laurel could live with Helen and Stephen, and, to ensure Laurel complies, pretends that she is marrying Ed Munn and moving to South America. Helen alone sees through the facade. In the film's final scene, Laurel is getting married inside Stephen and Helen's house while Stella watches from outside through the window (which Helen has insisted remain uncurtained). She turns and walks towards the camera, smiling through her tears.

What is Stella thinking, what is she feeling, as she walks away from Laurel, framed by a window as if by a cinema screen? For Williams, this is a moment of female 'self-sacrifice', in which Stella is erased both 'as a woman and as a mother'. She commences her reading with the experience of a female spectator (a spectator drawn from Marilyn French's 1977 novel *The Women's Room*), who describes the 'shock of recognition' in viewing this scene. Williams recounts the shock of recognition expressed in French's characters response to the scene: 'How they got us to consent to our own eradication!'. She argues that the film attempts to reconcile the sacrificial model of motherhood with Stella's social roles as a wife and a woman. The film in effect resolves the conflict between the roles of mother and woman by 'erasing' Stella from both. It is thus able to celebrate the institution of motherhood while devaluing the actual, lived experience of the mother (Stella) as a woman with an internal life and desires of her own. Stella is not only expendable; more than this, she must be dispatched so as not to trouble the patriarchal status quo. Nonetheless, Williams argues, female spectators of the film are far from unwitting victims of such ideology. She underlines the conflicted role of the female spectator in both 'recognising' the maternal conflict between self-sacrifice and independence while 'actively reflecting on these alternatives within the constraining social situation that Stella confronts'.[64]

But while Williams offers what may be called an 'against the grain reading' of how female spectators relate to Stella's sacrifice, Cavell challenges the universal assumption that her separation from her daughter is even a sacrifice in the first place. Rebuffing the feminist critique that posits Stella as an unwitting victim of social and cultural forces, Cavell argues instead that she is mistress of her own fate. According to Cavell, Stella, like the other women in the melodramas of the unknown women, deliberately rejects marriage as a path to education: neither Stephen Dallas nor Ed Munn is worthy partner, able to provide her with the 'meet and happy' conversation that is at the base of a good marriage. Neither of these men *sees* Stella for who she is, let alone who she could be. Nor does society at large. Stella is frowned upon by Stephen's society friends, snubbed by Laurel's teachers and mocked by the residents of the posh country club she visits with her daughter. And more than merely rejecting marriage, she also – like Nora – rejects motherhood, insofar as it is bound up with the norms of marriage and family life.

Standard readings of the film take Stella as the victim of her inability to read or make sense of polite society's rules of behaviour. Williams, for example, reads Stella as oblivious to the social transgressions she naively commits, unaware of the vulgarity of her dress sense and manners. In this reading, it is only when Stella overhears Laurel's friends gossiping about her that she realizes how she is perceived and, wishing to avoid ruining Laurel's chances of making a 'good match' with her well-off beau Richard, sacrifices her own happiness (which she finds in her role as mother to Laurel) by driving her daughter away. Cavell's reading of the film hinges on his claim that Stella 'makes a spectacle of herself' at the resort *on purpose*. He claims that Stella 'knows exactly what her effect is there, that her spectacle is part of a strategy for separating Laurel for her, not the catastrophe of misunderstanding that causes her afterward to form her strategy'.[65] He points out that Stella has shown herself, time and again, to be both aware of and able to manipulate clothing as a social tool: when she makes clothes for Laurel, for example, or when she deliberately removes the trims from a dress in order to present herself to Stephen according to his taste for simplicity and elegance. 'The evidence that Stella knows her effect turns simply on her massively authenticated knowledge of clothes', Cavell writes, 'she is an expert at their construction and their deconstruction'.[66] She knows, that is, what society expects of her, and her choice to flout those expectations is therefore a conscious strategy. Her decision to make a display of herself at the resort is an expression of both her taste (as opposed to received taste) and – as Robert Sinnerbrink puts it – her 'distaste for the life she thought she desired'.[67]

In Williams's reading, Stella's choices of attire are part of an attempt to gain acceptance into Stephen's world: a strategy that emphasizes her 'pathetic inadequacy' and ultimately backfires 'in the eyes of an upper-class restraint that values a streamlined and sleek ideal of femininity'.[68] Thus the film's final scene 'resolves' the contradiction of Stella's attempt to be a woman and a mother by eradicating both.[69] Her job is done, she has placed Laurel within the cinematic frame of life as Mrs Richard Grosvenor, and there is nothing left for her. This is her end. For Cavell, on the other hand, Stella, seeking an education, a life beyond the values of snobbish, small-minded Stephen and his friends, abdicates her role as mother on purpose. She walks *away* from Laurel *towards* something that might just be better (notably she is walking towards the camera, towards us). This is her beginning.

The difference turns on how seriously we take Stella's claim to Laurel that she desires to be 'something else besides a mother'. Williams claims that this a line rich with irony, since now there really is nothing else that she wants to be. Cavell takes Stella at her word (even if that 'something else' isn't what Stella implies to Laurel, i.e. to be Mrs Ed Munn). And is it so difficult, after all, to imagine that a woman might *actually* want to be something other than a mother?

This final scene is thus also, Sinnerbrink writes, a 'reflexive commentary on the communication between women that occurs via movies'.[70] Let's not forget that Helen – Stephen's new wife – has throughout the film been the sole character who seems to 'read between the lines' of Stella's behaviour and that it is she who leaves the curtains open for Stella to gaze upon the spectacle of her daughter's marriage, a marriage that resembles the happy ending of the film that Stephen and Stella watch on their first date. Helen assumes the role of author, framing the quasi-cinematic scene that Stella watches from her position as an anonymous spectator. As Stella walks away from the screen, gazing into the night with an enigmatic smile, she is herself transformed: from Stella to Stanwyck. Stella's walk towards us is allegorized as the presenting or creating of a star, an interpretation of stardom.

> This star, call her Barbara Stanwyck, is without obvious beauty or glamour ... stripped of ornament, in a nondescript hat and cloth overcoat. But she has a future. Not just because now we know – we soon knew – that this woman is the star of *The Lady Eve* and *Double Indemnity* and *Ball of Fire* ... but because she is presented here as a star (the camera showing her that particular insatiable interest in her every action and reaction), which entails the promise of return, of unpredictable reincarnation.[71] Both Stella (a name which means star) and the actress who plays her are thinking themselves into existence.

Figure 13 The controversial ending of *Stella Dallas*. *Stella Dallas* (King Vidor, 1937).

Irony

Cavell claims that critics such as Williams subject Stella to the same 'ironic misinterpretations' that other characters perpetuate against her when they misread her deliberate strategy of provocation as an unwitting display of ignorance. But how convincing is Cavell's interpretation of *Stella Dallas*? Even some of his most long-standing supporters have expressed reservations about his conclusion that Stella invents herself, deliberately embracing her unknownness as a strategy for living well in the world. Robert Sinnerbrink, for example, argues that Cavell's version of events faces the difficulty of explaining several earlier scenes in the film which contradict the idea that Stella makes a spectacle of herself on purpose, notably a key scene that takes place in the offices of Stephen's lawyer. In effect, it undermines the authenticity of not just the Christmas tree 'performance' but other moments that Stella shares with Laurel and Helen and as such undercuts the pitifulness of Stella's position. More than this, it overlooks certain socio-historical elements of the film: Stella's class, her gender and the manner in which they intersect. Sinnerbrink states that Cavell's approach to Stella Dallas and melodrama more generally 'struggles to articulate how the conditions of a character's world shape her quest for ethical self-transformation, and [...] the "impossible" desires that this social world stimulates yet cannot satisfy'.[72]

Sinnerbrink's lucid reading of the final scene argues that Stella's decision to separate herself from Laurel does not have to be either a sign of the film's erasure of Stella as mother and woman (Williams's reading) or autonomous decision that enables her to discover her new identity (Cavell's reading). Instead, we can think of it as both. Stella's display condenses many elements of her character and situation, and many conflicting features of the narrative arc, into a private space of viewing, emotional expression and bodily communication: 'Stella's self-sacrifice, her uneasy but independent manner of relating roles of mother and of (no longer married) woman, her sense of having traversed the fantasy of marrying ... only to find that this was not for her, not to her taste, not her style, however much it remains part of Laurel's world.'[73]

In a sense, the approaches to Stella by Cavell and Williams are aspectival. They allow us to see only one side of Stella. She is either erased or empowered (either a duck or a rabbit). And yet careful attention to Stanwyck's performance belies such easy divisions. While a lesser performer may have revealed the anguish behind Stella's sacrifice (so that the act is performed in spite of herself) or played up the triumph in her walk (so that the sacrifice is clearly a victory), Stanwyck's nuanced performance is finely calibrated so as to offer no such certainty. And this is how it should be, shouldn't it? Andrew Klevan puts it beautifully when he writes:

> The eloquence of particular films ... means that they will continually have a 'say' in their interpretation, ensuring that we will never know them, or know our experience of them; rather, we remain

in the process of knowing them and knowing our experience of them – forever guessing the unseen.[74]

Indeed Klevan hits the nail on the head in his star study of Stanwyck (published two years before Sinnerbrink's account of the film), when he suggests how strange it is that Cavell does not take the logic of unknownness to its conclusion when discussing Stella's behaviour, writing that 'by attributing to her "sure knowledge" and to us certainty concerning her motivations, Cavell may have inadvertently reduced the "unknownness" of Stella'.[75] In fine, that final action *must* be somewhat opaque, unresolvable, since it is only this way that Stella remains unknown not only to her fellow characters but also to us.

Perhaps though this double misunderstanding is to be expected of a genre whose subject is, as Cavell formulates it, the 'irony of human identity'.[76] That is, irony has a particularly important role within the melodramas, one that develops from remarriage comedies. In remarriage comedies, irony is the negation of conversation. The men and women of the melodramas speak at cross-purposes and misunderstand one another. In Cavell's words, they do not speak the same language. The finest description of such ironic incomprehension comes, Cavell claims, from 'Self Reliance'.

> Well, most men have bound their eyes with one or another handkerchief and attached themselves to some one of these communities of opinion. This conformity makes them false not in a few particulars, but false in all particulars. Their every truth is not quite true. Their two is not the real two; their four is not the real four: so that every word they say chagrins us, and we know not where to begin to set them right.[77]

But, of course, the couples of the remarriage comedies come to understand one another: reaching a point where they are able to acknowledge one another in a union of responsiveness, emblematized by their 'meet and happy conversation'. In the melodramas, however, communication and interaction are systematically negated. The woman fails to find a shared language with the men in her world and ultimately with any of the people in that world. Even Laurel misunderstands Stella eventually (and while figures such as Helen in *Stella Dallas* and Dr Jacquith in *Now, Voyager* seem able to understand something of our heroines, the relationships they share with the protagonists are not presented by the films as ones of easy mutuality). Irony serves to isolate the woman of the melodramas from almost everyone around her. So why not isolate her from us, her viewers, too?

Opera and the voice

We might ask, then, whether Cavell's claim to know Stella's intentions in this final scene – to have acknowledged her, when other women could not – is not precisely the kind of ironic misinterpretation that he accuses Williams of performing. What gives Cavell the right to speak for Stella? This is a particularly pressing question given that one of the themes of *Contesting Tears* is the matter of voicelessness, of finding one's voice, and in particular of the woman's discovery of her voice.

The matter of voice is a long-standing concern of Cavell. In the title of essay of *Must We Mean What We Say*, he expresses a concern with what he calls the *sound of philosophy*. In *The Claim of Reason* he states that the aim of his work – all his work – is to bring the human voice back into philosophy. He argues that the silencing of the voice is the goal of philosophical scepticism and that therefore the discovery or recovery of voice is at the heart of overcoming sceptical despair. His subsequent essays on literature (notably Shakespeare) and film examine how one might go about finding one's voice and what happens in the case of a failure to do so.

Almost always, it is the woman's voice, and the woman's fate, at stake. In Shakespeare's tragedies, for example, Desdemona and Cordelia die because voice comes too late.

In the films discussed in *Pursuits of Happiness*, the creation of the woman comes about as a result of her being able to join her voice with that of her male counterpart, engaging 'meet and happy conversation'. In the previous chapter I outlined Cavell's argument that in the remarriage comedies 'talking together is fully and plainly being together', that 'the central pair are learning to speak the same language'.[78] Also that the tone of that conversation is as important as the content. Cavell says that conversation within these films is a source of pleasure, for both the audience and the central couple alike: the couples in these films are not only able to talk together but to laugh together. But the form of discourse most readily associated with marriage is bickering: the 'characteristic sound of these comedies' is 'the sound of argument, of wrangling, of verbal battle'.[79] The female voice is raised *in contradiction* to the male voice. And this is, Cavell argues, a sign of caring: 'the hallmark of a willingness to bear up under an assault of words, to give as you get, where what is good must always, however strong, maintain its good spirits, a test of intellectual as well as spiritual stamina, of what you might call ear'.[80]

The Awful Truth shows what 'good' bickering looks like through a contrast with 'bad' lecturing, all the while foregrounding the woman's voice. After an early sequence in which Lucy and Jerry Warriner decide to part ways, Lucy's lawyer tries to persuade her to give marriage another chance. As he talks to Lucy, his wife harangues him about his dinner, which is rapidly growing cold; eventually he shouts at her to 'shut her mouth'. Here we are presented with the woman's voice as that of the harpy, harridan, virago, scold or shrew – a role presumably derived from *The Taming of the Shrew* and which is also assumed by, amongst others, *The Philadelphia Story*'s Tracy Lord and Amanda Bonner in *Adam's Rib*. (Their male equivalents are callous brutes who want their women to 'shut their mouths', a figure that recurs in the melodramas of the unknown woman, as we will see.) We do not even need to hear the voices of these women to see how their speech is coded visually as aggressive or pious – the hands on the hips, the tilted chins. Other women in the remarriage comedies meanwhile play dumb (like Dixie Belle or the cute competitors for Mugsy's affection in *The Lady Eve*). Or they are humourless and buttoned up (like *Bringing Up Baby*'s Miss Swallow or *The Awful Truth*'s ironically dubbed 'madcap heiress' Barbara Vance).

Lucy uses her voice quite differently. This is a woman who gives as good as she gets – and perhaps more. After Jerry embarrasses her by forcing her to dance with Dan Leeson, Lucy takes great glee in Jerry's own self-inflicted embarrassment when he bursts in on her singing recital having mistaken it for a romantic assignation. But in their game of one-up-manship Lucy has the last laugh because she can laugh not only at Jerry but also at herself. She is able to show Jerry up in front of his fiancée and her parents because she is willing firstly to make a fool of herself. In so doing she paves the way for their ultimate reconciliation, a reconciliation that takes place in a spirit of humour and humility.

It is important that in two of these incidents Lucy is singing. She's singing for – or at least before – Jerry. *Lucy is a singer.* Her relationship with her singing teacher Armand is the excuse for the pair's separation. Her inability to sing with Jerry's replacement Dan signals the death knell for their fledging relationship. And when she appropriates the song earlier performed by nightclub performer Dixie Belle, Cavell reads the gesture as Lucy proposing herself as 'a field on which [Jerry] may weave passion and tenderness', making both an offer of friendship and remarriage.[81] Perhaps we can go further than Cavell and argue that Lucy's singing here is more than an offer of friendship; it is a rebuke: a form of chastisement and a suggested corrective. A kind of bickering and an offer of education.

Figure 14 Lucy sings for Jerry in *The Awful Truth*. *The Awful Truth* (Leo McCarey, 1937).

Catherine Constable argues that Lucy teaches Jerry to see her as she wants to be seen.[82] Perhaps we might add to this: she teaches him to *listen to her voice*. Just so when Jerry repeats Lucy's words about faith in marriage to Barbara towards the film's end, adding 'I think I read it in a book or something', he is unconsciously revealing he has learned a lesson from Lucy. At the same time, both Cavell's and Jerry's misattribution of this vital quote seem to prove John Stuart Mill's suggestion that a vast number of supposedly original thoughts put forth by male thinkers belong to a woman by suggestion. Mill's is a vision, as Cavell puts it, of 'a very large proportion of Western culture as plagiarized, speaking with voices other than those it owns, implying *not* that culture does not listen to women, but that it very conveniently has'.[83]

In *The Awful Truth*, this usurpation of the female voice is played for comic effect. In the melodramas of the unknown woman, it is 'no laughing matter'. Quite to the contrary. As the heroine of *Gaslight* puts it, the matter of voice is serious: very serious. So serious that in Cavell's discussion of *Gaslight* he claims that voicelessness is 'tantamount to madness'.[84] The early sequences of *Gaslight* pose the question of whether Paula has a voice: which on a superficial level means whether she can sing, but on a more profound level it has to do with whether she can speak, or even think, for herself. Paula's mind is not on her singing, her tutor tells her. Her heart is not in it. The trouble is not with the voice alone, but with the lack of feeling behind it. Paula is distracted by her infatuation with her piano teacher, Gregory, who she will soon marry. Gregory's subsequent attempts to drive Paula mad are presented as his reducing her to silence. Throughout *Gaslight*, Gregory works to deprive Paula of her voice at the same time as he forces her to question her interpretation of the world, imposing on her the world as he would have her see it. The denial of voice is not (merely) the loss of speech but 'a loss of reason, of mind as such – say the capacity to count, to make a difference'.[85] (Bergman's beautifully gestural performance visually signals this loss of voice through the repeated motion of putting her hand to her mouth.)

At the climax of the film Paula however recovers her voice in a long speech that Cavell describes as a 'mad song', in which she confronts her husband with a knife. Cavell calls this speech Paula's 'aria', understanding her to be lifting her voice in song. Certainly Bergman delivers the monologue as if it were a sung performance: her voice raising through the octaves, her body opening out as if to project the words coming from her mouth. He translates it as her saying 'Now I *exist* because now I speak for myself'. It is therefore also her *cogito ergo sum*, her proof of existence not only to her husband but also – more importantly – to herself.

Cavell is building here on an idea developed in *A Pitch of Philosophy*, where he draws an equivalence between the melodrama of the unknown woman and opera, the Western institution in which, to Cavell's mind, 'the human voice is given its fullest acknowledgement'.[86] In both melodrama and opera, he claims, 'The woman's demand for

Figure 15 Paula confronts her tormentor in *Gaslight*: her speech is like a 'mad aria'. *Gaslight* (George Cukor, 1944).

a voice, for a language, for attention to, and the power to enforce attention to, her own subjectivity, say to her difference of existence, is expressible as a response to an Emersonian demand for thinking.'[87] He is clear that there are differences – especially ontological differences – between opera and film. Still, he suspects that opera has 'transformed itself into film, that film is, or was, our opera' (an idea floated in *Mr Deeds Goes to Town* and discussed in Chapter 2 of this book).

In particular melodrama and opera both push at the limits of linguistic expression, revealing something about the powers and limitations of the human capacity to raise the voice.[88] In opera, singing is a kind of abandonment: 'a spiritual achievement expressed as a willingness to depart from all settled habitation, all conformity of meaning.'[89] It embodies Thoreau's idea that being beside oneself in a sane sense – in other words, ecstasy – is that which proves one's humanity. Singing – *women's* singing – is to be understood as an ecstatic response: 'an irrupting of a new perspective of the self to itself'.[90]

But if singing exposes women as thinking, it also exposes her to the powers of those who do not want her to think, do not want autonomous proof of her existence. Cavell cites Catherine Clément's claim in her book *Opera, or the Undoing of Women* that opera – and by extension melodrama – is about the death of women, and women's self-expression, and the fact that women die, are driven mad or are ostracized because they express themselves. After all, as the philosopher Adriana Cavarero reminds us, patriarchy tells us that 'women should be seen and not heard'.[91] For Cavarero, the woman who sings is always a Siren, an outsider to the domestic order of daughter and wife. The female singing voice, she writes, cannot be domesticated: it disturbs the system of reason by leading elsewhere. No wonder Gregory is so swift to undermine Paula's self-assertion with his damning admonition, 'Don't get hysterical, Paula'. As Clément tells us: 'Men will tell you that hysteria is a sickness .... Do not believe it. Hysteria is a woman's principal resource' (176 Opera). (And it's perhaps for this reason that Cavell reads a key scene in *Stella Dallas* as expressing Stella's need to teach her daughter to cry.)

Cavarero and Cavell alike draw a link between the singing woman and homosexuality, arguing that the primacy of song over speech evokes the feminine, just as speech, understood as the power to signify, evokes the masculine. In Cavarero's words, 'where there is song, melody, and a voice, then there is generally a feminine experience, whether or not the composer or performer is a man'.[92] Both philosophers thus conflate the vocal with the feminine and the body on the one hand and the semantic with the masculine and the mind on the other. But there are a couple of potential problems with this way of thinking. On the one hand, the supremacy of music and song over speech in opera and melodrama may distract the audience from the plot of a story that is obsessively misogynist. The seductive power of opera consists in making these undomesticated heroines die singing. We watch the destruction of these women and *swoon*. On the other it risks abstracting the feminine: turning it into a category that can be co-opted by the male writer, director or spectator, arrogating the (embodied, real) female voice in the name of the (theoretical, philosophical) feminine.

This is precisely the charge that Modleski levels at Cavell in the introduction to her book *Feminism without Women*. Here, Modleski chides Cavell for his appropriation of female suffering. Cavell treats the female voice as a metaphor and metaphysics, she argues, or else he overidentifies with the beset femininity of his subjects: 'garrulously appropriating', in Modleski's words, the struggle of these women to make their voices heard. Cavell is however (perhaps as a result of listening to Modleski) not insensible to the risks that he runs in presuming to speak for his female subjects. Indeed throughout *Contesting Tears*, Cavell shows an almost painful awareness of his *own male voice*. For a man to notice the suffering of these women – who are suffering over what it is to be a woman – feels to Cavell as if it might be 'impertinent' or 'ignorantly expansive'.[93] Since the men in these films are judged and found over and again to be wanting, what exempts Cavell, a man, from the taint of male villainy? What gives him the right to intervene on behalf of these women? Cavell has already posed these questions in relationship to *Now, Voyager*, but they are especially pressing, he argues, in relationship to *Stella Dallas*, in which the male character's failing is manifested explicitly as 'perceptual incompetence', that is, 'in one man's affable crudeness and in another man's dulled conventionality'.[94]

What then, Cavell asks, is 'the pertinence of the male voice?'[95] Since this is an issue raised by the films themselves, it is something, Cavell speculates, that he must have been trying to get to for some time. Musing why it is that he has only just come to tackle the matter head on, Cavell finds an answer of sorts in autobiographical expression, which is the only mode, he feels, in which his encounter with feminism can take place. *A Pitch of Philosophy* is also linked to

Contesting Tears through this positing of autobiography as a self-conscious mode of criticism specifically in relationship to thinking about women in art. In the former, Cavell reminds us that his mother was a musician, that the language of music was her 'mother tongue'. He concludes 'Opera and the Lease of Voice' by asking whether he too is able to speak this language: 'Am I ready to vow', he asks, 'that I know my mother's mother tongue of music to be also mine?'[96] He seems to be picking up this same question when he opens and closes his essay on Stella Dallas with autobiographical references to his mother. The chapter opens as follows:

> When my mother asked for an opinion from my father and me about a new garment or ornament she had on, a characteristic form she gave her question was 'Too Stella Dallas'? The most frequent scene of the question was our getting ready to leave the apartment for the Friday night movies, by far the most important, and reliable, source of common pleasure for the three of us. I knew even then, so I seem to have always remembered it, that my mother's reference to Stella Dallas was not to a figure from whom she was entirely disassociating herself.[97]

As Rothman puts it, in this passage Cavell all but explicitly declares that his reading is guided by an intuition of his mother, by his intuition of her intuition, his recollection of knowing, even as a boy, that he identified with Stella – and more than this, that she identified with a Stella who knew that she was too much.[98] The male voice in this writing is thus attuned to his mother's way of thinking – and to Stella's as a reflection of his mother.

It seems that perhaps more than any other encounter with film, the writing of the chapters that come to make up *Contesting Tears* opens onto Cavell's own experience, as well as being a formative experience for the adult Cavell. It is as a result of the conversations – not always meet and happy, it must be said – that he enters into with Modleski,

Williams and others, that Cavell comes to turn back to himself, to consider the place of his own voice in these conversations, and to 'begin to write autobiographically'. So he writes:

> I do not say that it is because I was beginning to write autobiographically that I begin my thoughts on Stella with a moment of autobiography ... it is exactly as true that because I began this opening with a moment of autobiography that I have subsequently gone on to (in the first chapter of *A Pitch of Philosophy*) to take autobiographical expression distinctly further than I have ever done before. I trust this impulse will not be lost.

I trust this impulse will not be lost. With these words Cavell announces that something has changed – a new impulse has arisen – and he intends for that impetus to bear him forward. In the next two chapters we will consider how autobiography winds its way further into Cavell's work in tandem with a continued interest in ideas of perfectionism. It's just possible that what happens during the writing of *Contesting Tears* is a step in Cavell's own path of perfectionism: one that emerges from his experience of being unknown (or at least misunderstood) by other members of the Film Studies community, but also from his commitment to being part of this community, to making renewed efforts to understand and be understood.

Conclusion: On sharing pain

Why did it take Cavell so long – two decades nearly – to bring Emerson into conversation, or to bring out the conversation that was already taking place, with film? Rothman answers this question by pointing to Emerson's own (lack of) status within academic philosophy in the United States. It is in the writing of *Pursuits of Happiness* and *Contesting Tears* that Cavell's intuition that Hollywood movies have inherited the philosophical concerns of American transcendentalism, conjoined with his intuition that he has inherited these concerns, too, leads to the astonishing further intuition that his own philosophical procedures are underwritten by the way American movies think about society, human relationships and their own condition as films. It is in the very movies that were for so many years a normal part of Cavell's week that Emerson's ways of thinking remained alive within American culture, available as an inheritance. Apart from the role Hollywood movies played in Cavell's education, it would not have been possible for a philosopher who received his professional training within an Anglo-American tradition that has never acknowledged Emerson as a philosopher to have inherited Emerson's ways of thinking at all.[99]

The point that Rothman is making here is that these films don't illustrate or exemplify Emersonian thinking; they reveal it. What's more, they reveal its presence in the every day. In Cavell's works, Emerson's thought is 'preserved, is in existence, in works of lasting public power – world-famous, world-favoured films – while the Emerson text itself, so to speak, is repressed in the public it helped to found'.[100] Just so, the films discussed by Cavell in *Contesting Tears* turn Cavell towards perfectionism, allowing him to articulate concerns that were only implicit within *Pursuits of Happiness* and to think through the matter of how we relate to others and to ourselves. Above all, perhaps, they demonstrate that 'it is the logic of human intimacy ... that to exchange understanding with another is to share pain with that other, and that to take pleasure from another is to extend that pleasure'.[101]

Contesting Tears closes with an extraordinary image of isolation and pain, drawn once more from Cavell's own childhood:

> Now I am recapturing another of my mother's moods, somehow associated with the demand to be noticed (perhaps with its explicit failure, perhaps with the implicit failure of having to demand it). She named this state migraine – definable, I assumed, through

her therapy for it, which was to play the piano, in a darkened room (her eyes were evidently affected), alone. (I am interpreting the mood, after the fact, from the few times I came home from school late in the afternoon to enter such a scene.) What music she would play then (mostly Chopin, her favourite composer), and how she became a prominent pianist in Atlanta, then largely a culturally unprominent part of the country, and hence what her relation was to a certain stardom, and to her refusal of the chance for more, are pertinent matters. They must concern the relation between searching for the mother's gaze and being subjected to her moods. Hence they concern the question of what her moods are subjected to, to what scenes of inheritance. Was the music filling the loss or impoverishment of a self-abandoned ego (so speaking to melancholia), or was it remembering, say recounting, the origins, hence losses, of her reception, her glamourous talent for, the world of music (so speaking of dispossession and nostalgia)? Music, moods, worlds, abandonment, subjection, dispossession – of course; we are speaking of melodrama.[102]

Cavell tells us in 'Stella's Taste' that Stella is the most 'harrowing' for him of the unknown women melodramas, that it was distressing to him to have to watch it repeatedly. But he also says that the 'compensating knowledge' gained from the experience might be worth the price of the experience.[103] This closing image is very sad, but the sharing of it is a gesture of overcoming. It is a demand for friendship from the reader, a demand that might not always be met with uninterrupted good feeling, but one that, if taken up in the spirit in which it is meant, can be mutually enriching.

6

Perfectionism, Friendship, Education

There is nothing noble in being superior to your fellow man; true nobility is being superior to your former self.

– Ernest Hemingway

Our life is an apprenticeship to the truth that around every circle another can be drawn; that there is no end in nature, but every end is a beginning, and under every deep a lower deep opens.

– Ralph Waldo Emerson

Watching the women who populate the melodramas of *Contesting Tears* – Charlotte Vale, Bette Davis, Stella Dallas, Barbara Stanwyck, Paula Alquist Anton, Ingrid Bergman, Lisa Berndle, Joan Fontaine – Cavell learns what it looks like to be self-reliant. He sees their solitary struggles to find their voices. In the process of writing about them, he is faced with the problem of his own voice. What is it that Cavell wants to say about the films that he cares about and about film and philosophy more widely? How might he best say it? How can he, as a philosopher and a critic, enter into conversation with his readers in a manner that encourages – indeed demands – friendship?

These are the questions with which Cavell concludes *Contesting Tears*. Unsurprisingly, they are the same questions that open his next work on film, *Cities of Words*. This book is developed from a lecture course that Cavell delivered first at Harvard and then at the University of Chicago, a course which he called Moral Perfectionism.[1] In it, he pairs exegeses of some central texts of moral philosophy (by

Plato, Aristotle, Locke, Kant, Mill, Nietzsche, Rawls), or literary texts presenting moral issues bearing on perfectionist preoccupations (Shakespeare, Ibsen, George Bernard Shaw), or philosophical texts not usually considered by professional philosophers to be moral thinkers (Emerson and Freud), with readings of films, most of which are already covered within *Pursuits of Happiness* and *Contesting Tears*, the notable exceptions being *Mr Deeds* and Eric Rohmer's *Tale of Winter/Conte d'hiver* (1989). In the preface to the book, Cavell explains that he intends it to retain 'something of the sound of the original classroom lectures, as distinguished from the sound of a presentation to a scholarly organization or a formal talk to a general public',[2] that he thinks of it as a 'sequence of pedagogical letters'.[3] He compares *Cities of Words* (the subtitle of which is 'Pedagogical Letters on the Register of a Moral Life') to Friedrich Schiller's 'series of letters': *On the Aesthetic Education of Man* – a book that is similarly concerned with questions of perfectibility and authority, alongside morality and aesthetics.

The preface thus puts the notion of friendship into conversation with the notion of pedagogy. It raises the issue of authority, adding a further pair of questions to those that arose out of *Contesting Tears*: Who can help us to find our voices? Who has the authority to teach? These are questions that haunt both the earlier books on film genres.

As we discussed in the previous chapter, the unknown women approach a kind of perfectionism through the process of becoming self-reliant, by rejecting their male counterparts as unsuitable to educate them. But while *Pursuits of Happiness* gestures towards perfectionism through its invocation of Ibsen's Nora and Arnold's idea of 'the best self' existing in each of us, it remains an implicit theme. Returning to some of those films in *Cities of Words*, Cavell is able to pull perfectionism into the foreground, reframing those works in terms of what it is to live a moral life through a sustained dialogue with another person, a person who is both a friend and a teacher.

This chapter looks at how Cavell develops his conception of perfectionism in *Cities of Words*. In it, I place particular emphasis on the role of the friend and the role of the teacher – and the differences between these two roles. I ask how film might show us not only what perfectionism looks like but how it might bring about a transformation in us, as spectators. And I consider how Cavell himself thinks through his own role as friend and educator, returning to some of the concerns that were raised by his exchange with Tania Modleski.

In his response to Modleski's letter, Cavell worries that he has – inadvertently, through miscommunication and misunderstanding – refused an offer of conversation. 'I mean to do better,' he vows.[4] In *Cities of Words* he repeats this vow, acknowledging that 'interpretations I find convincing of lines and moments of films that I admire often do not at first find conviction in others',[5] but that there is a reason interpretations are difficult to arrive at and to accept: 'They are not to be believed as statements of fact are, or not believed. Accepting or rejecting them requires a work, a shift, of the self. Sometimes that shift is small, sometimes it is transformative.' To Cavell, this means that it is his 'never-ending task' to 'rediscover the reality of such work in one's experience', turning and returning to these films in order to test his own assertions against themselves or risk his interpretations being 'forever lost to culture'.[6] There is a sense in these words of writing, teaching and interpretation as a moral calling, one that Cavell feels bound to respond to.

What is moral perfectionism?

Cavell's version of perfectionism develops from Emerson and from the films discussed in *Pursuits of Happiness* and *Contesting Tears*. The resulting moral framework is a philosophy unlike any other. And yet he is not the first thinker to use the term 'perfectionism', and he is certainly not the first philosopher to think about questions of morality. It is important, then, to sketch out the background context of what is variously known as both Emersonian perfectionism and Cavellian perfectionism (since Cavell's work derives from Emerson but is informed by other thinkers and works of art, I shall use the latter when referring to the version of perfectionism he sets out in *Cities of Words*).

Historically, the philosophy of ethics has been split into three schools of thought: Kantian universalism (deontology), utilitarianism and Aristotelian virtue ethics. These theories are concerned with, respectively, doing one's duty, or maximizing the general happiness, or cultivating one's virtues. Cavellian perfectionism on the other hand, as Cavell explains both in the Carus lectures and in *Cities of Words* (and other writings), has to do with being true to oneself, with what Foucault refers to as the care of the self, and hence with a dissatisfaction with the self as it stands.[7] Romantics have spoken of the idea of becoming who you are. In the present day, we might say it has to do with self-improvement. For Stephen Mulhall, it is 'an understanding of the soul as on an onward or upward journey that begins by finding oneself lost to the world and requires a refusal of [current] society in the name of some further, more cultivated or culture, state of society and the self'.[8]

Perfectionism does not imply perfectibility – the attainment of some state of perfection. We cannot become perfect, unsurpassable. Rather, each attained state of the self (or society) always projects or opens up another state, the realization of which we must commit ourselves to anew. The Cavellian perfectionist is constantly striving for what Cavell calls 'the unattained yet attainable self'.[9] In this much, every attained state is effectively perfect just as it is – and yet it could still be *more* perfect. As Cavell explains:

> The soul's journey to itself, as if awakening out of a trance, is not pictured as a continuous path directed upwards to a known path of completion but rather as a zigzag of discontinuous steps [...] an

idea that projects no unique point of arrival but only a willingness for change, directed by specific aspirations that, while rejected, may at unpredictable times return within new power. The path is no more towards incorporation within a given condition of society than it is toward the capacity to judge that condition. The sage in us is what remains after our social positionings.[10]

Matteo Faloni's excellent exegesis of Cavellian perfectionism outlines the ways in which Cavell's use of the notion of perfectionism departs from the meaning the term has acquired elsewhere in contemporary moral philosophy.[11] Perfectionism has, Faloni reports, been associated with various moral theories. At the time that Cavell was writing the Carus lectures and *Cities of Words*, 'perfectionism' was associated with a certain type of teleological theory, one that, according John Rawls, has to do with maximizing 'the good of human excellence in art, science and culture'.[12] But, Faloni points out, Cavell's perfectionism should not be seen as a competing moral theory, rather 'as emphasizing the dimension of the moral life *any theory of it might wish to accommodate*'.[13] Any specific version of perfectionism, in Cavell's view, will provide its own specific concepts and methods of self-understanding. Hence the breadth of philosophers and philosophies whose work bears traces of perfectionism, including Aristotle, Augustine, Kant, Nietzsche, Heidegger and Wittgenstein.

In the period after Kant and Hegel, moral perfectionism, Cavell tells us, is identified less with canonical moral philosophers than with figures who work between philosophy and literature, such as Emerson, or with obviously literary figures such as Jane Austen, George Eliot, Matthew Arnold, Ibsen, George Bernard Shaw and Henry James. This shift in its articulation from philosophy proper to the arts is perhaps the reason that perfectionism has been somewhat maligned by figures such as Rawls, although there are other reasons, too, as we will discuss in due course. It also renders it impossible to enumerate a set of features that are possessed by all perfectionist writings. Thus Cavell, in much the same manner as he does with films, points instead to a founding myth of perfectionism, which he couches in terms taken from Plato's *Republic*, but which, as Stephen Mulhall points out, might well be differently articulated in different texts[14]:

> Obvious candidate features are its ideas of a mode of conversation between (older and younger) friends, one of whom is intellectually authoritative because his life is somehow exemplary of a representative of a life the other(s) are attracted to, and in the attraction of which the self recognizes itself as enchained, fixated, and feels itself removed from reality, whereupon the self finds that it can turn (convert, revolutionize itself) and a process of education is undertaken, in part through a discussion of education, in which each self is drawn on a journey of ascent to a further state of that self, where the higher is determined not by natural talent but by seeking to know what you are made of and cultivating the thing you are meant to do; it is a transformation of the self which finds expression in the imagination of a transformation of society into something like an aristocracy where what is best for society is a model for and is modeled on what is best for the individual soul, a best arrived at in the view of a new reality, a realm beyond, the true world, that of the Good, sustainer of the good city, that of Utopia.[15]

One can pull out some unifying threads, then. Each of the thinkers that Cavell discusses within *Cities of Words* perceives a split in the human self, seeing human nature as divided or double. The very conception of a divided self and a doubled world provides a perspective of judgement upon the world as it is, measured against the world as it may be. This tends to express, Cavell argues, 'disappointment with the world as it is, as the scene of human activity and prospects, and perhaps to lodge the demand or desire for a reform or transfiguration of the world'.[16] So common is this pattern of disappointment and desire that he thinks of it as the moral calling of philosophy: 'a register of the moral life that precedes, or intervenes in, the specification of moral theories which define the particular bases of moral judgments of particular acts or projects or characters as right or wrong, good or bad'.[17] Since it is grounded in this splitting, Cavell's perfectionism naturally also envisions the self as internally split or doubled, 'and part of what is both inspiring and frustrating about this vision is that our unattained state presents itself as attainable, as within our grasp if we will but admit its attractiveness and turn towards it'.[18] The unattained self is in us, not out there somewhere. This much should be familiar to us from the melodramas discussed in *Contesting Tears*. Nora and her daughters are sure that there is a better way of life for them. They are able to judge their present state and find it wanting and set about achieving a better, future state. They might call this an education, finding one's voice, a transformation or metamorphosis – an entry into 'a new mode of existence'.[19] Little matter. What is important is that these women can only arrive at this point by reaching inside themselves and enacting a process of self-betterment.

Accordingly, the greatest threat to perfectionism is not other versions of morality but rather debased versions of its own logic. If we come to believe that humans can be and remain perfect – that we are each perfect, just the way we are – then we fail to push ourselves onto the next stage of perfectionism. Cavell cautions against resting on our laurels or descending into sophistry.[20] Self-reliance's motto might well be 'to thine own self be true', but this isn't carte blanche to behave badly or carelessly. Let's not forget, he reminds us, who it is that utters this aphorism in Shakespeare's *Hamlet* – Polonius, a 'foolish prating knave' concerned only with maintaining the status quo.[21]

Film's discovery of perfectionism

In order to describe perfectionism, Cavell draws on the same methodology that he develops in his film books to describe the two genres that he has written about: describing what he sees as the founding myth of perfectionism, much as he describes the founding myths of the remarriage comedy and the unknown woman melodrama. Talking about film, that is, sets the template for talking about philosophy. Evidently perfectionism has something in common with film, something that is perhaps not shared by other philosophical models. We might say film is in perfectionism's DNA. In 'The Good of Film', the text of a December 2000 lecture presented at the Princeton University Center for Human Values, Cavell describes the origins of his interest in perfectionism as threefold. Firstly, in writing *The Claim of Reason*, he had the sense that Wittgenstein's *Philosophical Investigations* involved 'something like a moral or religious fervor'.[22] But while the *Philosophical Investigations* are works of ethical import, they are not generally considered to be works of ethical philosophy, a phenomenon that Cavell finds striking. Secondly, Cavell was dissatisfied with contemporary accounts of perfectionism, and in particular, John Rawls's reading of perfectionism as elitist. But thirdly and most importantly, Cavell recognized the working out of ideas of Emersonian perfectionism within the films covered in *Pursuits of Happiness* and *Contesting Tears*. It was this recognition that prompted Cavell to think that 'there may be a set of ideas *worth communicating here*'.[23]

Two features of the films that he writes about in *Pursuits of Happiness* and *Contesting Tears* are especially salient for Cavell's realization of perfectionism. Firstly, these films stress becoming, or being changed into, a certain sort of person. They explore the possibility of self-transformation, the characters' desires to reinvent themselves and to explore the possibility of a transfigured world in which new ways of being together might be possible. Robert Sinnerbrink states that 'they participate in the perfectionist quest for self-transformation within in a world that could be transformed, however partially, by reinventing our relationship with others'.[24] Secondly, and just as importantly, they do not fit readily within any of the other major categories of academic moral philosophy. In fact, the films in question show a clear disregard for explicit moral conversation, 'as if the perplexities of the conditions of ordinary moral life, matters of equality or of the conflict of inclination with duty, or of duty with duty, or means with ends, pose no intellectual hardships for these people'.[25] Cavell points to *His Girl Friday*'s brash dismissal of moral concerns, encapsulated in the line: 'Where do you get that ethics stuff? You're the only one who'll swipe any of it.' These films recognize, that is, that many moral situations arise 'not from an ignorance of your duties or a conflict of duties but from a confusion over your desires, your attractions and your aversions', a remark that very well describes the situation of the characters in *The Awful Truth*, for example, which we discussed in Chapter 4.

It will hardly be a revelation to readers who have followed me this far that the way in which Cavell brings film and moral philosophy together departs from more well-known iterations of what Robert Sinnerbrink has termed 'cinematic ethics': the idea, that is, that film explores ethical conundrums and that it involves us in this exploration.[26] In short, that film can 'do' ethics. Sinnerbrink argues that Cavell's account of moral perfectionism is, alongside Deleuze's existential account of film's provision of 'reasons to believe in this world', one of the key philosophical approaches to ethics in contemporary film theory.[27] But in other important works in the field, Cavell merits barely a mention, if indeed he is present at all. Lisa Downing and Libby Saxton, for example, dismiss his work as 'limited to a small corpus of films from a single national cinema'.[28] They argue that what is needed is more thorough-going ethics of cinema, one that 'broadens the scope of inquiry to include a wider range of both theoretical and filmic texts; and explores cinema's potential to constitute a genuinely ethical space of experience'.[29] Downing and Saxton's approach to cinematic ethics is typical to some extent of the field more widely, in that it tends to place existing ethical philosophies into conversation with film (although it admittedly extends beyond the dominant moral theories to take in alternative traditions of ethical inquiry such as existentialist and phenomenological approaches). Cavell, on the other hand, argues that film is at odds with philosophical ethics up to this point, and it therefore calls for a new articulation of ethics. He explains that

> when I thought about these eminent theories [of Kant, Mill, and Hegel] in connection with the lives depicted in the grand movies I had been immersed in, the theories and the depicted lives passed one another by, appeared irrelevant to each other. Yet these lives seemed and seem to me ones pursued by thoughtful, mature people, heavily in conversation with one another about the value of their individual or their joint pursuits. I could not understand my interest in them as unrelated to moral reflection. I claim for these films that they are masterpieces of the art of film, primary instances of America's artistic contribution to world cinema, and that their power is bound up in their exploration of a strain of moral urgency for which film's inherent powers of transfiguration and shock and emotionality and intimacy have a particular affinity.[30]

In particular, these films are concerned with the renunciation of a certain type of moral cynicism, 'a giving up on the aspiration to a life more coherent and admirable than seems affordable after the obligations and compromises of adulthood begin to obscure the promise and dreams of youth.'[31] In the remarriage comedies, for example, the principal pair are not especially concerned with moral dilemmas such as theft, murder or the death penalty ('that ethics stuff') but with the question of how to live their best lives, what kind of person they each want to be. These films turn on the question of divorce, on whether the central couple wish to continue being married, and what they are prepared to stake on this desire. 'They are deciding on what kinds of lives they wish to live and whether they wish to live them together, to consent to each other, to say yes to their lives and their life together.'³² What these couples show us is that every decision we make – however big or small – is in a sense a moral decision. In the words of Emerson, 'Character teaches above our wills. Men imagine that they communicate their virtue or vice only by overt actions, and do not see that virtue and vice emit a breath in every moment.'³³ Or, as Cavell puts it, these films show us that

> the moral life is not something constituted solely by consideration of isolated judgements of striking moral and political problems but is a life whose texture is a weave of cares and commitments in which one is bound to become lost and to need the friendly and credible words of others in order to find one's way, in which at any time choice may present itself (whether, or when, say, as in *The Lady Eve*, to confess an indiscretion, or whether, as in *The Awful Truth*, to take offense at an indiscretion), in pondering which *you will have to decide whose view of you is most valuable to you*.³⁴

Moral reasoning and the exemplar

According to Cavell then, to live a moral life, to endlessly become our best selves, we need 'friendly and credible words of others'. We need conversation. And we need to decide whose view of us is most valuable to us. We need to see ourselves through the eyes of another, another whose opinion we respect. The version of moral perfectionism that Cavell describes in *Cities of Words* is contingent on the presence of inspiring examples: figures who are able to hold themselves open to self-overcoming, whose orientation towards their own better selves is realized and displayed to us in such a way as to reveal our present state as dissatisfying and hence to encourage us to turn away from it: Emerson's 'friend' or 'true man' – 'a figure that may occur as the goal of the journey but also its instigation and accompaniment'.³⁵ Cavell also refers to this figure as the exemplar (a term developed from

Nietzsche) or 'the advanced figure who sets those who approach him on a path of education'.[36]

What exactly is the exemplar? He – and for Cavell it is always a he – is usually older and is essentially impersonal. Mulhall explains that although such a friend is always interested in his younger friend's state and fate, it is with a view to helping the younger friend to realize his own self-overcoming, not with a view to satisfying any of his own personal desires (in particular, not any romantic ones). Indeed, such an interest, according to Mulhall, 'would in fact sabotage the perfectionist impulse, in so far as it would impose demands on the befriended one to conform to the friend's desires, and thereby substitute one form of conformity with society's sense of what is possible with another (the friend's sense of what is necessary, and in particular for him)'.[37]

But if this is the case, then how is Cavell able to claim the remarriage comedies as examples of perfectionism in action? And what of the unknown women melodramas, since the exemplar is notably missing from Cavell's account of self-reliance in *Contesting Tears*? This absence comes despite the fact that Emerson describes this figure in 'Self-Reliance', referring to the 'true man', whose standard we are attracted to. It is curious then that Cavell makes little of it in *Contesting Tears*, even when, as in the case of *Now, Voyager*'s Dr. Jacquith, there seems to be an obvious candidate for this role. So how exactly can Cavell argue of either genre that 'the presence of friendship in the films (including the sometimes drastic lack of this relation in the melodramas) is *of the most specific importance* in establishing them as perfectionist narratives'?[38] It seems the question of what a friend is, and what friendship is, needs some attention.

Let's begin with *Pursuits of Happiness*. Here, Cavell explains that the remarriage motif is prompted by the changed situation of marriage, 'which is no longer assured or legitimized by the church or state or sexual compatibility or children' but rather by the 'willingness for remarriage, a way of continuing to affirm the happiness of one's initial leap'.[39] Marriage, in these films, is, in Sinnerbrink's words, 'at once a *romantic and ethical* relationship sustained by an existential will to repeat one's commitment to seek happiness through mutual acknowledgement with an equal'.[40] The central characters are engaged in the task of 'deciding what kinds of lives they wish to live and whether they wish to live them together, to consent to each other, to say yes to their lives and their life together'.[41] This decision-making plays out in the form of a series of dialogues or conversations between individuals who are striving to gain a place of mutual recognition. They need not agree on matters (remember *Adam's Rib*: vive le différence!) but they must come to see things as the other does. And the way in which they do this is to engage in a process of what Cavell calls moral reasoning: the giving of reasons for one's attitude, convictions or conduct.

The concept of moral reasoning is given extended consideration in *Conditions Handsome and Unhandsome* as well as *Cities of Words*, where Cavell gives voice to an intuition that has been haunting his work since *The Claim of Reason*. In a section of the earlier work entitled 'Knowledge and the Basis of Morality', Cavell explains that moral reasoning can be said to have been located with Socrates's explanation to Euthyphro that questions which cause hatred and anger – specifically unlike questions of science or measurement – are disagreements over the question of the just or the unjust, of the good and the bad, of the honourable and the dishonourable.

Socrates: But what kind of disagreement, my friend, causes hatred and anger? Let us look at the matter thus. If you and I were to disagree as to whether one number were more than another, would that make us angry and enemies? Should we not settle such a dispute at once by counting?
Euthyphro: Of course.

Socrates: And should we not settle a question about the relative weight of two things by weighing them?

Euthyphro: Of course.

Socrates: Then what is the question that would make us angry and enemies if we disagreed about it, and could not come to a settlement? Perhaps you have not an answer ready; but listen to mine. Is it not the question of the just and unjust, of the honourable and the dishonourable, of the good and the bad? Is it not questions about these matters which make you and me and everyone else quarrel, when we do quarrel, if we differ about them and can reach no satisfactory agreement?[42]

Cavell picks up this conversation again in an essay first presented in 2000 in Berlin, 'Philosophy the Day after Tomorrow'. In this short article, Cavell explains that it is still the case that the dominant professional pedagogy in moral philosophy proceeds by taking up questions of right and wrong (Kant) and questions of the good and bad (Mill). Issues here tend to emphasize matters of moral choice, of what action is to be done, and the reasons for doing it. The emphasis in Socrates's third pair, the honourable and the dishonourable, tends by contrast to emphasize the evaluation of a way of life, and it is this emphasis that perfectionism shares.[43] Argument is then a key feature of perfectionism, much like bickering is a key part of marriage. Argument here is not 'the attempt to persuade someone to a course of action' but 'responsiveness to and examination of one soul by another'.[44] It is aimed not at calculating principles or at finding universal truths but at acknowledging the need to make one's reasons for acting intelligible to others as well as to one's self.[45] That is, making oneself intelligible is the interpretation that moral perfectionism gives to the idea of moral reasoning. As Cavell writes, 'Perfectionism proposes confrontation and conversation as the means of determining whether we can live together, accept one another into the aspirations of our lives.'[46] In many ways, then, perfectionism is the moral equivalent of overcoming or acknowledgement, and it shares many of the same features, not least the fact that both are based on a kind of endless recommitment to doing one's best. Both place stress on transformation, conversation, confrontation. Both also emphasize uncertainty. We can never know the world, nor another's mind. Nor can we know that a course of moral action is incontrovertibly correct. In both cases, all we can do is put our case forward to the other as lucidly as possible.

So we can see now how the remarriage comedies might be said to turn around moral argument, an argument that takes place between friends. Indeed, in his introduction to *Cities of Words* Cavell states that marriage is an allegory (in these films, at least) of friendship.[47] But the question remains: why marriage? How do the matter of romance and the thorny problem of gender sit alongside the perfectionist model that Cavell draws from Emerson? In short, how is perfectionism gendered? For his part, Cavell is unforthcoming. Although he admits that the films he writes about involve gender as a central theme, Cavell disappointingly fails to take up the topic of gender explicitly in the pages of *Cities of Words*.[48] He dodges the question of same-sex marriages, moreover, by claiming that 'it is too early yet to know (or I am too isolated in my experience to tell) what new shapes such marriages will discover for their investments in imaginativeness, exclusiveness and equality'.[49] But we already know that Cavell does not see the relationship between the sexes in these films as being straightforwardly symmetrical, since the woman is in search not only of a friend but of a teacher, and it will be the man's job to rise to the challenge to being that teacher. Sometimes, as in the case of *The Awful Truth*, this will involve a significant transformation on his own part. In other films, as in *Adam's Rib*, the male character's flaws are not subject to the same scrutiny as his female counterpart's.

It seems that in perfectionism, as in the overcoming of scepticism, the 'creation of woman' remains the 'business of men'. A film such as *The Awful Truth* might offer a model of perfectionist argument in which the roles are rather less hierarchical. Jerry Warriner seems more friend than teacher, and as a result the relationship might be one of equals. Or, as Catherine Constable has it, we may even argue that Lucy Warriner is the exemplar in this pair. But by and large, Cavell's readings of films such as *Adam's Rib* and *The Philadelphia Story* suggest that the male character can be read more or less straightforwardly as an 'advanced figure' or 'exemplar' by whom the female character can be inspired to strive for her unattained yet attainable self. Robert Sinnerbrink points out for example that Dexter's drinking and other flaws, in *The Philadelphia Story*, do not appear to be subject to the same scrutiny or self-examination as Tracy's 'scolding' and her inflexible desire for 'perfection' rather than perfectionism.[50] Tracy's decision to divorce Dexter because of his drinking is not viewed as a valid response to marital discord but as evidence of her lack of sympathy, her intolerance or perfectionism. At the film's end, Tracy has been transformed as a result of her conversation with Dexter. But Dexter has not. And yet in Sinnerbrink's words, Cavell gives 'short shrift' to the problem of such inequality in gender relations.[51] The woman needs an education, and the man is there to give it her.

In the melodramas described in *Contesting Tears*, meanwhile, the female character lacks a male exemplar. Moral argument is forestalled. This is not an insurmountable obstacle to perfectionism: the woman must simply reach inside herself in order to find an exemplar. Indeed, in his chapter on Nietzsche, Cavell suggests that the rare and most valuable exemplar is not another person but 'your own higher self'.[52] Hence Stella Dallas's journey of self-reinvention and final moving walk into the night. Stella knows that the perfection of the self is not to be found in any point of arrival, but in departure, and that in Emersonian perfectionism the pain of departure can be overcome

Figure 16 *The Philadelphia Story*: the husband as moral model. *The Philadelphia Story* (George Cukor, 1941).

by the departure of the self, the act of leaving. 'Every end', Emerson writes, 'is a beginning.'⁵³ Still it is clear from the suffering that Stella and her sisters endure that the making of a suitable match would be a far more joyful path to self-improvement.

Two Tales of Winter

Cavell does, however, offer one example of a female character who embodies a perfectionist perspective but reaches this point neither by receiving an education at the hands of man nor through terrible suffering as a result of lacking such an education. This woman is Félicie, the heroine of Eric Rohmer's *Tale of Winter/Conte d'hiver* (1992). In 'Two Tales of Winter: Shakespeare and Rohmer', an essay included in *Cities of Words*, Cavell suggests that Rohmer's film is a variant on the remarriage comedy genre. It begins with a couple – Félicie and Charles – sharing a holiday romance – and after a series of obstacles, feints and misdirections, ends with them happily reunited. In order to get to this point, Félicie must, like all the characters in the remarriage comedies, 'overcome a series of internal obstacles', a process that requires 'not a moral reevaluation of particular actions or decisions' but 'the revision and transfiguration of a way of life'.[54]

At the end of the film's prologue, Félicie and Charles part ways and arrange to meet again. Charles is temporarily travelling outside France and can provide no usable address; unfortunately the address Félicie gives him proves to be incorrect. Five years later, Félicie is living in Paris with her mother and is a mother herself to a little girl, Elise, whose father is Charles. She is courted by two men: Maxence, the owner of the beauty salon where she works, and Loïc, a philosopher. Félicie discusses with each of them her ideas about her love, her regret at having given Charles the wrong address and her ongoing conviction that he loves her. She is fond of Loïc and is grateful to him for his friendship but does not find him physically attractive; she is attracted to Maxence physically and eventually agrees to move to the city of Nevers with him to start a new business and a family. Here, Félicie visits a cathedral with Elise and while there experiences something of a revelation. She tells Maxence she has changed her mind and returns to Paris. Loïc takes her to a performance of *The Winter's Tale*, which Félicie finds profoundly moving. Afterwards she and Loïc discuss the play and she relates to Loïc her experience in the cathedral. She describes her sense of true and false faith in a way that impresses Loïc (not least because he hears in her words an unlettered discovery of insights brought to philosophy by Plato, Pascal and Descartes) and she concludes that whether Charles returns or not, she will not live in a way that is incompatible with their finding one another again. Shortly afterwards, Félicie and Elise encounter Charles on a bus. They are reunited as a family, and Charles accompanies the pair to Félicie's mother's house, where he helps to prepare a meal.

Cavell's chapter on Rohmer's film both develops on and allows him to rethink arguments set out in his chapter devoted to Shakespeare's play, 'Recounting Gains, Showing Losses: Reading *The Winter's Tale*'. The final chapter in *Disowning Knowledge in Six Plays of Shakespeare*, this essay was republished the following year as part of *In Quest of the Ordinary*. *The Winter's Tale* meanwhile features as a key reference in *Pursuits of Happiness*. Rohmer's film bears many of the features of the genre's foundational myth, but intriguingly, the essay also sees Cavell shift for the first time from thinking about individual films in terms of genre to thinking about them in terms of auteurship. Rohmer's work contains consistent motifs, Cavell notes. These include, but are not limited to,

> demands for, and of specific places, particularly moving between two places; all are about measuring or marking time, or the lapse of time; and about nature or the normal or the trivial; about coincidence, loneliness or separation, chance and choice; about impressions you cannot put a word to; and all contain a moment of insight that has transformative power, and some fantastic thing that simply and blankly *happens* (a trick of the setting sun, a sudden onset of wind through high trees, an encounter).[55]

Most significantly, Rohmer's films all include what Cavell terms a transcendental moment, in which a character is transformed. This moment goes hand in hand with a cinema that focuses resolutely on the ordinary, a world in which nothing much happens: 'a visit, a drive, a talk in a shop, a broken appointment over the telephone, an encounter in a train station, a swim'.[56] Rohmer's films thus seem to Cavell to represent the threat of the ordinary that echoes Wittgenstein's sense of philosophy's craving at once to achieve it and to escape it.

Conte d'hiver is also concerned, at heart, with doubt. In *The Winter's Tale*, Leontes's doubt turns around the question of whether his children are his. In Rohmer's film, Félicie too suffers a crisis of doubt, one that, like Leontes's, is overcome by something 'that resembles faith but that is also to be distinguished from what we might expect of faith'.[57] Félicie reaches this overcoming, however, not through 'meet and happy' conversation with her former or current spouse but through a series of conversations with other men and women – Loïc, Maxence, her mother and sister – and through a moment of self-revelation which she arrives at almost spontaneously. There are two particularly important stations on her path: the moment in the cathedral in Nevers and the conversation that follows with Loïc. During the latter conversation, Félicie tells Loïc, 'Not everyone lives with hope.' She recounts her experience in the cathedral, describing 'an excitement in the brain': 'I didn't think. I saw my thoughts,' she tells him. She pledges to remain in place in the hope that Charles will find her. Little matter how slim the odds of it happening are: her discovery that this is what she wants is already enough for her. Cavell explains that since she has discovered her desire is for Charles, it does not really matter whether he actually returns: it will not affect how she lives now. Loïc is stunned by her, understanding what she says as what Cavell calls a 'secular Pascalian wager': 'This woman has placed her infinite stake in her life not on the theoretical rationality of God's existence, but on the rationality of her own desire.'[58] Indeed, he is so moved by her revelation that he tells her if he were God he would particularly cherish her. She replies that in that case, 'God ought to give me back Charles'. When Loïc indicates that this is too much to ask, she corrects him: 'I am not asking God to give him back.' That is, God ought to; it would make the world better. Cavell explains how Félicie comes to embody perfectionism:

> Félicie's interpretation of her prayer – intuiting Pascal's Wager on immortal joy and Plato's argument for the preexistence of the soul – is her way of marking the difference of Emersonian perfectionism from utilitarianism, whose calculation of pleasure is anything but

Figure 17 Félicie in *Conte d'hiver*: 'She exists, as her thoughts exist; she loves; she counts herself happy.' *Conte d'hiver* (Éric Rohmer, 1993).

Pascalian individual riskiness; and equally Kantianism, whose universalization by the moral law she denies when, as when Loïc said that her words were meaningless to him [...] she replies, 'I saw it; you did not'. She acts neither from reason (she once remarks that she doesn't like what is plausible), nor from inclination (she speaks instead of avoiding what is counter to her convictions) nor from hope (startling Loïc by saying that not everyone lives with hope, clearly not meaning that she lives with hopelessness). She exists, as her thoughts exist; she loves; she counts herself happy.[59]

Hierarchy and elitism

If Félicie is able to embody a form of perfectionism that takes place outside of marriage, outside of education by a man, free from suffering, then how does this recast the remarriage comedies and the unknown women melodramas? In particular, what does her childlike, joyous embrace of life's possibility offer to how we think about perfectionism?

In a first instance, Félicie's ability to be transformed without help from a male teacher puts the gender dynamics of the remarriage comedy into play and privileges conversation over education, the friend over the teacher. The texture and mood of the remarriage comedy, Cavell argues in *Contesting Tears*, are pervaded by conversation. Indeed, the willingness for conversation is the basis for marriage itself.[60] Rohmer's film is likewise pervaded by conversation, but here it does not attach itself to marriage.[61] Time and again, we see Félicie engaging in lengthy dialogues with Maxence and Loïc, testing out theories and trying to get to the bottom of her feelings. Her would-be husband Charles, meanwhile, is silent for the vast majority of the film's running time, and his sudden reappearance at the film's end aligns him more closely with the revivified Hermione than it does Leontes, undercutting the assertion that in the remarriage comedy it is mostly 'the man, and not the woman who doubts'.[62]

Cavell thus explains that Rohmer's film permits him to return to Shakespeare's play with new insights into its interest in the female protagonist who finds herself alone and who must come anew to an understanding of a reshaped world. He points out that one of the most unusual aspects of the film in terms of Rohmer's wider oeuvre is its attention to several generations (confirmed by the image of grandmother and grandchild sitting together on a sofa) and in particular in its attention to a young child (not a common feature of the Hollywood remarriage comedy). Cavell senses that Rohmer's camera's frequent cuts to five-year-old Elise by herself are 'as if to reassure itself of her existence', reminding us of how Shakespeare's *The Winter's Tale*, despite its comic motif of harmony, leaves a small child unaccounted for.[63] He argues that the timing of Leontes's jealous rage against Hermione – a sudden suspicion that she is having sexual relations with his friend Polixenes – coincides with her late pregnancy. Hermione is about to give birth to a second child, striking doubt into Leontes's heart about whether he is the father of Mamillus, his first child, too. He expresses this doubt when he asks Mamillus, 'Art thou my boy?', and attempts to reassure himself by remarking 'they say [your nose] is a copy of mine'. This is taken up by Rohmer, when Félicie, who hates her own nose, reassures Charles that Elise is indeed his daughter by pointing to the resemblance between their noses – an assertion he takes at face value. Charles is evidently not a man troubled by doubt or suspicion.

Cavell reminds us of the difference between women's experience of sceptical doubt and men's. Men, recall, can never truly know if they are the father of their child. A woman can never have a similar doubt. But she may have concerns or questions over the identity of her child's father. Indeed, Cavell suggests Félicie's pregnancy is in a sense an expression of her own doubts about Charles. His first words in the film are to tell Félicie that she is 'taking a risk' as they lie naked in bed together after having sex. Her mistake over the address becomes a test of Charles's ability to find her again. As Fiona Handyside puts it, it is not by coming into her life once but rather by coming back to her that he proves his suitability as a father and as a spouse.[64]

Félicie doubts. She throws down a challenge to the father of her child to overcome this doubt. And as she waits for him, she herself, by herself, learns to overcome her suspicions. None of the male figures in the film serve as educator, and none – with the exception of Charles, perhaps – seem to understand her. Several serve as sounding-boards, comforters, opponents, interlocutors – in short, friends. But ultimately, Félicie learns to rely on herself and on her instincts to allow her to change, to transform. As such, she has as much – if not more – in common with the heroines of the melodramas as she does the women who remarry in the comedies. Cavell describes, for examples, her 'strangeness to the world', 'her mystery', 'her unknownness' as 'something she feels in response to herself'.[65] Yet he calls her the 'antithesis' of Lisa in *Letter from an Unknown Woman*, a 'spiritual genius' able to demand that her uniqueness be recognized and to ask of men what she wants of them.[66] Félicie wants the men in her life

> to pray for her in church 'from the bottom of the heart', meaning to pray as if they *were* her; she wants them to know life from life, not from what others have said about life; she wants them masterful and submissive, intelligent and sweet; sometimes she wants to sleep next to them when she doesn't want to go home, yet does not then want to make love … she wants them to find her without her giving her address, she wants to be returned to, freely, to be found as herself, loved madly.[67]

She recounts her self-discovery not in terms of suffering but of joy. She has found herself. She tells her mother, 'There are no good or bad choices,' implying that she has moved beyond questions of traditional morality and embraced her choices as her choices, appropriate in the situation.

In a second instance, Félicie – although no doubt comfortably middle class – embodies a childlike naivety that seems to cut through the worldliness inherent to the remarriage comedies, with their reliance on double-entendre and innuendo. Cavell admits that both the genres he writes about, but in particular, the marriage comedies run the 'perpetual moral risk of snobbery'.[68] The remarriage comedies in particular seem to regard the more outstanding issues of moral complexity – abortion, euthanasia, poverty, taxation, capital punishment – as matters that will take care of themselves, preferring instead to focus on the romantic travails of a healthy, wealthy pair of upper-class white people. This is a reason, Cavell suggests, that the narrative of the films inevitably provides each of the pair with a moment of being humbled, or humiliated, hence with an opportunity for self-knowledge: 'The lives depicted can seem, from a philosophical perspective, too confined or aloof to provide moral inspiration or instruction for a rough world.'[69]

Such accusations of snobbery on the part of the film find an echo in John Rawls's claim that moral perfectionism is in itself elitist, since its focus on the state of one's own soul is inward looking and self-interested and therefore does little to improve society more broadly. As Stephen Mulhall puts it: 'The state of my soul might be of pressing importance to me, but why should it be of any concern to the arbitrators of what one might call public or social justice, i.e. to my fellow citizens?'[70] Does the focus on the individual's quest for happiness, acknowledgement and self-transformation leave these films open then to the charge of being elitist, bourgeois or apolitical?

In fact, whether Emersonian perfectionism is essentially elitist or on the contrary whether its imagination of justice is essential to the aspirations of a democratic society is, Cavell claims, 'a guiding question' of *Cities of Words*[71] and that 'the laboratory of film is one in which the elitism of perfectionism is tested'.[72] How is this the case? In the first instance, it has to do with the everyday. As Cavell explains, in these films, nothing legitimizes or ratifies marriage apart from the willingness for remarriage, and what makes remarriage worth reaffirming is 'a diurnal devotedness that involves friendship, play, surprise, and *mutual education*, all expressed in the pair's conversing with one another'.[73] In this much, perfectionism, like a commitment to ordinary language or to overcoming scepticism, is inherently democratic, turning as it does around a constant search for shared criteria against the threat of dissension and disagreement. For Cavell, in democracy we are always striving, against its inevitable failures and compromises, towards an increasing acknowledgement of the differences and idiosyncrasies of others. Indeed, in Rex Butler's words: 'Democracy is the political system more than any other that operates as its own self-criticism, that is never achieved as such but exists only in the process of its own endless testing and refinement.'[74]

Moreover for Cavell, our individual freedoms may be limited by the conditions that society imposes upon it, but whatever freedom is available to us, we should use wisely and with a view to improving both ourselves and the society that we live in. This is a variant on Rousseau's proposition that the realm of politics should be an extension of the realm of individual liberty: since the modern political community is understood to be the construction of its members, its laws (being determined by those members) are not heteronomous impositions on individual citizens but norms to which we as individuals consent or refuse. Cavell writes in *Conditions Handsome and Unhandsome*:

> [The] idea of the self must be such that it can contain, let us say, an intuition of partial compliance with its idea of itself, hence of distance from itself, space for consciousness of itself or of consciousness denied. The companion concept of society is such that partial compliance with its principles of justice is not necessarily a distancing of oneself from it, but may present itself as a sense of compromise by it or conspiracy with it.[75]

We might think of this sense of conspiracy or compromise with society as our having in a sense always already consented to society. The best works of art – such as the novels of Austen or Elliot – are, Cavell argues, born of this sense of compromise. They bear a certain respect for conformity and society as it is. They write 'as if out of the obligation to depict for their readers the truth of their condition, hence to awaken and confirm their knowledge of the brutalities of that condition, and to exemplify instances in which the soul can learn not to be crushed by the force of compromise'.[76] They ask us to maintain faith with one's desires even in the face of compromise. Such is the position that Félicie's commitment to waiting for Charles – even though the world is unlikely to deliver him – exemplifies. As Cavell explains, in perfectionism 'one's quarrel with the world need not be settled, nor cynically set aside as unsettlable. It is a condition in which you can at once want the world and want to change it'.[77]

Perfectionism embodies an idea of the individual's truth to humanity in herself that it sees as inseparable from a concern with society and the possibilities it holds out for others. In this much it is not self-interested but socially aware. In a second sense, though, it is democratic in the sense that – while it aspires to self-improvement – it is uninterested in ideas of culture, taste or intellectual prowess. To equate perfectionism with self-cultivation would, Cavell states wryly, 'be as much a debasement of the idea as any of the current popular philosophies that offer to release your potential for making a killing in real estate or the day trading or to provide you with the means to be all you can be'.[78] He writes: 'The Emersonian progress is not from coarseness to sophistication, or from commonness to prominence, but from loss to recovery, or, as Thoreau roughly says, from despair to interest, or as Kierkegaard and Heidegger and Wittgenstein more or less put the matter, from chatter to speech.'[79] Hence it is neither Maxence, with his good business sense and capitalist drive to do better for himself, nor well-read Loïc, with his encyclopaedic knowledge of the moral philosophers, who embodies perfectionism in *Conte d'hiver*. Indeed, one suspects that their very investment in these qualities leaves them fixed in place, conforming to a set of values which they have not yet thought through. Rather it is Félicie, who nervously witters throughout the film but who finally, eloquently, expresses her faith in the world in speech not chatter, that best serves as an exemplar of what it might look like to follow a perfectionist path. She embodies the democratization of perfectionism, displacing the need for education at the hands of man while making concrete an idea that Cavell intuited in *Conditions Handsome and Unhandsome*, that perfectionism's emphasis is, above all,

> upon becoming intelligible to oneself, as if the threat to one's moral coherence comes most insistently from that quarter, from one's sense of obscurity to oneself, as if we are subject to demands we cannot formulate, leaving us unjustified, as if our lives condemn us.

Perfectionism's emphasis on culture or cultivation is, to my mind, to be understood in connection with this search for intelligibility, or say this search for direction in what seems a scene of moral chaos, the scene of the dark place in which one has lost one's way.[80]

Cavell as teacher and friend

Film is an art form that calls our attention to the undramatic, the small, the repetitive, the quotidian: perhaps nowhere more so than in Rohmer's cinema. It shows us that morality is not something separate from us but is bound up in everyday lives, our smallest of choices. Watching it, we come to learn that

> our slights of one another, in an unexpressed or disguised meanness of thought, in a hardness of glance, a willful misconstrual, a shading of loyalty, a dismissal of intention, a casual indiscriminateness of praise or blame – in any of the countless signs of skepticism with respect to the reality, the separateness, of another – we run the risk of suffering, or dealing, little deaths every day.[81]

Film thus returns us to Wittgenstein and to the idea that everything matters. In our every word and every gesture, we bear responsibility for the world we share. If we are disappointed by our inability to live up to this responsibility, it is because we know that there is a better way, a better world to be had. To borrow Robert Sinnerbrink's words, 'the moral calling of film may begin with disappointment in the world, but it offers the prospect of transforming ourselves and our relationship with it'.[82]

The films about which Cavell writes not only give rise to his conception of perfectionism, but they serve as exemplars in and of themselves. They do this through the actions of the characters on screen: Félicie models what it is to strive for a better world; Stella shows us how to find the courage to be self-reliant; the Warriners show us what it might look like to commit and recommit to a marriage that could, itself, be better, if only the individuals making it up might try a little harder to share their vision of the world with one another. But of course there are non-cinematic characters – such as Ibsen's Nora, or Shakespeare's Leontes and Hermione – who behave in much the same way as these characters. It is the unique existence of Félicie, Stella, Jerry and Lucy as cinematic characters, embedded in an egalitarian medium particularly well placed to capture the ordinariness of their lives – that lends them their peculiar power. Film transfigures these men and women, expressing perfectionism – the unending zigzag of steps towards a better self – physically. As David Rodowick puts it, 'One of the powers of photogenesis is to express the transformation of fixation *as* metamorphosis, to show that subjects do become, or become-other, on film.'[83] More than this, these works of art do not just show us transformation, but they bring about transformation, in the spectator. Film is, in Cavell's words, a philosophical accompaniment to everyday life, but it might also affect the everyday life. In the film *Pennies from Heaven*, one character puts it like this: 'Every time you walk out of a movie, the world has changed.'[84] In the next chapter we will examine how, exactly, this change might be accomplished.

But there is something that might intervene between the film and the viewer: the critic. Robert Sinnerbrink has described Cavell as a 'mediator': a go-between who places film into dialogue with philosophy.[85] This seems to me wrong. For Cavell, film is philosophical – or at least the films he writes about are. They don't need him to 'do' philosophy, since as William Rothman puts it, 'they reveal themselves to be self-evidently consequential'.[86] Cavell defines a 'good film' as

> one that bears up under criticism of the sort that is invited and expected by serious works within the classical arts, works that attest that film is the latest of the great arts, so works in which an audience's passionate interest, or disinterest, is rewarded with an

articulation of the condition of the interest that illuminates it and expands self-awareness.[87]

And the best of these films do all this without tipping the hand of their artistry.

Cavell is not a mediator. What Cavell is, however, is a critic and a teacher. He explains that it was a revelation to him 'to discover the intellectual depth and artistic conscience in the Hollywood comedies and melodramas that I had devoted a book each to studying'.[88] What Cavell discovers over the course of writing the film books is that he had taken attachment and memories of these films for granted, 'namely assumed that their value could be accounted for otherwise than by understanding film writers, actors, directors, designers, and photographers to be following and adapting and contesting ancient crafts'.[89] His work is aimed at forestalling just such a taking-for-grantedness on our part, leading us to think about how we respond to these films and what to make of these responses. So before we move on to further consider the question of how film engages the spectator in a perfectionist relation, and how Cavell's criticism is reflective of this, we must first think about Cavell's own role as teacher and as friend.

The teaching of Cavell's course on perfectionism was another revelation for him. It allowed him to connect great texts of moral philosophy whose power to inspire thought had, in some cases, lasted for millennia, with a thoroughly contemporary art form: 'a body of films whose experience has been found to survive the changing tastes of generations and *which minimizes the degree of expertise required to respond to them intelligently*, so that the differences between generations can become interesting and discussible from all sides'.[90] Once more, Cavell emphasizes film as the most democratic of art forms: a medium of which one needs no specialist knowledge in order to talk authoritatively about it. At first glance, this position might appear risible – especially to scholars studying and teaching in Film Studies departments where the degree of expertise often needed to talk lucidly about film is very evident. Let's read Cavell with the same generosity of spirit that he offers to so many of his subjects, though, and imagine that what he means here is that film has a visceral power to move audiences that prefigures articulation or theory. That it is film's privileged relationship to the ordinary – to ordinary words, worlds, actions, speech and events – that makes it so special.

For Emerson, thinking is a double process, which consists of two steps: transfiguration and conversion, or intuition and tuition.[91] This is the process by which experience is converted into thought, the process by which it is articulated. It is the process undergone by Félicie when she first intuits a kind of grace moment in Nevers Cathedral, and when she retrospectively describes this experience to Loïc, crystallizing a feeling that she had not yet given voice to and in the process transforming herself. There is a sense in which Cavell sees the viewing of film as an intuitive experience: the role of the student of film and of the teacher of film alike is to put this experience into words. In an essay entitled 'Moral Reasoning: Teaching from the Core', Cavell compares both himself and his graduate students to 'guides'. Teaching a text, Cavell explains, has less to do with checking on a beginner's mastery of knowledge and more to do with guiding the student through texts that the teacher will continue to read indefinitely and that they are prepared to read again with more understanding this time than the last. It is, he says, 'a relationship of tact and trust'.[92]

The image that Cavell conjures, of both student and teacher striving to articulate their responses to film, is one of mutual acknowledgement and overcoming. It is analogous, perhaps, with marriage – at least as Cavell conceives of it. That is, there is an asymmetry to the relationship of teacher and student, of course. And there is also parity between individuals striving to best communicate their ideas and feelings about the film. In the chapter on *The Awful Truth* featured in *Cities of Words*,

Cavell explains that between men and women, love must be spoken to be known: a feeling or intuition must be articulated in order for the object of that love to understand that it exists. And someone has to go first. In the remarriage comedy, it is the man who claims his right to speak of love to the woman, to ask for reciprocation. Hence Jerry must cross the threshold first. So too, the teacher makes the opening gambit in an ongoing conversation, a conversation that flows both ways. A Cavellian education emphasizes an encounter with one's uniqueness through the pain of individuation as much as the joy of communion. It encourages the cultivation of self-knowledge (or self-reliance) amongst teachers and students, as well as the acknowledgement of otherness. As Naoko Saito puts it, the Cavellian classroom is a place to cultivate 'the art of patient listening and imaginative seeing'.[93] It is only then that students and teachers come to acquire the sense of responsibility for their own words and to learn what it means to join the city of words.

Conclusion: From the classroom to the page

In the classroom, then, Cavell may assume the role of educator, exemplar *and* friend. He describes a room full of not only undergraduate students and graduate students but also visitors and auditors and other teachers and recounts having the sense that 'anyone, destined for any achievement, may be a member of the group sitting in your classroom, weighing the value of what you have to offer'.[94]

> I had the feeling one could say anything one had it at heart to say about major moments of our shared culture, and if one got it clear enough and interesting enough, one would be understood, and not just by this group but by what the group represented for

me, the body of citizens of good will with time for thought and imagination. This permanently affected the way I write books.[95]

Cities of Words is, however, Cavell's final scholarly monograph. His subsequent two books comprise *Little Did I Know* (2010), an autobiography, and *Philosophy the Day after Tomorrow* (2006), a collection of essays written between 1996 and 2006. In the final chapter of this book, I will go on to examine how Cavell's own perfectionist education – arrived at via the acts of writing and teaching – shapes these two works. But I will also consider how we as students and readers of Cavell might be shaped by this work. In the introduction to *Cities of Words* Cavell is clear that there is a difference between attending a class and reading a book, just as there is a difference between lecturing and writing. What is it to read Cavell? To think about – and write about – film in his wake? For, like the best teachers, he does not tell us anything new but helps us to *understand* something that is already in plain view, since this, as Wittgenstein has it, is what we seem 'in some sense not to understand'.[96] To put it simply, Cavell teaches those who read him to trust their own voice. It is my belief that this is nothing short of an act of love.

Love's Work

For years I've been thinking aloud – and often wondering if I've made myself ludicrous in one way or another. I think the anxiety comes from knowing I have no real qualifications to write as I do. […] My evidence – such as it is – is almost always intimate. I feel this – do you? I'm struck by this thought – are you? Essays about one person's affective experience have, by their very nature, not a leg to stand on. All they have is their freedom. And the reader is likewise unusually free, because I have absolutely nothing over her, no authority. She can reject my feelings at every point, she can say: 'No, I have never felt that', or 'Dear Lord, the thought never crossed my mind!'

Why am I telling you this? Because it happened to me. Let me tell you what happened to me.

– Zadie Smith, *Feel Free*

This is what I see. Can you see it too?
– Stanley Cavell, *Must We Mean What We Say?*

Towards the conclusion of 'The End of Myths', Cavell discusses the nature of modern love, via the late films of Alfred Hitchcock.[1] These films, produced after the Second World War, inhabit according to Cavell a world of stolen love, love neither earned nor freely given. Watching them, we no longer take it for granted that their characters – male or female – are capable of intimacy, that their cool, calm surfaces belie the 'fires banked within'. *To Catch a Thief*'s vision of love is merely convention; *Marnie*'s central figures are thieves of love.[2] In *The Birds*, human yearning can only be satisfied by something superhuman, by 'all the birds of the heavens'.[3]

This is in contrast with Hitchcock's earlier *Notorious*, in which love is still a possibility. Ingrid Bergman may try her best to deny her feelings, but she is not detached from them, and at the film's end, she stands facing her lover, their relationship on an equal footing. Hitchcock's later heroines, however – played by Grace Kelly, Kim Novak or Tippi Hedren – will never make their matches. In the films that they inhabit 'all modern love is perverse, because now tangential to the circling of society', so 'the promise of love depends upon the acceptance of perversity, and that in turn requires the strength to share privacy, to cohabit in one element, unsponsored by society. This fancy lady's private element is unsharable: no man is a bird of her feather'.[4] *Psycho* perhaps best embodies the modern relation to love, 'in which our capacity for feeling, our modulation of instinct, is no longer elicited by human centers of love and hate, but immediately by the theories we give ourselves of love and hate'.[5] Cavell concludes that 'knowledge has not replaced love as our address to the world, but knowledge has replaced the world as the object of our passion'.[6] And indeed, some thirty years later, in an essay titled 'The Future of Possibility', Cavell draws on three very different films – Bergman's *Smiles of a Summer Night*, Alain Resnais and Marguerite Duras's *Hiroshima, Mon Amour*, and Michelangelo Antonioni's *L'Avventura* – to ask whether, in the modern age, love is an exhausted possibility.[7] He wonders whether the age of scepticism has destroyed our potential for love. What would be at stake if so?

Love is not a word commonly associated with Cavell. Education, conversation, attention. Friendship, marriage, romance. Care. Even passion. These are the terms which surface repeatedly within Cavell's writing and the scholarship surrounding it. But love? Love is barely spoken of. Ironically, it perhaps receives its most extended treatment in Cavell's early essay on *King Lear*, titled 'The *Avoidance* of Love' (my emphasis): an essay which turns around Cordelia's decision to love and be silent – that is, precisely *not* to speak of love. The marriages that Cavell describes in *Pursuits of Happiness* are sexless, childlike: they culminate in odd, awkward kisses and cold draughty bedrooms that seem ill-suited to a night of lovemaking. Cavell describes marriage itself in terms of friendship or fellowship, as 'a condition in which a kinship is to be recognised and then an affinity established'.[8] Still, this passionless kinship is far more desirable than the fanatic ardour of Lisa for Stefan, Stella for Stephen or even perhaps Charlotte for Jerry, described in *Contesting Tears*. In the melodramas, even maternal love is at best problematic, and at worst just as destructive as romantic love.

Yet at the heart of all Cavell's writing are two great loves. Philosophy: the love of wisdom. And cinephilia: the love of film. Time and again Cavell describes his *care* for film. 'Film is an interest of mine,' he writes, '*or say a love*, not separate from my interest in, or love of, philosophy'.[9] Film *matters*, that is, and that mattering demands something of him. This something takes the form of writing, perhaps Cavell's third love. Recalling being asked as a young man by Arthur Danto whether his slowness to publish was because he didn't like to write, Cavell explains:

> I could not protest that I had written more than I had published because I seemed to recognise that that might only prove the truth of Arthur's surmise, not that I hadn't in some sense written, but that what kept me from offering it to strangers was not simply the fear that it wasn't good enough but, compounded with that, *the fear that my pleasure in it would show*, which for some reason would constitute a worse exposure.[10]

Cavell loves to write; it is one of his great joys. In writing, he finds a place in which he could 'with a certain constancy encounter times of lucid happiness'.[11] Through writing, he connects with the world.

This chapter asks, then, what it is for Cavell to write about film; to write, as he puts it in his autobiography *Little Did I Know*, 'for friends and strangers'. It looks at Cavell's film criticism as what Robert Sinnerbrink has called 'romantic film-philosophy', Andrew Klevan 'philosophical film criticism' and the feminist philosopher Toril Moi 'ordinary language criticism': a responsive form of writing about film that allows the film to 'speak first'.[12] It also considers Cavell's criticism as what Cavell himself has called a 'passionate utterance', a claim on his reader's conscience.[13] Both romance and passion are intimately bound up with love. I want finally to argue that Cavell's writing, even as it refuses to name itself as such, is an act of love and that to write philosophy and to write film criticism are to do love's work.

Cavellian film criticism

In separate essays, all published in 2011, Robert Sinnerbrink, Andrew Klevan and Toril Moi attempt to get to grips with what is so unique about Cavell's approach to film criticism. Sinnerbrink's chapter, published in Havi Carel and Greg Tuck's *New Takes in Film Philosophy*, situates Cavell within the romantic tradition by referring to his writing about film as 'romantic film-philosophy'. Sinnerbrink argues that many philosophers 'disenfranchise' film (to borrow a phrase from Arthur Danto) by subsuming it within a preexisting framework that typically reduces its aesthetic complexity. Cavell's romantic film-philosophy, however, 'does not presuppose the conceptual superiority of philosophy over cinema, avoids the temptation to translate film into a philosophical metalanguage, and thereby opens up the possibility that philosophy might be transformed through its encounter with film'.[14] In this model, film and philosophy 'become active partners in a "thinking dialogue"; a transformative engagement that helps elaborate the philosophy immanent within particular films, while promoting philosophy to respond creatively to the kind of thinking that cinema allows us to experience'.[15]

Sinnerbrink frames this mutually enriching exchange between film and philosophy as romantic, drawing on Nikolas Kompridis's use of the term in his collection *Philosophical Romanticism*. For Kompridis, philosophical romanticism is a self-reflective, critical response to the Enlightenment version of modernity: at once a critique of modern philosophy and a cultural critique of modernity itself. He explains that philosophy is part of modernity, and so it is asked to make sense of the conditions in which it exists, as well how it responds to these conditions. As such, philosophical romanticism is in a constant state of self-questioning and transformation, posing questions about, amongst other things, the form through which philosophy should express itself: 'questions about the nature, sources and limits of its expressivity, of how it can "speak" in a voice of its own', become paramount.[16] And this preoccupation with problems of expressivity draws philosophical romanticism ever closer to the humanities – including, of course, the study of film. As it comes to recognize that philosophy's fate is bound up with the culture to which it belongs, philosophical romanticism engages in a critique of culture that is continuous with its critique of philosophy. Philosophical romanticism does not seek absolutes; rather it looks to the emergence of non-standard and pluralistic forms of arguments. 'Ultimately', writes Kompridis, 'the purpose of such arguments is to get us to see things in a different light, and that light can shine only when a new perspective is made available to us'.[17]

The primary task of philosophy, according to philosophical romanticism, is to enlarge the cultural conditions of intelligibility and possibility and thereby open the horizon of the future. In short, philosophical romanticism is responsive to new ways of thinking and open to change. To romanticize the world is to make way for change, with the emphasis on making way: while philosophical romanticism ushers in change, it does not impose it. As Cavell puts it, 'What happens in the world ... is always happening.'[18] Receptivity is essential to 'making' the new possible – receptivity to the present, to the difference between today and yesterday, to as yet undisclosed possibilities, and thinking about receptivity in this way reframes how we see agency. Agency, that is, becomes a matter of what we let ourselves be affected by, rather than a matter of what we exercise control over. Related to this, philosophical romanticism has a special interest in the everyday, not just as it is now, but as it might be. This is, in part, because the ordinary opens onto – if not the transcendent – then at least the possibility of a meaningful universe, one that exists beyond the crippling conditions of fragmentation, anomie and scepticism ushered in by modernism. Cavell, drawing on Heidegger, puts it thus: 'The redemption of the things of the world is the redemption of human nature, and chiefly from its destructiveness of its own conditions of existence.'[19]

While all of these concerns are integral to philosophical romanticism, there is, according to Kompridis, one overarching concern that distinguishes philosophical romanticism from other traditions of modern philosophy: the concern with realizing a form of freedom that the conditions of modernity make possible and thwart at the same time. This is a non-individualistic form of freedom, in which one is able to recognize one's words and actions as one's own, as spontaneously originating from oneself, at the same time as acknowledging the social and political relationships which we are part of.[20] What this amounts to is a process of looking backwards in order to look forward and of looking inward in order to look outward. Philosophical romanticism thinks the *new*: it looks for alternative possibilities of being, different ways of seeing. Sinnerbrink thus concludes that art, literature and film are essential to this task, 'for they provide alternative forms of aesthetic disclosure that opens up new possibilities of thought, meaning and action'.[21] Cavell himself characterizes these art forms as 'thinking for the future'.[22]

In her article, 'The Adventure of Reading: Literature and Philosophy, Cavell and Beauvoir', Toril Moi perceives a similar kind of 'making way for the new' in what Cavell does. Moi argues that a key feature of Cavellian criticism is its avoidance of the assumption that there is a ready-made conceptual framework or theoretical approach that should be applied to film to yield meaning or which the film is supposed to illustrate. Instead, she argues, both the object of criticism and criticism itself allow us to think beyond existing paradigms.

Moi's analysis of what she calls 'ordinary language criticism' is focused in the main on literature, but she is inspired by Cavell's practice of 'checking one's experience' against the work of art by paying careful attention, an idea that he sets out in *Pursuits of Happiness*.[23] 'Films and plays and books can help us overcome, or undo, our existing beliefs,' Moi writes. This means 'reading (and viewing) can expand our understanding of the world, and of ourselves, if we let it'.[24] Opening ourselves up to a film or a book requires attention: a concept that Moi points out comes from the Latin *ad-tendere*: to stretch or reach towards something. To attend to something is 'to direct the mind or the senses toward something, to apply oneself; to watch over, minister to, wait upon, follow frequent; to wait for, expect'.[25] An attentive gaze, Moi writes (drawing on Iris Murdoch), is a 'just and loving gaze'.[26] It strives to understand, to be responsive, to see things in a new manner. It *acknowledges* the work of art, in much the same way as the husbands and wives described in *Pursuits of Happiness* come to acknowledge one another.

In this much, Moi argues Cavell's practice of ordinary language criticism is diametrically opposed to what is often known as 'critical theory', a practice which Cavell describes as offering readings of films that claim to be 'the only game in town'.[27] Such theories are anathema to conversation: they are inward looking and isolating and cause 'uncreativeness and parochialism more often than [making] for anything better'.[28] Theory closes down possibilities. Cavell's philosophically inflected criticism opens them up.

Cavell's criticism thus conjoins film and philosophy, in the sense of seeing how ideas of scepticism or self-reliance may illuminate film, but it also understands film *as* philosophy, discovering and dramatizing philosophical matters themselves. More than that, Moi argues, for Cavell criticism – literary criticism, music criticism, film criticism – is philosophical: 'the work of reading, thinking and writing about literature and other art forms – can be part of philosophy ... Criticism is an activity in which the philosopher, encountering the work of art, can attempt to get clear on questions he couldn't get clear on in any other way'.[29] Thinking about *The Awful Truth*, *Stella Dallas* or *Conte d'hiver*, Cavell pushes his understanding of scepticism and self-reliance further than he could have done otherwise. Crucially, this understanding comes to him through writing. Moi cites a passage written by Cavell in 2002, as part of a foreword to a new edition of *Must We Mean What We Say?*:

> Only in stages have I come to see that each of my ventures in and from philosophy bears on my ways of understanding the extent to which my relation to myself is figured in relation to my words. This establishes from the beginning my sense that in appealing from philosophy to, for example, literature, I am not seeking illustrations for truths philosophy already knows, but illumination of philosophical pertinence that philosophy alone has not surely grasped – as though an essential part of its task must work behind its back. I do not understand such appeals as 'going outside' philosophy.[30]

Moi stresses Cavell's emphasis here on his relation to his words: a phrase which she believes gestures towards Cavell's desire to understand language as something we do, 'so that our words reveal us, our values and commitments, and what we take ourselves to be responsible for'.[31] Hence Moi's emphasis on Cavell's criticism as ordinary language. If questions of expression, of the words we use to capture our experience, are at the heart of philosophy, then criticism – the act of accounting for one's experience of a work of art – can *be* philosophy.

As Andrew Klevan expresses it in his article 'Notes on Stanley and Philosophical Film Criticism', also published in Carel and Tuck's collection, Cavell's very *approach* to film is philosophical.[32] Klevan, whose own style of textual analysis and appreciation is heavily influenced by Cavell (along with V.F. Perkins), dubs Cavell's film writing 'Philosophical Film Criticism' and characterizes it as a six-step process of 'discovering', 'revealing', 'describing', 'returning', 'investigating' and 'appreciating'.[33] For Klevan, Cavell's criticism takes the form of a 'disclosure of the everyday'[34]: of revealing or uncovering what was always before our eyes, of seeing a new aspect of something familiar (a practice akin to Moi's idea of paying attention). He writes:

> Unlike most contemporary forms of textual scholarship which derive meaning from a work's origins, its historical, cultural, or national context, Cavell's criticism emphasizes those meanings that are *discovered* during *this* moment of engagement with the text, and with each other (through dialogue, during teaching). It tends not to rely on information of facts … in order to propose a 'truth' and instead stresses 'responsiveness' as a way of learning of learning (about something).[35]

Something of this process is captured by Wittgenstein's observation in point 89 of the *Investigations*, where he writes: 'We want to understand something that is already in plain view. For this is what we seem in some sense not to understand.'[36] According to Klevan, film continuously reminds us of this because it presents people, places and objects in plain view.

There is a moral imperative to this revelation of the everyday, since when we miss the things before us, we fail to pay attention to the world that surrounds and by extension to our experience of it. The result is that our lives go not exactly unexamined, but that we miss them, that they are lost to us: a moral that Cavell sees as being at the heart of *Letter from an Unknown Woman* as well as Henry James's short novella, *The Beast in the Jungle*.[37] In both, a man takes for granted, or overlooks, the enduring love of an unassuming woman and hence misses out on the adventure of their lives. Klevan makes an astute connection between the missable and the dismissible – to miss something is a failure to appreciate it. 'We may simply miss a moment, it may simply pass us by, but we may also think we have seen a moment, seen all there is to see.'[38] That is, it has not had its full effect upon us. Thinking about this problem of oversight, Cavell is led to quote Henry James, on 'The Art of Fiction':

> The power to guess the unseen in the seen, to trace the implications of things, to judge the whole piece by the pattern, the condition of feeling life in general so completely that you are well on your way to knowing any particular corner of it – this cluster of gift may almost be said to constitute experience … Therefore, if I should certainly say to a novice, 'Write from experience and experience only,' I should feel that this was a rather tantalising monition if I were not careful immediately to add, 'Try to be one of the people on whom nothing is lost'.[39]

To Cavell's mind, the work of criticism is to reveal the object we've been missing, to show that we have not yet appreciated it fully. He admits that until he came to write about the films covered in *Contesting Tears* and *Pursuits of Happiness*, he had taken his 'attachment and memories of these films for granted', not realizing 'the intellectual depth and artistic conscience' in them.[40] This was a mistake, he comes to see. It is the role of the critic to think about how a good film makes sense to us, what it means to us and whether it has its desired effect upon us. Of course, it is the most humdrum or everyday objects that usually go overlooked. Film, perhaps more than any other art, can slip by unnoticed or at least unappreciated (hence the feminist theorist Sandra Laugier is led to argue that 'attention to the everyday is ... the first definition of *caring*', a word which as we know has a great significance for how Cavell understands his relationship to film).[41]

Ultimately Klevan understands Cavellian film criticism then as engagement with a film that is 'not simply about interpreting it, or excavating it, but *appreciating* it'.[42] Like Moi, he emphasizes that good criticism requires a certain quality of attention towards the object, akin to what the Wittgensteinian philosopher has called 'a willingness to participate in the adventure of the text'.[43] Like Moi, too, he asks that the critic work to '*find the words to praise* the film'.[44] Implicit within such engagement is the exercise of taste, but also the desire to forge a connection with one's interlocutor, to start a conversation. In Klevan's words:

> We 'praise' not only because we feel that we might owe it to the creators of the work but because of this 'compulsion to share'.[...] I choose this moment to discuss because I value it and you may value it too. You may have missed it, or you sensed it but let it go, or you saw it too. You are not alone.[45]

The Band Wagon

The question of praise was introduced in *Contesting Tears*. It is taken up again in *Philosophy the Day after Tomorrow* (2006), a collection of essays written between 1996 and 2006. *Philosophy the Day after Tomorrow* features two essays devoted to film: 'Something out of the Ordinary' and 'Fred Astaire Asserts the Right to Praise', both devoted to the same film, Vincente Minnelli's 1953 *The Band Wagon*. Since the former was written in 1997, the latter in 1998, they are contemporaneous with the writing and publication of *Contesting Tears*, and indeed, these works bear the mark of the lessons Cavell learned during the preparation of his book on the female voice. Here, as in the essays that make up *Contesting Tears*, Cavell foregrounds the question of who has the right to speak for whom (and for whom *he himself* has the right to speak), and what is at stake in speaking up, all the while knowing full well that our words are open to misinterpretation and to rebuke.

The Band Wagon opens on Tony Hunter (Astaire), once a famous star of musical comedies on stage and later on screen. Now largely forgotten after three years without a movie, he returns from Hollywood to New York. Arriving at Grand Central Station, he is greeted enthusiastically by his good friends Lester and Lily Marton, and they tell him they have written a stage show, a light musical comedy, that will be a perfect comeback for Tony. They will also act in it, and they have already caught the interest of Jeffrey Cordova, who they say can do anything. As soon as Jeffrey hears Lily outline the play, he declares it to be a brilliant reinterpretation of the Faust legend, which should star Tony and himself as the characters corresponding to Faust and the Devil. Tony is dubious about the Faust idea but signs on nonetheless, and Jeffrey has the Martons rewrite the play as a dark, pretentious musical drama. Jeffrey also arranges for ballerina Gabrielle Gerard (Cyd Charisse) to join the production, along with her snobbish boyfriend, choreographer and manager Paul Byrd (James Mitchell). Upon meeting, Tony and Gaby are sarcastic and hostile to each other, but as time passes it becomes clear they are falling in love. When the first out-of-town tryout in New Haven proves disastrous, Tony demands that Jeffrey convert the production back into the light comedy that the Martons had originally envisioned. Jeffrey agrees on condition that Tony is in charge of it. Paul says the show is no longer suitable for Gaby and walks out, expecting her to follow, but she is now pleased to stay and work with Tony. After some weeks on tour to perfect the new lighthearted musical numbers, the revised show proves to be a hit on its Broadway opening. Afterwards, Gaby and Tony kiss in front of the entire cast and crew.

Cavell's focus in the essays on *The Band Wagon* is on the fact and possibility of praise, on the 'little deaths' activated when praise is unfairly denied or too casually given. In 'Something out of the Ordinary' he foregrounds the missability of film moments, offering praise to a moment that might otherwise go neglected. The essay is devoted to just ninety seconds of film: an earlier scene in which Astaire sings a short song, 'By Myself'. The short number consists of Tony/Astaire walking down a train platform at Grand Central Station and into the main concourse of the station, singing as he goes. According to Cavell, this is as 'uneventful as a photographed song can be',[46] yet his reading of this short clip is richly detailed, taking in dialogue, camera movement, choreography, composition and performance. He notes such 'missable' features as the song's opening chord progression, which can be said to allude to Wagner's Tristan and Isolde, and Astaire's rather jaunty walk, 'the walk of a man who is known to move in dance exactly like no other man'.[47] While this walk is ordinary enough, it is no ordinary walk. 'Recall to begin with its jauntiness', he writes, 'the slight but distinct exaggeration of his body swinging from side to side as he paces along the platform'. This is a walk which at any moment might turn into a dance, and if his walking does turn into dancing, 'then isn't what we see of his delivery revealed to have been already dancing, a sort of limiting case, or proto-state, of dancing?'[48] Still, Cavell notes we only actually see Astaire's feet towards the end of the clip, as a cut shows Astaire walking into a station (this is, as Klevan points out, worth noting, since Astaire is so rarely fragmented on screen: the power of his performance depending on the synchronicity and grace of his whole body.)[49]

Figure 18 *The Band Wagon*: Fred Astaire walks 'the walk of a man who is known to move in dance exactly like no other man'. *The Band Wagon* (Vincente Minnelli, 1953).

After Astaire has finished singing in earnest, he continues to sound out the song's tune, 'not precisely by humming it but with the kind of syllabification, or proto-speech, that musicians sometimes use to remind themselves of the exact material of a passage of sound': Da; da da da; da da da.⁵⁰ This not-quite-singing, Cavell argues, is, in its 'distraction, disorientation, dispossession', an unguarded expression of consciousness.⁵¹ It is not unlike that other ordinary moment Cavell singles out – Deeds, on his bed, rubbing his foot. Or indeed all those small, fidgety gestures Deeds himself is smart enough to notice. In both cases, Cavell takes the unremarkable (the missable) and sees it as an emblematization of the ordinary, those little details to which we so often fail to pay proper attention.

False praise, too, is a form of inattention, and *The Band Wagon* is full of moments of generic praise that says little about its object, as when producer Jeff Cordova is described by his show business friends as 'a genius', 'fabulous, phenomenal, fantastic', 'the greatest writer/

producer in town'. Or when Tony himself describes his leading lady, Gabrielle, as 'fabulous, sensational, the loveliest thing I've ever seen', only to reveal the insincerity of these statements when he actually encounters her. Minnelli may be mocking the hype that surrounds Hollywood productions, but there is a serious point here too. Such moments threaten at all times to 'occlude the sincere or negate the natural', to replace authentic praise with simpering hyperbole.[52] In 'Fred Astaire Asserts the Right to Praise', though, Cavell takes the question not so much of whether praise is sufficient or accurate as whether it is earned or acceptable. Cavell calls this unearned praise 'blasphemous': praise that is 'not so much false as vain'.[53]

To demonstrate what he means, he turns to a sequence that has, as Cavell acknowledges, already received considerable attention within Film Studies and Cultural Studies, Astaire's famous 'shoeshine number'. This sequence follows on almost immediately from the one considered in 'Something out of the Ordinary'. Having left the station, Tony strolls down 42nd Street, site of his former glory. He wonders aloud what has happened to the Broadway theatres and wanders into an amusement arcade that was once the Elgin Theatre. Once inside, he examines the various entertainments, part amused, part bemused. Then he trips over the outstretched foot of a black shoeshine man (played by the real-life shoeshiner Leroy Daniels)[54] and is inspired to embark upon a musical number, 'When There's a Shine on Your Shoes', which opens with the following lines:

When you feel as low as the bottom of a well
And can't get out of the mood,
Do something to perk yourself up
And change your attitude.

The shoeshine man at first seems uninterested in Tony's performance, but as Tony introduces the notion of a shoeshine as a way of perking oneself up, he stands and joins in the dance, using his brushes as percussion. In the second chorus of the song, the shoeshine man shuffles around the stand while Tony, poised above, turns with him, as if in response. At the completion of the circle Astaire leaps over Daniels's head and begins what Cavell calls 'an ecstatic weaving of frenzy': an almost manic dervish around the arcade, during which he rapidly repeats 'shoe shine, shoe shine, I've got a shoe shine'. There is a destructive, dangerous, unhinged quality to this solo dance, which terrifies passers-by and spills out into the scenery. Tony recovers himself, though, and returns to the shoeshine to finish the number, as they execute a 'walk-off' that leaves the shoeshine man on his knees while Tony struts out of the arcade.

What are we to make of this strange, chaotic song and dance? According to Cavell, what we witness is a dance of praise: an acknowledgement of the genius of black dancing of which Astaire is the legatee. The dance is an acknowledgement of debt, a recognition that another's dancing has been appropriated. But other critics take quite the opposite view. Cavell himself acknowledges for example

Figure 19 *The Band Wagon*: the beginning of the shoeshine dance. *The Band Wagon* (Vincente Minnelli, 1953).

Figure 20 *The Band Wagon*: as Astaire exits the scene, Daniels is left on his knees (Vincente Minnelli, 1953).

Michael Rogin's *Blackface, White Noise*, in which Rogin makes the argument that America has established its national identity and culture through the appropriation of black culture (constituting 'racialized entertainment as commodity').[55] For Rogin, what *The Band Wagon* shows 'is acknowledgment as domination, for Astaire dances on a platform above the African American shoeshine boy, an old man who flips his rag, dances, and blacks (up) Astaire's shoes'.[56] In a similar vein, Utz McKnight, in his book *The Everyday Practice of Race in America*, argues that the racial subjectivity established in *The Band Wagon*'s shoeshine scene demonstrates an obvious 'social subordination' of the black man to the white.[57] McKnight sees Daniels's role as facilitating Astaire's (re)discovery of his voice; he himself gains little from the exchange. He criticizes Cavell for overlooking Daniels as a subject in his own right, one who might have his own voice to find (notably Daniels dances but remains mute), his own discoveries to make. Áine Kelly's response to the scene likewise focuses on 'numerous details ... that agitate', including Astaire's elevated position and instructive, 'arguably patronising' poses; Daniels's gormless, open-mouth gazing, initial inaction, and lack of responsiveness, turning to wide-eyed servility; the attention of passers-by to the white man but not the black man, and – the ultimate problem – that it is only as a type, rather than an individual – that Daniels moves Astaire to dance.[58] Robert Gooding-Williams goes further still, arguing that the sequence relies on offensive constructions of black masculinity (as a threatening and barbaric force, as a source of sexual potency) and on the distortion of racial stereotypes. 'With his shoe shined, Astaire mirrors Daniels just as Daniels mirrors Astaire', Gooding-Williams writes, 'each equally manifesting the black masculinity that joins them, each legislating, let us suppose, not as Cavell imagines, for the republic of all rational beings ... but for a republic of all the white men who crave black manhood'.[59]

Cavell admits in 'Fred Astaire Asserts the Right to Praise' that the shadow of racism looms over the scene, pointing out, amongst other things, that the noun 'shine' was historically used as a derogatory name for a black man. But, he argues, this is deliberate strategy on the part of the film: Astaire's praise is not a straightforward homage to black culture but an acknowledgement of the potential pitfalls inherent in offering such praise from a position of white privilege. Astaire's dance of praise, that is, 'is itself to be understood specifically as about this painful and potentially deadly irony of the white praise of a black culture whose very terms of praise it has appropriated'.[60] Now the audience for this number has a choice: 'You can either understand Astaire, and the establishment of talent implicated in the production of such a work', and therefore to be using the word conformably accepting its derogatory association, 'or you can understand Astaire to be mentioning this word as part of risking the full sense of what it means for him to be singing this song to this man'.[61] Cavell continues:

Since in this dance of identity Astaire provides himself with an occasion for acknowledging his indebtedness for his existence as a dancer – his deepest identity – to the genius of black dancing; and since I grant to Astaire the knowledge that he must face the knowledge that this acknowledgement, or homage, or the right to it on his part must be open to being contested, since this very man, taken differently, represents a perfect case of an American profiting from the conditions of injustice under which black creativity manifested itself on these shores; hence that his dance must throughout consist in contesting this contesting of it, hence in manifesting the contesting of his right to dance: I am bound to ask: May we take the details of this remarkable routine into account in thinking through this fateful ambiguity?[62]

In his defence of Cavell's reading, 'On Stanley Cavell's Band Wagon', William Rothman evokes Astaire's celebrated 'Bojangles number' from George Stevens's 1936 *Swing Time* in support of Cavell's claims that the shoeshine number is a dance of praise. The Bojangles number, Rothman argues, pays homage to the great black dancer Bill Robinson, aka Bojangles, but also to John Sublett, known professionally as 'John Bubbles', one of Astaire's early dance teachers. In it we see Astaire, clad in white, dancing solo but matched step by step by three long black shadows, that are 'surely', to Rothman's mind, 'stand-in for the great black dancers in whose footsteps Astaire was literally following'.[63] In the America of *Swing Time*, and even the America of *The Band Wagon*, gifted black performers toiled in relative obscurity while whites reaped rewards by 'covering' their work. Thus, Rothman argues, the 'Bojangles of Harlem' routine was as explicit and sincere acknowledgement as was allowable in 1930s Hollywood of an unjust reality, in which society consigned black dancers to anonymity, no matter how worthy they may have been of the fame – and financial rewards – that Astaire had indisputably earned by dint of his hard work and genius. The irony of this tribute to the legion of unrecognized black dancers, of course, is that much like in *The Band Wagon* the spotlight is on Astaire. The shadows are faceless, nameless, just as Leroy Daniels is voiceless. Indeed, they appear to be Astaire's shadows. On the other hand, these black shadows dwarf Astaire, and he is dancing in blackface. Are they shadows he casts? Or are they pulling his strings? These sequences are so ambiguous as to be irresolvable. As Cavell writes, in parenthesis, of *The Band Wagon*:

> Is transferring a black shine to Astaire's shoes a mockery of Astaire's pretension to black dance, or a sign of permission to make of it what he, with his own genius, must? I take this as posing irreducibly a historical question concerning black dancers' perceptions of Astaire's work. This shoeshine man poses this question precisely because he was not a professional dancer but was in fact, in his day, a shoeshine man by the name of Leroy Daniels, embodying the fate and genius of black culture but not in a position to speak with, or to confer, specific authority to participate in it.[64]

Both Rothman's and Cavell's readings are nuanced, thoughtful. They are attentive to the detail of the film and of its production. And yet the remonstrations from McKnight, Kelly and Gooding-Williams suggest that there is a risk here that Cavell courts similar accusations of appropriation to those levelled at Cavell by Modleski: only now, what is at stake is not the male philosopher's 'garrulous appropriation' of the female voice but the white man's fantasy of black masculinity's ability to overcome scepticism. This is not necessarily Cavell's fantasy, but it is arguably a fantasy that *The Band Wagon* buys into, and therefore Cavell's praise of Astaire's praise may well be misplaced. As Robert Gooding-Williams has it, 'the blackening of Astaire's shoes at the hands of a black man relieves him of the melancholic hovering he personifies in the first routine'.[65] He continues:

> In *Swing Time*, Astaire pays homage to the tradition and genius of black dance by blackening his face and performing 'Bojangles of Harlem'. If,

in *The Band Wagon*, he gets his shoes rather than his faced 'blacked up', the substance of the performance remains the same: homage that cannot separate itself from the legacy of blackface minstrelry's myths and fantasies about black masculinity. *The Band Wagon*'s reiteration of these myths and fantasies – specifically its suggestion that blackness and especially black masculinity is a magical force that can bring alienated, melancholic white men to earth – suffuses and saturates its gestures towards homage, thus compromising, fatally, our ability to see in Astaire's 'dance of praise' anything more than a form of idolatry that superstitiously mistakes a myth about black manhood for the rich artistic tradition to which Astaire owes his existence as a dancer.[66]

Gooding-Williams makes a direct comparison between Astaire's dance of praise and the masculine imaginary's appropriation of the feminine. While he doesn't mention Modleski's critique of Cavell specifically, he draws parallels between the presentation of blackness – 'pitched to white fantasies and expectations of black serviceability' and 'a general tendency in the West to pitch presentations of femininity to male fantasies and expectations of women's serviceability'.[67] In both cases the risk is a recuperation of the other into an economy of the same, an economy that is at once instrumental and reductive, since it at once makes blackness/femininity an instrument of masculinity and at the same time reduces it to a horizon of possibilities that serve white male concerns.[68] Gooding-Williams is finally led to ask: Is it possible for 'white praise of a black culture whose very terms it has appropriated' – Cavell's words – to persuade us that it is not false praise?[69] The question poses itself once more: who has the right to speak for whom?

Passionate utterances

Gooding-Williams's critique of Cavell's essays on *The Band Wagon* seems to have a similar effect on Cavell to Modleski's criticisms of certain sections of *Contesting Tears*. In an eight-page response to

Gooding-Williams that features in the same volume as the latter's original essay (Andrew Norris's *The Claim to Community*), Cavell responds to Gooding-Williams's suggestion that, rather than read black culture through the lens of white, Western philosophy, he listen more carefully to African American philosophical thought, in terms that bear a striking resemblance to his reply to Modleski. 'I have no defense against my having not tried to listen to and respond to [black philosophy] before now, other than … as with feminism, I seem to have needed an invitation to feel entitled to take it up – to go beyond autobiographical responses to isolated events,' he writes.[70] And yet, at the same time, he once more situates his response to the film as an autobiographical response, one that is bound up with his subjective experience of the film, with Cavell as an individual critic who is writing for an unknown audience:

> In claiming the right, or standing, of Astaire to praise here, I am claiming my right, or standing, to praise Astaire. I recognize no established convention as grounding me; the utterance is not performative but passionate, its act irreducibly perlocutionary. Its acceptability is exposed to the other. And here I am not in a position to single out the other to whom I address myself. Why take so stacked a risk? I suppose because I have already taken it, I have in my life taken Astaire to heart as part of my education by film and by music. It is understandable that another may claim the standing to contest it.[71]

This passage goes to the heart of Cavell who understands criticism as a personal response to film that is written for someone. As such criticism is not merely a statement (about what film is). It is an action: an approach to the reader. In writing criticism, Cavell is doing something. He is making, in his own words, a 'passionate utterance'.

Cavell opens 'Something out of the Ordinary' with two quotations, one from John Dewey on the importance of self-reliance and one from

Nietzsche on the vanishing of intelligent criticism. These quotations lead Cavell to reflect on the question of aesthetic judgement. Cavell offers his readings of the two Astaire routines as adaptations of Kant's notion of aesthetic judgement. According to Cavell, 'Kant's location of aesthetic judgement ... makes room for a particular form of criticism, one that supplies the concepts that, after the fact of pleasure, articulate the grounds of that experience in particular objects.'[72] Thus criticism is the critic's rebukable attempt to justify and so show to be acceptable the pleasure he or she takes in some work of art. It is a judgement that the critic expounds in order to express her wish that others take pleasure from where she has taken it. Writing, for example, of that first scene, he says: 'The utterance or delivery of Astaire's song and proto-dance has singled me out for a response of pleasure [...] In my wish to share the pleasure I judge the scene of walking and of melodic syllabification as appropriate expressions of the ordinary as the missable.'[73] He recalls that in an early essay published in *Must We Mean What We Say?* ('Aesthetic Problems of Modern Philosophy'), he made an analogy between Kant's characterization of aesthetic judgement and the claim of ordinary language philosophers to voice what we would ordinarily say when and what we should mean in saying it.[74] But, Cavell admits,

> I was not able ... to surmise why there should be this intuitive connection between the arrogation of the right to speak for others about the language we share and about works of art we cannot bear not to share. I gestured at comparing the risk of aesthetic isolation with that of moral or political isolation, but what I could not get at, I think now, was the feature of the aesthetic claim, as suggested by Kant's description, as a kind of compulsion to share a pleasure, hence as tinged with an anxiety that the claim stands to be rebuked. It is a condition of, or threat to, that relation to things called aesthetic, that something I know and cannot make intelligible stands to be lost to me.[75]

This passage introduces into Cavell's work the possibility – and threat – of rebuke: a word that implies not only disagreement but also disapproval, the sense that someone is not only wrong but has made a moral error. It is worth repeating in this context that this essay is published around the same time as *Contesting Tears*, the drafting of which had led to numerous rebukes for Cavell from the likes of Tania Modleski. It is no great stretch, then, to suppose that Cavell's unpleasant encounter with feminist film theory raises this possibility for him: that an aesthetic pleasure he feels prompted to share might stand to be rebuked, but also that the rebuke might itself have a positive potential.

One way of reframing rebuke is as a matter of alternative interpretations. Cavell argues that for any interpretation to be significant, there must be at least one other interpretation possible. For what is an interpretation? It is a way of explaining – a scientist's interpretation of the data – but it can also be stylistic representation of a creative work or dramatic role – Oliver's interpretation of Hamlet, for example. For Cavell, an interpretation is 'seeing an aspect': it is seeing something *as* something.[76] Let's think once more of Wittgenstein's duck-rabbit. This figure may be seen as a duck or as a rabbit. At any point, we see either the duck or the rabbit. But it cannot exist as a duck-rabbit without both possibilities existing. That is, for us to see anything *as* something, there *must* be another way of seeing it.[77]

Film seems to court a particularly vehement level of disagreement. The films that Cavell writes about – in *Pursuits of Happiness* but elsewhere too – are ones 'that some people treasure and others despise'.[78] So the difficulty of interpreting them is 'the same as the difficulty of expressing oneself satisfactorily, of making oneself find the words for what one is specifically interested to say, which comes to the difficulty, as I put it, of finding the right to be thus interested'.[79] Cavell thus announces to his readers 'a difference in my approach to aesthetic matters from that of most, of course not all, work in aesthetics in the Anglo-American ways of philosophy ... I mean the sort of emphasis I place on the criticism, or reading, of individual works of art'.[80] He characterizes this emphasis as 'letting a work of art have a voice in what philosophy says about it'[81] and tells his readers that 'the judgement I make in discussing the sequence here expresses my pleasure and sense of value in it and awaits your agreement upon this'.[82]

It is in this sense that Cavell's criticism becomes a kind of 'passionate utterance'. A passionate utterance, Cavell explains in several of the articles collected in *Philosophy the Day after Tomorrow*, is, to put it simply, an expression of feeling. It is moreover an expression of feeling aimed at provoking an appropriate response from an interlocutor. Cavell draws examples from A.J. Ayer: 'You acted wrongly in stealing that money', 'Tolerance is a virtue', 'I am bored' – the latter of which, if said to you by a child, is perhaps an appeal for an interesting suggestion or offer of amusement and, if by a friend (romantic or not), 'is apt to still be an appeal and still to set a stake on some piece of your future together'.[83] In either case, Cavell cautions, 'You had better answer, and carefully.'[84]

Cavell compares passionate utterances to Austin's performative utterances, saying that there are a number of conventions or conditions that are necessary for passionate utterances to take effect.

> There is no conventional procedure for appealing to you to act in response to my expression of passion (of outrage at your treachery or callousness, of jealousy over your attentions, of hurt over your slights of recognition). Call this absence of convention the first condition of passionate utterance; and let's go further. Whether, then, I have the standing to appeal to or to question you – to single you out as the object of my passion – is part of the argument to ensue. Call standing and singling out the second and third conditions of passionate utterance. These conditions for felicity, or say appropriateness, are not given *a priori* but are to be discovered

or refined, or else the effort to articulate it is to be denied. There is no question therefore of executing a procedure correctly and completely, but there are the further unshiftable demands, or rules, that (fourth) the one uttering a passion must have the passion, and (fifth) the one singled out must respond now and here, and (sixth) respond in kind, that is to say, be *moved* to respond, or else resist the demand.[85]

A performative utterance, Cavell surmises, is an offer to participate in the law; a passionate utterance is an invitation to improvisation in the disorders of desire. Kant's aesthetic judgement (in radical contrast with his moral judgement) is a form of passionate utterance: 'One person, risking exposure to rebuff, singles out another, through the expression of an emotion and a claim of value, to respond in kind, that is, with appropriate emotion and action (if mainly of speech), here and now.'[86]

So praise is a mode of aesthetic judgement, and aesthetic judgement is a mode of passionate utterance. So it is that Cavell understands Astaire's 'dance of praise' as a passionate utterance, one that risks being read as an expression of white privilege. Likewise his praise for this scene, his appreciation of it, is Cavell's own passionate utterance, which he addresses to us, his readers. Whether Cavell is right to praise Astaire is 'a question to be held open throughout'.[87] Cavell offers to us, his readers, his praising of Astaire, his aesthetic judgement of the chosen routine, but he never moves beyond offering. He does not insist on his right to praise (though neither does he ask for permission, for who has the right to grant it?). It is his responsibility to convince the reader of the worthiness of his claims. 'When I praise I do not ask others to praise, to imitate me,' he writes, 'but to see or hear'. It entails a sense of possibility but also 'a grave risk'.[88]

Passionate utterances leave the expresser fully exposed, at risk. Philosophical criticism is thus a matter of risk, 'a work of determining, as it were after the fact, the grounds of (the concepts shaping) pleasure and value in the working of the object. In this light criticism becomes a conduct of gratitude, one could say, a specification and test of tribute, a test in which I am inherently exposed to rebuke'.[89] What is the risk inherent in making a passionate utterance? Not that the philosophical or critical claim will be met with disagreement but with dismissal. Early in *Little Did I Know*, Cavell remarks upon the close connection between philosophy and autobiography (a connection that develops in no small part out of his work on *Contesting Tears*) and on that connection's grounding the philosopher's speaking for other (making claims about 'we', say, for example). He finds a 'trouble' in this idea:

> I am not sure that those who write out of a sense of history of oppression would be glad to adopt this posture. I believe that certain women I know who write philosophically would not at all be glad to adopt this posture or feel spoken for by one who does.

As we have seen, the question of authority, of who has the right to speak for another, has long been a central thread in Cavell's work, stretching back even before his work on the voice in *Contesting Tears* and *A Pitch of Philosophy*.[90] In Cavell's work on Austin, for example, and with regard to ordinary language, Cavell discusses the problem and advantage of the first-person plural. It may seem, he admits, that to use the first-person plural is to speak for others (a particular problem when one is a white, male Harvard Professor). However, Cavell reconfigures the use of a phrase like 'When we say … we mean … ' so that the speaker is not making a unilateral statement but is rather offering something for others to register their thoughts or their responses against: in short, he invites the response 'yes we do' but also 'no we don't' – or even, 'you may, but I do not'. As such, Cavell's ordinary language philosophy is inherently political: it suggests that there must be an assent to the political realm within which one finds oneself and that the offering of the words is a continual attempt to express or test the possibilities of that assent, not just on the level of overt political discussion but on the level of our ordinary words.[91] What's more, to ask someone 'in what circumstances would we say ....' is to ask that person something about themselves. That is, we ask them to describe something that they do. Hence, Cavell's use of the first-person plural is, paradoxically, an invitation to his interlocutor to acquire self-knowledge. But it is also an invitation to see oneself as a part of a community (if only a community of two) to agree that we understand one another, that we agree on what we might say when.

In his thinking on criticism as passionate utterance, this matter comes into the foreground in a hitherto unprecedented manner. Cavell takes passionate utterance to call for 'acceptance [which] does not only mean that it is agreed with, only that disagreement must claim for itself the standing of philosophy'.[92] What is troubling to him is the possibility of certain others' refusing to meet on that ground, 'not contesting the claim that this is what we say but disdaining the idea that there is a "we" at all', as Naomi Scheman puts it.[93] To rebuke someone is to enter or to acknowledge already being entered into a community, a culture. It is to say that her opinion, her reading, matters, if only by dint of his wrongness. Bickering is the sign of a good marriage. Dissent is the sign of a good classroom. Rebuke, retort, response – these are all forms of conversation, and conversation, we know, is the first step to overcoming isolation. But to dismiss someone is to plunge into scepticism. It is, in the words of Áine Kelly, an 'outright annihilation' of the other person.[94]

Cavell acknowledges that it is a human tendency not to embrace our shared uncertainties but to avoid them, to close our eyes to other human persons in their separateness and complexity, a tendency that he is as guilty of as anyone else.

> In the everyday ways in which denial occurs in my life with the other – in a momentary irritation, or a recurrent grudge, in an

unexpected rush of resentment, in a hard glance, in a dishonest attestation, in the telling of a tale, in the believing of a tale, in a false silence, in a fear of engulfment, in a fantasy of solitude of self-destruction – the problem is to recognise myself as denying another, to understand that I carry chaos in myself. Here is the scandal of scepticism with respect to the existence of others; I am the scandal.[95]

To make a passionate utterance is to recognize the person whom we're addressing as an individual, to acknowledge their existence: to speak not just in terms of 'we' but also in terms of 'I' and 'you'. Taking risks entails, of course, acknowledging that they might not always pay off. Whether Cavell can, in good conscience, enter a claim on another's behalf depends on a complex initiation of acknowledgement and recognition. It depends, in the words of Scheman, 'not just on the content of what I say but, crucially, on the relationship between us, on whether we can meet each other, be each other's companion, whether you can – or should – trust me, and me you'.[96] How we take Cavell's reading of the arcade scene will, of course, depend not only on our personal reaction to the film but on our experiences and subjectivities in general. Still, as Kelly puts it, 'a certain degree of intellectual openness – the indulgence we might grant a trusted companion – might mitigate against questions of race, gender, and sexuality limiting too strictly our inclination toward acceptance, our inclination toward praise'.[97] In the words of Toril Moi, '"we" can be used in myriad ways, very few of which are objectionable':

> Ordinary language philosophy often talks 'about what we should say'. The usual rejoinder is to reject the 'we' as normative, as an attempt to tell others what they must say. But this we is neither an order nor an empirical claim. It is, rather, an invitation to the reader to test something for herself, to see if she can see what I see. If she can't, we try to figure out why. The claims of ordinary

language philosophy are invitations to a conversation, invitations to do philosophy together.[98]

Cavell's method, he asserts, 'has nothing to do with – is a kind of negation of – an idea of reading as a judicious balancing of all reasonable interpretations. My reading is nothing if not partial.'[99] Elsewhere he states that

> I have nothing more to go on than my conviction that I make sense. It may prove to be the case that I am wrong, that my conviction isolates me, from all others, from myself. That will not be the same as a discovery that I am dogmatic or egomaniacal. The wish and search for community are the wish and search for reason.[100]

The partiality of his utopian accounts of *The Band Wagon*'s shoeshine scene or *Stella Dallas*'s final walk away from the camera may strain against other analyses, written by feminist critics or anti-racist thinkers, and might be more or less convincing to us as ways of accounting for what is going on in these moments. But they are resolute in their commitment to overcoming solipsism, silence and scepticism. At the end of *The Philadelphia Story*, as Tracy Lord and C.K. Dexter Haven talk their way to remarriage, Dexter says to Tracy: 'I'll risk it. Will you?' Such is the offer Cavell makes to his readers. What is at stake is the possibility of a shared future, a world that together, we might make better.

And so we are back to love. At the end of 'The Future of Possibility', Cavell invokes the spirit of Phillip Pirrip, best known to most of us as Pip, from Charles Dickens's *Great Expectations*. 'Pip is said to be a young man of "great expectations" yet he can be said to have no expectations great or small, but simply to have formed his character on a love quite independent of its fate in the world – on love, in short; a figure, therefore, with some hard things to earn, yet who survives the learning.'[101] He contrasts Pip, quite naturally, with Miss Havisham, a woman who expected love and who, when that demand was thwarted, gave up on the future. Miss Havisham 'shows possibilities not to be everywhere exhausted but everywhere untried, which suggests that the step to the future is closed not through depletion but through fixation, through the withholding or theft of love'.[102] Here, we are in the veins of perfectionism: fixation is the opposite of possibility. But more than this, to take steps without a path is a risk. And that risk is the acknowledgement of a future, 'the fact of futurity'.[103] Love replaces expectation with a promise, something that we open to the world without knowing what the world will – or will not – give us back.

Conclusion: 'I write for friends and strangers'

The fact that the black man is left on his knees at the end of the shoeshine scene is in Cavell's reading a deliberate gesture towards the invisible labour of black dancers. He reads the moment as utopian in that it offers us, for a moment, the vision of two men – one white, one black – dancing together. But he also sees it as a moment of realism, in that it reminds us that in the America of 1953, these men cannot exit the scene as equals. Ultimately, Astaire's dance changes nothing within the film. But it may yet be a call for change: a call that is made to *us*, the film's viewers. The diegetic audience for Tony's performance may not be able to recognize the part of the shoeshine man in inspiring and participating in the dance, that is, but we – the film's spectators – can. The evidence for it is there, on screen. It is therefore 'up to us to recognise that this routine is as much about the appropriation of another's dancing as it is about the origin of dancing in ecstasy. Then it is up to us to determine whether we can accept pleasure on this basis'.[104] For Cavell, this crystallizes as a question of consent: just as the couples of the remarriage comedies and the women of the melodramas have to determine whether they can be happy in an imperfect society, so both Astaire and his audience ask what it is to call attention to racial injustice in an unjust society. As Cavell admits, the fact is we are left with a black man on his knees. Can we consent to that? Tony leaves him there. Do we consent to that? Astaire leaves the scene holding out his arms towards Daniels, as if torn away, as if beckoning. There is regret, Cavell believes, in this gesture. Also a beckoning – towards a better future? Still, he writes, 'It is not him that I am concerned for, but for us.'[105]

Why praise Astaire? Why not chalk up the experience of pleasure and value to an idiosyncrasy of my own and of whomever happens to share it? 'But', Cavell writes,

> as an idiosyncrasy is in fact not the way the experience so far comes to me. And as Kant more or less puts the matter, heard particularly after a course of Emerson and of Walter Benjamin: If I am to possess my own experience I cannot afford to cede it to my culture as that culture stands. I must find ways to insist upon it.[106]

As early as *Pursuits of Happiness*, Cavell explains that his film books are made of his 'readings' of films, readings that, to all intents and purposes, constitute accounts of his 'experience of a film'.[107] He continues:

> To take an interest in an object is to take an interest in one's experience of the object, so that to examine and defend my interest in these films is to examine and defend my interest in my own experience, in the moments and passages of my life I have spent with them. This means, in turn, defending the process of criticism, so far as criticism is thought of, as I think of it, as a natural extension of conversation.[108]

This passage opens onto several important points. Firstly, it makes the claim that criticism is a matter of subjective experience. The film *I* see may not be the film that *you* see. To write critically about the film is therefore, secondly, to reflect upon one's own subjectivity. Thirdly, it is an attempt at overcoming that subjectivity by communicating, as precisely as possibly, in words, what my experience of the film was to you, the reader. So fourthly, criticism is an acknowledgement of the other and a form of conversation. This is a conversation that is subject, of course, to delays of time and space. Discussing the process of transcribing his moral perfectionism lectures as *Cities of Words*, Cavell admits that the book must, naturally, differ from the lectures, since the relationship of the writer to his reader is different from that of the teacher to his students. 'It is the same man saying "I" here as said "I" there, but the you, whom I address here, unlike the students and friends in the classroom, are free to walk away from any sentence or paragraph of it without embarrassment to either of us, and indeed to drop the course at any time without penalty other than its loss.'[109] Writing is in this case a leap of faith, a plea for readers to bear with the critic through the thornier or more complex passages to treat the object before them (the book) with the same care and attention that Cavell treats those before him (the films). Cavell's writing costs him something. He feels it should cost the reader something too,[110] a position that finds echoes in a remark of the British author and essayist Zadie Smith:

> Writing exists for me at the intersection of three precarious, uncertain elements: language, the world, the self. The first is never wholly mine; the second I can only ever know in a partial sense; the third is a malleable and improvised response to the first two. [...] It's this self – whose boundaries are uncertain, whose language is never pure, whose world is in no way 'self-evident' – that I try to write from and to. My hope is for a reader who, like the author, often wonders how free she really is, and who takes it for granted that reading involves all the same liberties and exigencies as writing.[111]

At heart, then, Cavellian spectatorship turns not around matters of ontology, absence and presence but on matters of attention, acknowledgement and responsiveness. Ontologically, film invokes our situation to the world, since on the one hand it tells us that a certain powerlessness is natural to us, and on the other, it invites us to think that it is not natural to assume that we are always naturally powerless. In other words, our displacement from the events of the screen tells us the story of our responsibility towards the world.[112] But in terms of a response, the film courts the same thoughtfulness as the world itself. The film speaks first, and we are called upon to look and to listen. As Cavell puts it, film

> asks of us, not exactly more in the way of response, but one which is more personal. It promises us, not the re-assembly of community, but personal relationship unsponsored by that community; not the overcoming of our isolation, but the sharing of that isolation – not to save the world out of love, but to save love for the world, until it is responsive again. 'Ah love, let us be true to one another.'[113]

That this contract, in which art asks its interlocutor for something and promises her something else, bears a resemblance to a marriage contract is not unimportant. Cavell closes the passage cited above with a quote from Arnold's 'Dover Beach': a poem supposedly written by Arnold to his wife during their honeymoon and which muses on the melancholy withdrawal of faith and religion in the industrial age. The world has no longer 'joy, nor love, nor light / Nor certitude, nor peace, nor help for pain'; these things can now perhaps only be found in the mutual faith of husband and wife in one another: the metaphor that Cavell takes up in *Pursuits of Happiness*. Film spectatorship models acknowledgement; it shows us what it might look like to really see someone; to see the tiny, ordinary details that make up lived life; to 'measure the bearing of another's life [by] seeing it from that other's perspective'.[114] It teaches us to look attentively, responsively, lovingly upon one another. Robert Sinnerbrink has suggested that in Cavell's work the relationship between film and philosophy is a marriage of sorts[115]; I believe, rather, that it is from the meeting of film and viewer – a meeting that need not be framed in terms of marriage but of friendship, perhaps of love – that a 'meet and happy conversation' might be sprung.

That the form that this response takes is fraught with risk – of rebuke, misunderstanding, of dismissal – is what makes it a moral act. To practise Cavellian criticism is to do what the philosopher Gillian Rose has called 'love's work'. To do love's work is 'to stay in the fray, in the revel of ideas and risk; learning, failing, wooing, grieving, trusting, working, reposing – in this sin of language and lips'.[116] It means recognizing and identifying conflicts which are ignored or overlooked and, crucially, refusing to identify the different positions as 'guilty' or 'innocent'. To do love's work is to experience the impossibility of reconciling different positions, to refuse to take sides and so to look guilty to everyone, to satisfy no one, to be torn apart.

Cavell has long felt outside, exceptional yet desperate to not be so. Too young, too old, too Jewish, too American, too philosophical or serious, too literary or excitable ... a dreamer.[117] Time and again he describes his affinity, or identification, with 'the stranger'.[118] His work on film, seen as an idiosyncrasy amongst his philosophical colleagues, was met with outright hostility amongst some scholars in Film Studies. Still, he persists in writing for 'friends and strangers', in doing what Emerson refers to as 'standing for humanity'. To understand humanity, for Cavell, is

> to bear up under my consideration, under the weight of my representation of humanity, under the measure of it, under the way, for examples, I am whatever I may be said to be, the way I am a father, a grandfather, a son, an American, a depressed patriot, a Jew, a white man, a professor, knock-kneed, bald, divorced, married, temperamentally inclined to both disappointment and to joy, to solitude and to love, to high and major art and to minor and low, to scorn and to forbearance. To know others is to know not the things

they are (rich butchers or French bakers or tall candlestick makers) but all the ways in which they are what they simultaneously or successively are, or partially are, or deny they are.[119]

Cavell's work – love's work – is endless. As Andrew Klevan expresses it, 'The eloquence of particular films means that they will continually have a say in their interpretation: we will never know them but remain always in the process of knowing them, left forever guessing the unseen from the seen.'[120] Just so, Cavell writes that 'a work one cares about is not so much something one has read as something one is a reader of, one's connection with it goes on, as with any relation one cares about'.[121] The acknowledgement of the otherness of others is both painful and pleasurable, and come what may we are always – always – trapped within our own subjectivities. We are both alone and not alone, mysteries to one another, eternal puzzles – but ones that, nevertheless, we should strive to solve, all the while acknowledging that we never will. The effort, Cavell tells us, will be worth it.

Postscript: The End. The Beginning

Berkeley, 1960

Open on the bright parks of Berkeley. Our hero is in his mid-thirties. He is completing a fourth year as an assistant professor in the philosophy department. He has good friends, good colleagues, with whom he can share a few laughs, but he is recently separated from his wife and is juggling the shared care of a bright-eyed little girl with his academic responsibilities, and it is taking its toll. He is struggling to complete his now very overdue doctoral thesis, and under notice from his department that unless it is submitted within the coming academic year, his promotion to tenure will not be recommended and his position will terminate. He sighs to a friend that he is 'pretty securely wrapped in general sentiments of guilt and failure'.[1]

Cut to a cinema, the hoarding of which advertises Ingmar Bergman's *Smiles of a Summer Night*. Our hero exits, bemused but elated. Naturally perhaps, he feels an immediate affinity with its characters: the isolated father Fredrick; his unoriented, unclaimed wife Anne; his turbulent, seminarian son Henrik; his former and future love Desiree. His response to the film is immediate and almost overwhelming.

Stockholm, 1994

Cavell is now sixty-eight years old. Through good fortune, he finds himself at Stockholm's Royal Dramatic Theatre attending a performance of Bergman's production of *The Winter's Tale*. The performance strikes him as cinematic, as somehow studying film. That evening, Cavell considers his 'overevaluation' of the Bergman film that once meant so much to him, his 'infatuation' with it. He wonders, how can he be sure that the film he recalls now – after several viewings – is the same as the one he saw then? That he is being faithful to his original experience of the film? Of course, he concludes, he cannot. And so he must find new reasons to love the film, new points of entry. He must stake a field on which to await fresh impressions. This thought inspires him to write an essay, entitled 'Seasons of Love: Bergman's *Smiles of a Summer's Night* and *The Winter's Tale*', in which he considers the kind of love of the film inspired in him, the kind that film is apt, for Cavell to inspire. It is a beautiful essay, rich in autobiographical detail, and the kind of gentle insight that Cavell makes look so easy, but which, one suspects, is hard won.

In an essay written thirty-five years after that first viewing of *Smiles of a Summer Night*, when Cavell is twice the age that he was upon first encountering the film, he writes:

> *Smiles of A Summer Night* was not the first film I loved, but it was the first in which I came away from the experience of a film with the sense or revelation that, as in instances of the great arts, everything means something, and took that experience home to spend, it turned out, all night inviting my journal to continue telling what everything came to in this particular case, or whether there is a something that an everything could come to, and whether we should desire such a thing. [...] I seem to recall pretty well the treasures of romantic excess with which I wished to greet each discriminable motion, each change of light, each posture and juxtaposition taken by old, or rather new, love.[2]

Without *Smiles of a Summer Night*, there may never have been *Pursuits of Happiness*, Cavell tells us: within it lies what we might call the prototype for the remarriage genre. But more than this, without this film, which teaches Cavell what love for a film is, there may also not have been *The World Viewed, Contesting Tears, Cities of Tears* or the myriad short articles and paragraphs in which film shapes Cavell's philosophy. There might not even have been *Conditions Handsome or Unhandsome*, *In Quest of the Ordinary*, or *Philosophy the Day after Tomorrow*. Almost certainly, the landscape of Cavell's philosophy would have been terribly different.

The film, Cavell writes, 'represented to me … some new standard to which the articulation of the response to film had to rise'. Put otherwise, *Smiles of a Summer Night* teaches Cavell not only how to love but how to give voice to that love. It changes his view of film and of the world. In turn, if we let him, Cavell might just change ours.

Notes

Introduction

1. Such events are described by Stanley Cavell in his autobiographical work, *Little Did I Know: Excerpts from Memory* (Palo Alto, CA: Stanford University Press, 2010), p. 21.
2. Stanley Cavell, *The World Viewed: Reflections on the Ontology of Film* (enlarged edition) (Cambridge, MA: Harvard University Press, 1979), p. xix.
3. Katrina Forrester, review of Cavell, *Little Did I Know*, Cambridge Literary Review 2/5 (Summer 2011), pp. 153–174.
4. Harry Kreisler, 'Interview with Stanley Cavell: Conversations with History', Institute of International Studies, UC Berkeley, 2002. Transcript: http://globetrotter.berkeley.edu/people2/Cavell/cavell-con1.html
Video: https://www.youtube.com/watch?v=eIIKqEl8xEw

Chapter 1

1. Cavell, *Little Did I Know*, pp. 21–22.
2. Ibid., p. 155.
3. Cavell describes the pair's late-night dissections of the film with relish: 'Our reconstructions of a film (often in the larger Hart's cafeteria in Sacramento, where musicians would often around midnight begin wandering in after playing a date) invariably began, and usually ended, by remembering, and judging, all we could of the music, or the film's sounds more generally, working up considerable enthusiasm over such details as the pitch of the doorbell that initiates the opening sequence of the film echoes the pitch on which the title music ended' (*Little Did I Know*, p. 160).

4   Cavell describes the impetus for and eventual decision to change his name in both *A Pitch of Philosophy* and *Little Did I Know* (see esp. pp. 199–203 of the latter).
5   James Conant, 'An Interview with Stanley Cavell', in *The Senses of Stanley Cavell*, R. Fleming and M. Payne (eds.) (Lewisburg, PA: Bucknell University Press, 1989), pp. 21–72 (23).
6   Cavell, *Little Did I Know*, p. 408.
7   In particular, Cavell cites *Smiles of a Summer Night* (Ingmar Bergman, 1955), *Hiroshima Mon Amour* (Alain Resnais and Marguerite Duras, 1959) and *L'Avventura* (Michelangelo Antonioni, 1960) as films that suggested to him new possibilities of philosophical thought and expression. See Stanley Cavell, 'The Future of Possibility', in *Philosophical Romanticism*, Nikolas Kompridis (ed.) (Oxford and New York, NY: Routledge, 2006), pp. 21–31.
8   Cavell, *Little Did I Know*, p. 423.
9   Ibid., p. 425.
10 Daniel Morgan's article, 'Stanley Cavell: The Contingencies of Film and Its Theory' – a very useful starting point for anyone interested in Cavell's work but lacking the patience for a whole book – sketches out these connections succinctly and insightfully. In *Thinking in the Dark: Cinema, Theory, Practice*, Murray Pomerance and R. Barton Palmer (eds.) (New Brunswick, NJ: Rutgers University Press, 2016), pp. 162–173.
11 Leo Braudy, 'Review: The World Viewed by Stanley Cavell', *Film Quarterly* 25/4 (Summer, 1972), pp. 28–29.
12 Michael Fischer, *Stanley Cavell and Literary Skepticism* (Chicago, IL: University of Chicago Press, 1989).
13 Garrett Stewart, 'The Avoidance of Stanley Cavell', in *Contending with Stanley Cavell*, Russell B. Goodman (ed.) (Oxford: Oxford University Press, 2005), pp. 140–156.
14 Russell B. Goodman, 'Introduction', in *Contending with Stanley Cavell*, Russell B. Goodman (ed.) (Oxford: Oxford University Press, 2005), pp. 3–9.
15 Fischer, *Stanley Cavell*, p. xii. Fischer notes of Cavell's 'dim hearing' amongst literary theorists: 'Despite Cavell's longstanding indebtedness

to literature, not very much has been written about him.' Reasons are sought in the remaining chapters on theory's refusal of the 'ordinary', a concept central to Cavell's deliberations.

16 Stephen Melville, 'Oblique and Ordinary: Stanley Cavell's Engagements of Emerson', *American Literary History* 5/1 (Spring, 1993), p. 172.
17 Timothy Gould, *Hearing Things: Voice and Method in the Writing of Stanley Cavell* (Chicago, IL: Chicago University Press, 1998).
18 Stewart, 'Avoidance', p. 142.
19 One of Cavell's most vigorous defenders, Stephen Mulhall, has devoted an entire chapter to this paragraph. Stephen Mulhall, 'On Refusing to Begin', in *Contending with Stanley Cavell*, Russell B. Goodman (ed.) (Oxford: Oxford University Press, 2005), pp. 140–156.
20 Stanley Cavell, *Themes out of School: Effects and Causes* (San Francisco, CA: North Point Press, 1984; Chicago, IL: University of Chicago Press, 1988), p. 141.
21 Robert Sinnerbrink, 'Re-enfranchising Film: Towards a Romantic Film-Philosophy', in *New Takes in Film-Philosophy*, Greg Tuck and Havi Carel (eds.) (Basingstoke: Palgrave Macmillan, 2011).
22 Braudy, 'Review', p. 29. Braudy in fact writes that it is 'difficult not to attack Cavell personally'.
23 Anthony Kenny, '"Clouds of Not Knowing", review of *The Claim of Reason* by Stanley Cavell', *Times Literary Supplement* 19 (April, 1980), p. 449. Cited in Robert Sinnerbrink, 'Cavellian Meditations: How to Do Things with Film and Philosophy', *Film-Philosophy* 18 (2014): Special Section on Stanley Cavell, pp. 50–69 [53].
24 Sinnerbrink, 'Meditations', p. 53. Sinnerbrink notes that these criticisms of Cavell's style were also repeated by other philosophers, including Mark Glouberman, in the *Review of Metaphysics*, who calls Cavell's style 'inexcusable'; and Dan Ducker, in *International Philosophical Quarterly*, who writes that 'the pattern of withholding judgement, of putting off closure, builds certain frustrations in the reader. There are moments in Cavell's book where one wants to scream, "Good God, come to the point!"'. See also Jonathan Culler, 'Bad Writing and Good Philosophy', in *Just Being Difficult? Academic Writing in the Public Arena*, Jonathan

Culler and Kevin Lamb (eds.) (Stanford, CA: Stanford University Press, 2003), pp. 43–67.
25 Mulhall, 'On Refusing', p. 32.
26 Stewart, 'Avoidance', p. 141.
27 Stanley Cavell, *Disowning Knowledge in Six Plays of Shakespeare* (Cambridge: Cambridge University Press, 1989), p. 72.
28 Stewart, 'Avoidance', p. 146.
29 Yet, as William Rothman rightly says, any reader tempted to accuse Cavell of being naive about racism, or even for being an unwitting racist himself, would do well to read the sections of his autobiography *Little Did I Know*, in which he recounts his experience as a high school student in the early 1940s, playing piano in a nearly all black jazz band. Rothman also points out that Cavell was instrumental in the establishment of Harvard's African American Studies Department, a fact often noted by Cornel West, one of his former teaching assistants. See William Rothman, 'On Stanley Cavell's Band Wagon', *Film-Philosophy* 18 (2014): Special Section on Stanley Cavell, pp. 9–34 (22).
30 Stewart, 'Avoidance', p. 141.
31 Stanley Cavell, *Conditions Handsome and Unhandsome: The Constitution of Emersonian Perfectionism* (Chicago, IL: University of Chicago Press, 1990), p. 12. This is a difficulty in the assimilation of the Americanist Cavell that Cary Wolfe also draws out in 1994 essay: Cary Wolfe, 'Alone with America: Cavell, Emerson, and the Politics of Individualism', *New Literary History* 25/1 (Winter, 1994), pp. 135–157. For more on Cavell and his relationship to American politics, see also James Conant and Simon Critchley's essays in Russell B. Goodman's edited collection.
32 Cavell, *Little Did I Know*, p. 303.
33 Ibid., p. 304.
34 Cf. David N. Rodowick, 'An Elegy for Theory', *October* 122 (Fall, 2007), pp. 91–109 and John Mullarkey, *Refractions of Reality: Philosophy and the Moving Image* (London: Palgrave MacMilllan, 2009).
35 Rodowick, 'Elegy', p. 101.

36 This explanation is necessarily reductive. Both terms – analytic and continental philosophy – lack clear definition and are highly contested. For more see Simon Critchley, 'Introduction: What Is Continental Philosophy?', in Simon Critchley and William Schroder, *A Companion to Continental Philosophy*, Blackwell Companions to Philosophy (Malden, MA: Blackwell Publishing, 1998), p. 4.

37 Áine Kelly, 'Stylists in the American Grain: Wallace Stevens, Stanley Cavell and Richard Rorty', *European Journal of Pragmatism and American Studies* 2/2 (2009), pp. 211–223 (215).

38 Noël Carroll, 'Review: Pursuits of Happiness', *Journal of Aesthetics and Art Criticism* 41/1 (1982), pp. 105.

39 Ibid., p.106.

40 William Rothman, 'Introduction', in *Cavell on Film* (Albany, NY: SUNY Press, 2005), p. xii.

41 See for example Rodowick, 'Elegy' and Fischer, 'Stanley Cavell', 1989.

42 Morgan, 'Stanley Cavell: The Contingencies of Film and Its Theory', p. 165.

43 Cavell, *The World Viewed*, p. 16.

44 Stanley Cavell, *Pursuits of Happiness: The Hollywood Comedy of Remarriage* (Cambridge, MA: Harvard University Press, 1981), p. 16.

45 Rothman, 'Introduction', in *Cavell on Film*, p. xii.

46 Cited in Rothman, *Cavell on Film*, p. xiv.

47 Stanley Cavell, 'The Good of Film', in *Cavell on Film*, William Rothman (ed.) (Albany, NY: State University of New York Press, 2005), p. 344.

48 Cavell, *Little Did I Know*, pp. 303–304.

49 Ibid., p. 304.

Chapter 2

1 Andrew Klevan, 'What Becomes of Thinking on Film?', interview with Stanley Cavell, in *Film as Philosophy: Essays on Cinema after Wittgenstein and Cavell*, Rupert Read and Jerry Goodenough (Basingstoke/New York, NY: Palgrave MacMillan, 2005), p. 167.

2. Ibid., p. 173.
3. Cavell himself emphasizes the appeal of Austin's storytelling to him, drawing a connection to his father's notoriety as a raconteur, in conversation with Harry Kreisler:

   > A completely unlettered man, but in love with learning. Always spoke with an accent, which he hated. Loved eloquence, which he didn't possess, except in the form of being able to tell Yiddish jokes. He was famous in our small circle of acquaintances for being able to spellbind any crowd, especially at the dinner table, with stories, sometimes as brief as a few seconds with a saying, sometimes that would last twenty minutes. Now, to tell a joke and keep people spellbound for twenty minutes is an important matter, that's important talent.

   I mention that about him because my most influential teacher in my life was J.L. Austin, whose philosophy consisted utterly, essentially, in an ability to imagine stories that could describe and make concrete various philosophical concepts. So Austin was completely fastidious and an impeccable speaker of English, and my father was anything but that. They had in common this ability to tell pertinent stories.
4. Cavell, 'The Good of Film', p. 125.
5. Andrew Klevan, *Film Performance: From Achievement to Appreciation* (London: Wallflower, 2005), p. 169.
6. Ibid., p. 167.
7. Stanley Cavell, *Must We Mean What We Say? A Book of Essays* (Cambridge: Cambridge University Press, 2002 [1976]), p. 99.
8. Wittgenstein, *Tractatus Logic-Philosophicus*, trans. D.F. Pears and B.F. McGuiness (London: Routledge and Kegan Paul, 1961 [1921]).
9. Ibid.
10. Diane Collinson and Kathryn Plant, 'Wittgenstein', in *Fifty Major Philosophers* (Oxford: Routledge, 2008), p. 218.
11. Ludwig Wittgenstein, *Philosophical Investigations*, trans. G.EM. Anscombe (Oxford: Blackwell, 1953), p. 109.
12. Guy Longworth, 'John Langshaw Austin', in *The Stanford Encyclopedia of Philosophy*, Edward N. Zalta (ed.) (Spring 2017 Edition) Available at https://plato.stanford.edu/archives/spr2017/entries/austin-jl/>

13 J.L. Austin, *Philosophical Papers* (Oxford: The Clarendon Press, 1979 [1961]), pp. 181–182 (cited in Longworth).
14 Longworth, 'John Langshaw Austin'.
15 J.L. Austin, *How to Do Things with Words*, 2nd Edition (Cambridge, MA: Harvard University Press, 1975 [1962]), p. 7.
16 Longsworth, 'John Langshaw Austin'. Longsworth offers a perspicacious, if by his own admission, somewhat bald explanation of Austin's arguments about knowledge in the same article.
17 Cavell, *Must We Mean What We Say?*, p. 104.
18 Ibid.
19 Ibid.
20 Ibid., p. 93.
21 Ibid., p. 264.
22 Ibid., p. 94.
23 Ibid., p. 96.
24 Ibid.
25 Ibid., p. 271.
26 Ibid., p. 272.
27 Ibid., p. 180.
28 Klevan, *Film Performance*, p. 169.
29 Cavell, *Must We Mean What We Say?*, p. 228.
30 Ibid., p. 229.
31 Ibid., p. 230.
32 Ibid., p. 236.
33 Ibid., p. 235.
34 Ibid., p. 236.
35 Intriguingly, film pops up again when Cavell returns to the question of intention in 'Being Odd, Getting Even', an essay published some twenty years later. Here he draws a comparison between an analogy that Austin draws between intention and headlights and the work of the comic W.C. Fields, *In Quest of the Ordinary: Lines of Skepticism and Romanticism* (Chicago, IL: Chicago University Press, 1988), p. 117.
36 Cavell, *Must We Mean What We Say?*, p. 237.
37 Ibid., p. 270.

38 Mary Devereaux, 'Neighbouring the World: Movies as a Subject for Philosophy', *The Bucknell Review* 31/1 (1 January 1989), p. 195.
39 Cavell, *Pursuits*, pp. 11–12.
40 Cavell, *Cavell on Film*, p. 183.
41 Ibid.
42 Ibid., p. 184.
43 Ibid.
44 Ibid., p. 185.
45 Ibid., p. 187.
46 Ibid., p. 191.
47 Ibid., p. 125. Cavell revisits *Deeds* in a chapter of *Cities of Words*, and again in conversation with Andrew Klevan.
48 Ibid., p. 126.
49 Emerson, 'Behaviour', from *The Conduct of Life*, cited in Cavell, *Cavell on Film*, p. 127.
50 Cavell floats but does not answer the question as to whether fidgetiness as a marker of humanness is true of humanity in all its incarnations or whether it may be true only of human creatures in the modern age and in particular the period of late capitalism that constitutes the setting of *Mr Deeds Goes to Town*.
51 Stanley Cavell, *Cities of Words: Pedagogical Letters on a Register of the Moral Life* (Cambridge: Harvard University Press, 2004), p. 204.
52 Ibid., p. 206.
53 Cavell, *Cavell on Film*, p. 126.
54 Klevan, 'What Becomes of Thinking on Film?', p. 181.
55 Ibid., p. 181.
56 Ibid., p. 182.
57 Cavell, *Cities*, p. 203.
58 Cavell, 'The Thought of Movies', in *Cavell on Film*, pp. 87–106 (92).
59 Opera is a personal and professional passion of Cavell: it features as a structuring concern in his 1994 autobiographical work *A Pitch of Philosophy: Autobiographical Exercises* (which includes a section entitled 'Opera and the Lease of Voice') and is often grouped thematically with television and film in overviews of Cavell's work (see for example Mulhall, Eldridge).

60 'Opera in (and as) Film', in Cavell, *Cavell on Film*, p. 306.
61 Cavell, *Must We Mean What We Say?*, p. xxxvi.
62 Rex Butler, 'Stanley Cavell', in *Film, Theory, Philosophy: The Key Thinkers*, Felicity Colman (ed.) (Durham, NC: Acumen, 2009), p. 146.
63 Stanley Cavell, *The Claim of Reason: Wittgenstein, Skepticism, Morality, and Tragedy* (Oxford: Clarendon Press, 1979; Oxford: Oxford University Press, 1982), p. 123.
64 Cavell, *Must We Mean What We Say?*, p. 230.

Chapter 3

1 Stanley Cavell, *The World Viewed: Reflections on the Ontology of Film* (New York, NY: Viking Press, 1971), p. xix.
2 Ibid., pp. 4–5.
3 One wonders to what extent Cavell is being wilfully ignorant of a whole swathe of film culture here. In the UK, cine-clubs and societies had been placing film in a hierarchy of value since the 1920s, for example, while in the United States, Jonas Mekas had founded the magazine *Film Culture* in 1954, and in 1962, he co-founded the Film-Makers' Cooperative and the Filmmakers' Cinematheque which eventually grew into Anthology Film Archives, one of the world's largest and most important repositories of avant-garde film. Mekas was of course part of the New American Cinema, alongside Hollis Frampton and Kenneth Anger. There is then an entire film history that runs counter to Cavell's assertions here, one that it is hard to believe he was entirely oblivious to.
4 Cavell, *World Viewed*, pp. 5–6.
5 See for example Rosalind Krauss's review of *The World Viewed*: 'Dark Glasses and Bifocals, a Book Review', in *Artforum* (May 1974), pp. 59–62.
6 Cavell, *World Viewed*, p. xix.
7 Cavell, *Cavell on Film*, p. 282.
8 Cavell, *World Viewed*, p. 9.
9 Ibid., p. 11.

10 An instructive comparison can be made between Cavell's thoughts on the relationship between the film and the theatrical viewing situation and those of Roland Barthes, in 'On Leaving the Movie Theatre'. Barthes does not comment on the timing of one's entrance and exit into the theatre but likewise emphasizes the importance of public anonymity. 'In the darkness of the theatre (anonymous, populated, numerous – oh, the boredom, the frustration of so-called private showings!) lies the very fascination of the film (any film). Think of the contrary experience: on television, where films are also shows, no fascination; here darkness is erased, anonymity repressed… television doomed us to the Family, whose household instrument it has become – what the hearth used to be, flanked by its communal kettle.' (Roland Barthes, 'Leaving the Movie Theatre', in *The Rustle of Language*, trans. Richard Howard (New York, NY: Hill and Wang, 1986), p. 346.
11 William Rothman and Marian Keane, *Reading Cavell's The World Viewed: A Philosophical Perspective on Film* (Detroit, MI: Wayne University Press, 2000), p. 48.
12 Cavell, *Must We Mean What We Say?*, p. 99.
13 Mullarkey, *Refractions of Reality*, p. 111.
14 Andre Bazin, 'Ontology of the Photographic Image', in *What Is Cinema?*, trans. Hugh Gray (Berkeley, CA: University of California Press, 1967), p. 110.
15 Cavell, *World Viewed*, p. 16. My emphasis.
16 Austin, *How to Do Things with Words*, p. 181.
17 Cavell, *World Viewed*, p. 17.
18 Ibid., pp. 18–19. Emphasis in original.
19 Rothman and Keane, *Reading*, p. 29; Morgan, 'Stanley Cavell', p. 164.
20 Morgan, 'Stanley Cavell', p. 164.
21 Daniel Shaw, 'Stanley Cavell on the Magic of the Movies', *Film-Philosophy* 21/1 (2017), p. 199. The philosopher Noël Carroll likewise describes Cavell as an 'advocate' of Bazinian realism.
22 Cavell, *World Viewed*, p. 20.
23 Bazin, 'Ontology of the Photographic Image', p. 12.
24 Ibid.

25 Cavell, *World Viewed*, p. 21.
26 Ibid., p. 25.
27 Ibid.
28 Thomas Hilgers, *Aesthetic Disinterestedness: Art, Experience, and the Self* (Oxford: Routledge, 2016).
29 Christian Metz, *Film Language: A Semiotics of the Cinema* (New York, NY/Oxford: Oxford University Press, 1974), p. 10.
30 Ibid., p.10.
31 Both Sesonske's review article of *The World Viewed* and Cavell's response originated in a symposium held in Autumn 1972, in Sarasota, Florida. For more, see Cavell, *World Viewed*, p. 161.
32 Cavell, *World Viewed*, p. 155.
33 Ibid., p. 26.
34 Ibid., p. 20.
35 Lisa Trahair, 'Being on the Outside: Cinematic Automatism in Stanley Cavell's *The World Viewed*', *Film-Philosophy* 18 (2014): Special Section on Stanley Cavell, pp. 128–146.
36 Ibid., p. 130.
37 Cavell, *World Viewed*, pp. 72–73.
38 Ibid., p. 103.
39 Ibid., p. 69.
40 Richard Dyer, *Stars* (London: BFI Education, 1979); Metz.
41 See for example D.N. Rodowick, *The Virtual Life of Film* (Cambridge, MA: Harvard University Press, 2007).
42 The openness of Cavell's understanding of automatism has led in part to a renewed interest in Cavell's work in an age of digital cinema. Daniel Morgan argues that Cavell's engagement with modernism is what lends his work relevance in this context: in *The World Viewed* Cavell argues that while for much of film history photography was film's central automatism, the rise of new kinds of films in the 1960s suggests that it was never more than a convention, its importance appearing as necessary but in reality historically contingent. This recognition, Morgan claims, 'is what not only enables Cavell's theory to survive the emergence of digital media, a post-photographic condition,

but gives it explanatory force in these new circumstances. We don't leave the cinema, or its appeals, even as those appeals are transformed'. See, for example, Rodowick, *The Virtual Life of Film*, Rosalind Krauss, '*A Voyage on the North Sea*': *Art in the Age of the Post-medium Condition* (London: Thames and Hudson, 1999), and Morgan, 'Stanley Cavell', p. 171.
43 Cavell, *World Viewed*, p. 36.
44 Ibid., p. 60.
45 Ibid., p. 61.
46 Ibid., p. 50.
47 Ibid., p. 22.
48 Fritz Novotny, *Painting and Sculpture in Europe, 1780–1880 (Pelican History of Art)* (New Haven, CT: Yale University Press, 1971).
49 Cavell, *World Viewed*, p. 22.
50 Ibid., p. 23.
51 Ibid., p. 21.
52 Ibid., p. 22.
53 Rothman and Keane, *Reading*, p. 64.
54 Cavell is commonly agreed to be working within a secular framework; nonetheless Espen Dahl has produced some brilliant work on the relationship between Cavell's thought and theology, and in relation to the loss of the natural relation in particular. Lisa Trahair draws a link between Bazin's emphasis on aesthetics as the domain of the spiritual and Cavell's claim that 'the human condemnation to intention and sequence is the sequel, if not the meaning, of original sin' (Trahair, 'Being on the Outside', pp. 132–133).
55 William Rothman and Marian Keane, 'Toward a Reading of The World Viewed', *Journal of Film and Video* 49 (Spring/Summer 1997), p. 13.
56 Trahair, 'Being on the Outside', p. 133.
57 Martin Shuster, 'The Ordinariness and Absence of the World: Cavell's Ontology of the Screen – Reading the World Viewed', *Modern Language Notes* 130/5 (December 2015), pp. 1070–1071. Shuster is citing Heidegger's 'The Age of the World Picture'. There are numerous accounts of the relationship between Cavell and Heidegger, and many

the works offer lucid and indeed persuasive accounts of the importance of reading Cavell alongside Heidegger. However, it is my contention, following Shuster, that while Cavell relies on elements of Heidegger's account to advance an understanding of 'world' and human agency, notably an impulse to resist viewing our relationship to the world as one of knowing, he fundamentally rejects other elements of Heidegger's work. Heidegger is not a structuring influence on Cavell's philosophy in the same way than that Austin, Wittgenstein, Emerson or Thoreau are, hence his somewhat marginal place within this account of Cavell's work.

58 Cavell, *World Viewed*, p. 22. Lisa Trahair expands this point articulately in 'Being on the Outside'.
59 Cavell, *World Viewed*, p. 216.
60 Ibid., p. 107. My emphasis.
61 Shuster astutely compares the situation to Cavell's description of language and meaning making: 'You can no more tell beforehand whether a line of argument will convince you, or an answer raise your laughter. But when it happens, it will feel like a discovery of the a priori, a necessity of language, and of the world, coming to light.' Shuster, 'The Ordinariness and Absence of the World', p. 1093. The quote is from *The Senses of Walden* (San Francisco, CA: North Point Press, 1981), p. 43.
62 Cavell, *World Viewed*, p. 104.
63 Ibid., p. 32.
64 Cavell, *The Claim of Reason*, p. 123.
65 Cavell, *World Viewed*, p. 32.
66 Ibid., p. 40.
67 Ibid., p. 135.
68 Trahair, 'Being on the Outside', p. 137.
69 Morgan, 'Stanley Cavell', pp. 163–164.
70 Both John Mullarkey and David Rodowick have investigated the correlation between Cavell and Deleuze in greater detail. See Mullarkey, *Refractions of Reality* and Rodowick, 'Elegy', pp. 91–109 and *The Virtual Life of Film*.
71 Cavell, *World Viewed*, pp. 62–63.

72 Ibid., p. 62.
73 Shuster, 'The Ordinariness and Absence of the World', p. 1093. My emphasis.
74 Cavell, *World Viewed*, p. 60.
75 Ibid., p. 105.
76 Shuster, 'The Ordinariness and Absence of the World', pp. 1093–1094.
77 Cavell, *The Claim of Reason*, p. 236.
78 Cavell, *World Viewed*, p. 189.
79 Ibid., p. 226.
80 Ibid., p. 131.
81 Ibid., pp. 131–132.
82 Ibid., p. 132.
83 See for example Andrew Sarris, 'Notes on the Auteur Theory in 1962', *Film Culture* 27 (Winter 1962–1963), pp. 1–8.
84 Cavell, *World Viewed*, p. 219.
85 Ibid., p. 118.
86 Ibid., p. 128.
87 Ibid., p. 127.
88 Ibid., p. 123.
89 Trahair, 'Being on the Outside', p. 143.
90 Cavell, *World Viewed*, p. 125.
91 Cavell, *Pursuits of Happiness*, p. 207.
92 Trahair, 'Being on the Outside', p. 143.
93 Cavell, *World Viewed*, p. 188.

Chapter 4

1 Rothman and Keane, *Reading*, p. 42.
2 Cavell, *Must We Mean What We Say?*, p. xxxvi.
3 Cavell, *The Senses of Walden*, p. 172.
4 Karen Hanson, 'Being Doubted, Being Assured', in *Images in Our Souls: Cavell, Psychoanalysis and Cinema* (Baltimore and London: The John Hopkins Press, 1987), pp. 187–201 (187).

5 Cavell, *The Claim of Reason*, p. 442.
6 Cavell, *Cavell on Film*, p. 345.
7 As expressed by Mulhall, 'On Refusing, pp. 22–36.
8 Cavell, *The Claim of Reason*, pp. 82–83. Emphasis in original.
9 Cavell, *Must We Mean What We Say?*, pp. 263–264.
10 Ibid., p. 257.
11 Stanley Cavell, *In Quest of the Ordinary: Lines of Skepticism and Romanticism* (Chicago, IL: University of Chicago Press, 1988), p. 83.
12 David MacArthur, 'What Goes without Seeing: Marriage, Sex, and the Ordinary in *The Awful Truth*', *Film-Philosophy* 18 (2014): Special Section on Stanley Cavell, p. 93.
13 Cavell, *Themes out of School*, p. 14.
14 Ludwig Wittgenstein, *Philosophical Investigations*, trans. G.E.M. Anscombe, Third Edition (Oxford: Blackwell, 1978), p. 187, note 129.
15 Andrew Klevan, *Disclosure of the Everyday: Undramatic Achievement in Narrative Film* (Trowbridge: Flicks Books, 2000), p. 12.
16 Ibid., p. 12.
17 Cavell, *Must We Mean What We Say?*, p. 323.
18 MacArthur, 'What Goes without Seeing', p. 95.
19 Fischer, *Stanley Cavell*, p. 83.
20 Klevan, *Disclosure of the Everyday*, p. 12, citing Fischer, *Stanley Cavell*, p. 85.
21 Stanley Cavell, 'Epistemology and Tragedy: A Reading of Othello', *Daedalus* 108/3, 'Hypocrisy, Illusion, and Evasion' (Summer 1979), pp. 27–43.
22 Cavell, *Must We Mean What We Say?*, p. 324.
23 Stanley Cavell, *Contesting Tears: The Hollywood Melodrama of the Unknown Woman* (Chicago, IL: University of Chicago Press, 1996), pp. xi–xii.
24 Cavell, *Pursuits of Happiness*, p. 1. Cavell is referring to Frye's article 'The Argument of Comedy', available in *Northrop Frye's Writings on Shakespeare and the Renaissance*, Troni Y. Grande and Garry Sherber (eds.) (Toronto: University of Toronto Press, 2010).
25 See Andrew Sarris, *You Ain't Heard Nothin' Yet: The American Talking Film, History & Memory, 1927–1949* (New York, NY/Oxford: Oxford

University Press, 1998) and David R. Shumway, 'Screwball Comedies: Constructing Romance, Mystifying Marriage', in *Film Genre Reader III*, Barry Keith Grant (ed.) (Austin, TX: University of Texas Press, 2003).

26 Steve Neale, 'Comedy', in *The Cinema Book*, Third Edition (London: BFI, 2007), pp. 270–276.
27 See for example Christine Gledhill on standardization and differentiation in 'History of Genre Criticism: Introduction', in *The Cinema Book*, Third Edition, Pam Cook (ed.) (London: BFI, 2007), pp. 252–259.
28 Cavell, *Pursuits of Happiness*, p. 24.
29 Ibid., pp. 31–32.
30 Stephen Mulhall, *Stanley Cavell: Philosophy's Recounting of the Ordinary* (Oxford: Oxford University Press, 1994), p. 234.
31 Cavell, *In Quest of the Ordinary*, p. 176.
32 Cavell, *Pursuits of Happiness*, p. 2.
33 Mulhall, *Stanley Cavell*, p. 235.
34 In William Rothman, 'Cavell on Film, Television and Opera', in *Stanley Cavell*, Richard Eldridge (ed.) (Cambridge: Cambridge University Press, 2003), p. 212.
35 Cavell, *Pursuits of Happiness*, p. 113.
36 Cavell pursues the return to childhood in detail on p.103 of *Pursuits of Happiness*, and again throughout chapters on *Bringing Up Baby* and *The Awful Truth*.
37 Cavell, *Pursuits of Happiness*, p. 54.
38 Cavell, *Contesting*, p. 30.
39 Stanley Cavell, 'The Incessance and the Absence of the Political', in *The Claim to Community: Essays on Stanley Cavell and Political Philosophy*, Andrew Norris, (ed.) (Stanford, CA: Stanford University Press, 2006), pp. 263–317 (300).
40 Cavell, *Cities of Words*, pp. 164–207.
41 Robert Sinnerbrink, *Cinematic Ethics: Exploring Ethical Experience through Film* (London: Routledge, 2015), p. 45. Sinnerbrink is citing *Cities of Words*, p. 75.
42 Cavell, *Pursuits of Happiness*, p. 102.
43 Butler, 'Stanley Cavell', p. 146.

44 Ibid., p. 147.
45 Cavell, *Must We Mean What We Say?*, p. 263.
46 Cavell, *Pursuits of Happiness*, p. 14.
47 Ibid., p. 86.
48 Ibid., p. 32.
49 Ibid., p. 88.
50 Ibid., p. 239.
51 Ibid., p. 132.
52 Ibid., p. 239.
53 Ibid.
54 Ibid.
55 Ibid., p. 86.
56 Mulhall, *Stanley Cavell*, p. 235.
57 Cavell, *Pursuits of Happiness*, p. 127.
58 Klevan, *Disclosure of the Everyday*, p. 22.
59 Ibid., p. 23.
60 Cavell, *Must We Mean What We Say?*, p. 350.
61 Cavell, *Pursuits of Happiness*, p. 233.
62 MacArthur, 'What Goes without Seeing', p. 98.
63 Cavell, *Themes out of School*, p. 192.
64 Mulhall, *Stanley Cavell*, p. 235.
65 Klevan, *Disclosure of the Everyday*, p. 25.
66 Cavell, *Pursuits of Happiness*, p. 16.
67 Ibid.
68 Ibid., p. 56.
69 Ibid., p. 84.
70 Ibid., p. 56.
71 Kathrina Glitre, '"The Same, but Different": The Awful Truth about Marriage, Remarriage and Screwball Comedy', *Cineaction* 54 (2001), p. 9.
72 Ibid., p. 56.
73 Cavell, *Pursuits of Happiness*, p. 57.
74 Catherine Constable, 'Seeing Lucy's Perspective: Returning to Cavell, Wittgenstein and *The Awful Truth*', *New Review of Film and Television Studies* 9/3 (2011), p. 361. In a footnote to this article, Constable

acknowledges a debt to Andrew Klevan whose paper at the 'Film-Philosophy' conference in Bristol 2008 inspired her line of thought. She notes that parts of Klevan's paper were since revised and published as 'Notes on Stanley Cavell and Philosophical Film Criticism', in *New Takes in Film-Philosophy*, H. Carel and G. Tuck (eds.) (Basingstoke: Palgrave Macmillan, 2011), pp. 48–64. It is worth adding, however, that Klevan advances a similar argument concerning Jerry rather than Lucy needing to reform in his 2005 book *Film Performance*, pp. 35–37.

75 Glitre, 'The Same, but Different', pp. 7–10.
76 Cavell, *Pursuits of Happiness*, p. 260. My emphasis.
77 Constable, 'Seeing Lucy's Perspective', p. 366.
78 Cavell, *Contesting*, p. 10. My emphasis.
79 Cavell, *Pursuits of Happiness*, p. 32.
80 Mulhall, *Stanley Cavell*, p. 234.
81 Rothman, 'Cavell on Film, Television and Opera', pp. 206–238 (215).
82 Klevan, *Disclosure of the Everyday*, p. 182.
83 Cavell, *Pursuits of Happiness*, p. 88.
84 Stanley Cavell, 'What Becomes of Things on Film?', *Philosophy and Literature* 2/2 (Fall, 1978), p. 249.
85 Ibid., p. 257.
86 Cavell, *Pursuits of Happiness*, p. 130.
87 Ibid.
88 Ibid., pp. 118–119.
89 Cavell, *Must We Mean What We Say?*, p. 330.
90 Cavell, *Pursuits of Happiness*, p. 12.
91 Rothman, *Cavell on Film*, p. xvii.
92 Ibid., p. 13.

Chapter 5

1 Cavell, *Contesting*, p. 118.
2 Rothman in Richard Eldridge (ed.), *Stanley Cavell* (Cambridge: Cambridge University Press, 2003), p. 221.

3   Cavell, *Pursuits of Happiness*, p. 157.
4   Cavell, 'The Politics of Interpretation', in *Themes out of School: Effects and Causes* (San Francisco: North Point Press, 1984; Chicago: University of Chicago Press, 1988).
5   Cavell, *Conditions Handsome and Unhandsome*, p. 4.
6   Ibid., p. 5.
7   Cavell, *The Senses of Walden*, p. 145.
8   Stanley Cavell, *This New yet Unapproachable America: Lectures after Emerson after Wittgenstein* (Chicago, IL: University of Chicago Press, 1989), p. 81.
9   Cavell, *In Quest of the Ordinary*, p. i.
10 Ibid., p. 6.
11 Ibid., p. 4.
12 For an excellent discussion of the ways in which Cavell takes up Thoreau, see Stephen Mulhall, *Stanley Cavell: Philosophy's Recounting of the Ordinary* (Oxford: Oxford University Press, 1998). Áine Kelly and Andrew Taylor's edited volume is very useful on the links between Thoreau, Emerson and Americanness: *Stanley Cavell, Literature, and Film: The Idea of America* (London: Routledge, 2013).
13 Cavell, *Senses of Walden*, p. 142.
14 Ibid., p. 147.
15 Ibid., p. 147.
16 Cavell, *In Quest of the Ordinary*, p. 130.
17 Ibid., p. 107.
18 Cavell, *Pursuits of Happiness*, p. 15.
19 Cavell, *In Quest of the Ordinary*, pp. 129–130.
20 Cavell, *Contesting*, p. 9.
21 Cavell brings up Emerson in order to answer a question about whether it is somehow irresponsible to make a film about the problems of leisure in an age of desperation, quoting the line 'Do not tell me, as a good man did today, of my obligation to put all poor men in good situations.' 'It is not I who make them and who keep them poor; and so far as I can better the situation of whoever is poor I can do it only by answering my genius when it calls,' Cavell explains (*Pursuits of Happiness*, pp. 6–7).

22 Cavell, *Contesting*, p. 220.
23 Mulhall, *Stanley Cavell*, p. 237.
24 Henrik Ibsen, *A Doll's House, The Wild Duck, Lady from the Sea*, trans. R Farquharson Sharp and Eleanor Marx-Aveling (London: Dent, 1958), p. 68. I follow Alice Crary's reworked translation as given in her article 'Austin and the Ethics of Discourse', in *Reading Cavell*, Alice Crary and Sanford Shieh (eds.) (New York, NY: Routledge, 2006). The emphasis is mine.
25 Cavell, *Contesting*, p. 10.
26 Ibid., p. 11.
27 Ibid., pp. 87–88.
28 Ibid., p. 11.
29 Ibid., p. 6.
30 Ibid., p. 5.
31 Ibid., p. 6.
32 Peter Brooks, *The Melodramatic Imagination: Balzac, Henry James, Melodrama and the Mode of Excess* (New Haven, CT: Yale University Press, 1976).
33 Joseph Smith and William Kerrigan (eds.), *Images in Our Souls: Cavell, Psychoanalysis, and Cinema* (Baltimore, MD: Johns Hopkins University Press, 1987), p. 22.
34 For a concise yet comprehensive overview of theories of psychoanalysis and film, see Barbara Creed, 'Film and Psychoanalysis', in *The Oxford Guide to Film Studies*, John Hill and Pamela Church Gibson (eds.) (Oxford: Oxford University Press, 1998).
35 Cavell recognizes that this is something of a generalization: Chaplin, Keaton and Gary Cooper are obvious exceptions. But on the whole, he argues, men are of interest to the cinema in crowds and in conflict, but women 'bequeath psychic depth to film's interest' (Smith and Kerrigan, *Images in Our Souls*, p. 29).
36 Ibid.
37 Ibid., p. 4.
38 Indeed Cavell conveys something of the unplanned nature of this latter connection in *Contesting*, when he writes: 'My project, through

its origin in an effort to bring in to play, and relate, a small number of comedies and a smaller number of melodramas, is shaped by a set of preoccupations of mine with intersections between cinema and philosophical skepticism, between tragedy and melodrama, hence (it turned out) between skepticism and gender.' Cavell, *Contesting*, p. 99.
39 Ibid., p. 30.
40 Smith and Kerrigan, *Images in Our Souls*, p. 31.
41 Ibid., p. 34.
42 Wittgenstein, *Philosophical Investigations*, p. 187.
43 Ralph Waldo Emerson, 'Behaviour'.
44 Mulhall, *Stanley Cavell*, p. 240.
45 Cavell, 'What Photography Calls Thinking', in *Cavell on Film*, pp. 115–135 (126).
46 Ibid., p. 131.
47 Ibid., p. 13. My emphasis.
48 Ibid., p. 132.
49 Mulhall, *Stanley Cavell*, p. 242.
50 Cavell, *Contesting*, p. 106.
51 Hanson, 'Being Doubted', p. 191.
52 Cavell, *Contesting*, p. 106.
53 Cavell, *Contesting*, p. 105.
54 Mulhall, *Stanley Cavell*, p. 242.
55 Ibid., p. 245.
56 Cavell, *Contesting*, pp. 246–247.
57 Tania Modleski, 'Letter to the Editor', *Critical Inquiry* 17/1 (Autumn 1990), p. 237. Modleski subsequently expanded her charge against Cavell in the opening chapter of her book *Feminism without Women: Culture and Criticism in a 'Postfeminist' Age* (London: Routledge, 1991), where she connects Cavell's misunderstanding of feminist concerns to a rather marginalizing attitude towards women in Emerson.
58 Modleski, *Feminism without Women*.
59 Cavell, 'Response to Tania Modleski', *Critical Inquiry* 17/1 (Autumn 1990), p. 242.
60 Sinnerbrink, *Cinematic Ethics*, p. 114.

61 See Modleski, 'Letter to the Editor'; E. Ann Kaplan, 'The Case of the Missing Mother': Maternal Issues in King Vidor's Stella Dallas', *Heresies* 16 (1983), pp. 81–85; Mary Ann Doane, *The Desire to Desire: The Woman's Film of the 1940's* (Bloomington, IN: University of Indiana Press, 1987); and Linda Williams, 'Something Else Besides a Woman: *Stella Dallas* and the Maternal Melodrama', *Cinema Journal*, 24/1 (Autumn 1984), pp. 2–27.
62 William Rothman, 'Pathos and Transfiguration in the Face of the Camera: A Reading of Stella Dallas', in *The 'I' of the Camera: Essays in Film Criticism, History and Aesthetics* (Cambridge: Cambridge University Press, 1988), pp. 85–94.
63 Cavell, *Cities of Words*, p. 269.
64 Sinnerbrink, *Cinematic Ethics*, p. 116.
65 Cavell, *Contesting*, p. 203.
66 Ibid., p. 196.
67 Sinnerbrink, *Cinematic Ethics*, p. 119.
68 Williams, 'Something Else', p. 13.
69 Ibid., p. 17.
70 Sinnerbrink, *Cinematic Ethics*, p. 119.
71 Cavell, *Contesting*, p. 219.
72 Sinnerbrink, *Cinematic Ethics*, p. 123.
73 Ibid., p. 124.
74 Andrew Klevan in Russell Goodman (ed.), *Contending with Stanley Cavell* (Oxford: Oxford University Press, 2005), p. 119.
75 Andrew Klevan, *Barbara Stanwyck* (London: BFI/Palgrave MacMillan, 2013), p. 50.
76 Cavell, *Contesting*, p. 210.
77 Smith and Kerrigan, *Images in Our Souls*, p. 31.
78 Ibid., p. 88.
79 Cavell, *Pursuits of Happiness*, p. 86.
80 Ibid., p. 33.
81 Ibid., p. 253.
82 Constable, 'Seeing Lucy's perspective', p. 366.
83 Stanley Cavell, *A Pitch of Philosophy: Autobiographical Exercises* (Cambridge, MA: Harvard University Press, 1994), pp. 16–17.

84   Cavell, *Contesting*, p. 66.
85   Ibid., p. 58.
86   Williams, 'Something Else', p. 15.
87   Ibid., p. 220.
88   Cavell, Pitch, p. 155.
89   Ibid., p. 144.
90   Ibid., p. 145.
91   Adriana Cavarero, *For More than One Voice: Toward a Philosophy of Vocal Expression* (Stanford, CA: Stanford University Press, 2005), p. 117.
92   Ibid., p. 122.
93   Cavell, *Contesting*, p. 199.
94   Ibid., p. 198.
95   Ibid., p. 199.
96   Cavell, *Pitch*, p. 169.
97   Cavell, *Contesting*, p. 200.
98   Rothman in Eldridge, *Stanley Cavell*, p. 225.
99   Rothman, *Cavell on Film*, p. xxii.
100 Cavell, *Contesting*, p. 220.
101 Ibid., p. 221.
102 Ibid., p. 222.
103 Ibid., p. 200.

Chapter 6

1   Cavell, *Cities of Words*, p. ix.
2   Ibid.
3   Ibid., p. x.
4   Cavell, 'Response to Tania Modleski', p. 242.
5   Cavell, *Cities of Words*, p. 245.
6   Ibid., p. 246.
7   Michel Foucault, *The Care of the Self* (London: Penguin, 2009).

8 Mulhall, *Stanley Cavell*, p. 265.
9 Cavell, *Conditions Handsome and Unhandsome*.
10 Cavell, 'The Good of Film', p. 337. Kristen Boudreau observes that Cavell develops the idea of the zigzag journey through inconsistency from Emerson, who writes that 'the voyage of the best ship is a zigzag line of a hundred tacks. See the line from a sufficient distance, and it straightens itself to the average tendency. Your genuine action will explain itself, and will explain your other genuine actions', as well as Henry James, who in *The Portrait of a Lady* describes his erratic heroine thus: 'In matters of opinion she had her own way, and it led her into a thousand ridiculous zigzags.' See Kristen Boudreau, 'The Haunting of History: Emerson, James, and the Ghosts of Human Suffering', in *Stanley Cavell, Literature, and Film: The Idea of America*, Áine Kelly and Andrew Taylor (eds.) (London: Routledge, 2013), p. 82.
11 Matteo Faloni, 'Perfectionism and Moral Reasoning', *European Journal of Pragmatism and American Philosophy* 2 (2010).
12 John Rawls, *A Theory of Justice* (Cambridge, MA: Belknap Press/ Harvard University Press, 1971).
13 Cavell, *Conditions Handsome and Unhandsome*, p. xxxi. My emphasis.
14 Mulhall, *Stanley Cavell*, p. 266.
15 Cavell, *Conditions Handsome and Unhandsome*, pp. 6–7.
16 Cavell, *Cities of Words*, p. 2.
17 Ibid.
18 Stephen Mulhall, 'Film and Philosophy: Digital Cinema and Moral Philosophy', Karlsruhe ZKM Lecture, [unpublished], p. 27.
19 Mulhall, *Stanley Cavell*, p. 237.
20 Cavell, 'The Good of Film', p. 340.
21 Ibid.
22 Cavell, *Cavell on Film*, p. 336.
23 Ibid., p. 337. My emphasis.
24 Sinnerbrink, *Cinematic Ethics*, p. 36.
25 Cavell, 'The Good of Film', p. 338.
26 Sinnerbrink, *Cinematic Ethics*.
27 Ibid., p. xii.

28 Lisa Downing and Libby Saxton, *Film and Ethics: Foreclosed Encounters* (Abingdon and New York: Routledge, 2010), p. 19.
29 Ibid., p. 20.
30 Cavell, *Cities of Words*, p. 9.
31 Ibid., p. 11.
32 Ibid., p. 39.
33 Ibid.
34 Ibid., p. 16. My emphasis.
35 Ibid., p. 27.
36 Cavell, 'The Good of Film', p. 337.
37 Mulhall, 'Film and Philosophy: Digital Cinema and Moral Philosophy', p. 35.
38 Cavell, *Cities of Words*, p. 27.
39 Stanley Cavell, 'A Capra Moment', in *Cavell on Film* (Albany, NY: SUNY Press, 2005), p. 137.
40 Sinnerbrink, *Cinematic Ethics*, p. 40. My emphasis.
41 Cavell, *Cities of Words*, p. 15.
42 Cavell, *The Claim of Reason*, p. 253.
43 Cavell, 'Philosophy the Day after Tomorrow', in *Cavell on Film*, p. 325.
44 Cavell, 'The Good of Film', p. 339.
45 Cavell, *Cities of Words*, p. 42.
46 Ibid., p. 25.
47 Ibid., p. 15.
48 Ibid., p. 16.
49 Ibid.
50 Sinnerbrink, *Cinematic Ethics*, p. 44.
51 Ibid.
52 Cavell, citing Nietzsche, *Cities of Words*, p. 220.
53 Emerson, 'Circles', in *The Portable Emerson* (London: Penguin Classics, 2014).
54 Cavell, *Cities of Words*, p. 421.
55 Cavell, 'On Eric Rohmer's *Conte d'hiver*', in *Cavell on Film*, p. 288.
56 Cavell, 'The Good of Film', p. 346.
57 Cavell, *Cities of Words*, p. 426.
58 Cavell, *Cavell on Film*, p. 291.

59 Cavell, *Cities of Words*, p. 426.
60 Cavell, *Contesting*, p. 5.
61 Lawrence F. Rhu points out that Rohmer's film better exemplifies the structural characteristic of the remarriage comedy where the central couple gets back together again, than it does the overcoming of problems internal to communication between the couple.
62 Cavell, *Cities of Words*, p. 442.
63 Ibid., pp. 423–424.
64 Fiona Handyside, 'Words for a Conversation: Speech, Doubt and Faith in the films of Eric Rohmer and Mia Hansen-Løve', *Studies in French Cinema*, forthcoming.
65 Cavell, *Cities of Words*, p. 426.
66 Ibid., p. 441.
67 Ibid.
68 Ibid., p. 17.
69 Cavell, 'Philosophy the Day after Tomorrow', p. 325.
70 Mulhall, *Stanley Cavell*, p. 267.
71 Cavell, *Cities of Words*, p. 14.
72 Cavell, 'The Good of Film', p. 339.
73 Cavell, 'Philosophy the Day after Tomorrow', p. 325. My emphasis.
74 Butler, 'Stanley Cavell', p. 147.
75 Cavell, *Conditions Handsome and Unhandsome*, p. 31.
76 Cavell, 'Philosophy the Day after Tomorrow', p. 326.
77 Cavell, *Cities of Words*, p. 18.
78 Cavell, 'The Good of Film', pp. 339–340.
79 Ibid., p. 340.
80 Cavell, *Conditions Handsome and Unhandsome*, pp. xxxi–xxxii.
81 Cavell, 'The Good of Film', p. 340.
82 Sinnerbrink, *Cinematic Ethics*, p. 34.
83 David Rodowick, *Philosophy's Artful Conversation* (Cambridge, MA: Harvard University Press, 2015), p. 270.
84 I am grateful to Philip Ehrenberg for pointing out this wonderful line. His blogpost on Perfectionism can be found here: https://dnrodowick.wordpress.com/author/phehrenberg/. Last accessed 18 January 2018.
85 Sinnerbrink, *Cinematic Ethics*, p. 43.

86 Rothman, 'On Stanley Cavell's Band Wagon' Special Section on Stanley Cavell, p. 15.
87 Cavell, 'The Good of Film', p. 334.
88 Ibid., p. 335.
89 Ibid.
90 Cavell, 'Moral Reasoning: Teaching from the Core', in *Cavell on Film*, p. 358. My emphasis.
91 Emerson, 'Self-Reliance'. Discussed in *Conditions Handsome and Unhandsome*, p. xxxi, 36.
92 Cavell, 'Moral Reasoning: Teaching from the Core', p. 351.
93 Naoko Saito, 'Awakening My Voice: Learning from Cavell's perfectionist education', *Education Philosophy and Theory* 36/1 (2004), p. 87.
94 Cavell, 'Moral Reasoning: Teaching from the Core', pp. 358–359.
95 Ibid.
96 Wittgenstein, *Philosophical Investigations*, p. 89.

Chapter 7

1 Cavell, *The World Viewed*, pp. 64–68.
2 Ibid., p. 65.
3 Ibid., p. 66.
4 Ibid., pp. 67–68.
5 Ibid., p. 67.
6 Ibid., p. 65.
7 Cavell, 'The Future of Possibility', pp. 21–59.
8 Cavell, *Pursuits of Happiness*, p. 102.
9 Stanley Cavell, 'Naughty Narrators: Negation of Voice in Gaslight', in *Languages of the Unsayable: The Play of Negativity in Literature and Literary Theory*, Sanford Budick and Wolfgang Iser (eds.) (New York, NY: Columbia University Press, 1989), p. 340. My emphasis.
10 Stanley Cavell, 'Crossing Paths', in *Cavell on Film*, William Rothman (ed.) (Albany, NY: State University of New York Press, 2005), pp. 361–374. My emphasis.

11 Cavell, *Little Did I Know*, p. 443.
12 Sinnerbrink, 'Re-enfranchising Film', pp. 25–47.
13 Stanley Cavell, 'Performative and Passionate Utterance', in *Philosophy the Day after Tomorrow* (Cambridge, MA: The Belknap Press of Harvard University Press, 2005).
14 Ibid.
15 Ibid., p. 36.
16 Ibid., p. 4.
17 Ibid.
18 Cavell, *Conditions Handsome and Unhandsome*, p. 20.
19 Cavell, *In Quest of the Ordinary*, p. 66.
20 Nikolas Kompridis (ed.), *Philosophical Romanticism* (London/New York, NY: Routledge, 2006), pp. 4–6.
21 Sinnerbrink, 'Re-enfranchising Film', p. 37.
22 Cavell, 'The Future of Possibility', p. 23.
23 Cavell, *Pursuits of Happiness*, p. 12.
24 Toril Moi, 'The Adventure of Reading: Literature and Philosophy, Cavell and Beauvoir', *Literature and Theology* 25/2 (June 2011), pp. 125–140 (131).
25 Toril Moi, *Revolution of the Ordinary: Literary Studies after Wittgenstein, Austin, and Cavell* (Chicago: Chicago University Press, 2017), p. 227.
26 See Iris Murdoch, *The Sovereignty of Good* (London: Routledge, 2001), p. 33.
27 Cavell, *Pursuits of Happiness*, p. 273.
28 Ibid., p. 274.
29 Moi, 'The Adventure of Reading', p.128.
30 This quotation comes from the preface to the updated edition of *Must We Mean What We Say?*, published by Cambridge University Press in 2002, pp. xxiv–xv.
31 Moi, 'The Adventure of Reading', p. 129.
32 Klevan, 'Notes on Stanley Cavell', pp. 48–64.
33 Ibid.
34 See Klevan, *Disclosure of the Everyday*.

35 Klevan, 'Notes on Stanley Cavell', p. 50.
36 Wittgenstein, *Philosophical Investigations*, p. 36.
37 Cavell, *Cities of Words*.
38 Klevan, 'Notes on Stanley Cavell', p. 60.
39 Henry James, 'The Art of Fiction'. Originally published in *Longman's Magazine* 4 (September 1884). Quoted in Cavell, *Themes out of School*, p. 6.
40 Ibid.
41 Sandra Laugier, 'The Ethics of Care as a Politics of the Ordinary', *Literature and Theology* 25/2 (June 2011), pp. 217–240 (220). My emphasis.
42 Klevan, 'Notes on Stanley Cavell', p. 60. My emphasis.
43 Cora Diamond, 'Missing the Adventure: Reply to Martha Nussbaum', in *The Realistic Spirit: Wittgenstein, Philosophy, and the Mind* (Cambridge, MA: MIT Press, 2005). p. 313. Cited in Moi, 'The Adventure of Reading'.
44 Klevan, 'Notes on Stanley Cavell', p. 60. My emphasis.
45 Ibid., p. 61.
46 Ibid., p. 22.
47 Ibid., p. 23.
48 Ibid.
49 Andrew Klevan, 'Internalising the Musical: *The Band Wagon*', in *Film Moments*, Tom Brown and James Walters (eds.) (London: BFI, 1951), p. 12.
50 Stanley Cavell, 'Something Out of the Ordinary', in *Philosophy the Day after Tomorrow* (Cambridge, MA: Harvard University Press, 2006), pp. 7–27.
51 Ibid.
52 Áine Kelly, '"A Dance of Frenzy, a Dance of Praise": Fred Astaire Acknowledges America', in *Stanley Cavell, Literature and Film: The Idea of America*, Andrew Taylor and Áine Kelly (eds.) (Oxford and New York: Routledge, 2013), pp. 152–169. Kelly's article offers a comprehensive overview of rebukes to Cavell, as well as a lucid and elegant reading of *The Band Wagon*.

53 Stanley Cavell, 'Fred Astaire Asserts the Right to Praise', in *Philosophy the Day after Tomorrow* (Cambridge, MA: Harvard University Press, 2006), pp. 61–82.
54 Daniels was not just a professional shoeshiner but a shoeshiner who danced while performing his business. His story is fascinating. For more see Ronald E. Franklin, 'Real Shoeshine Man Leroy Daniels Danced with Fred Astaire' in *The Band Wagon*. Available at: http:https://reelrundown.com/movies/Real-Shoeshine-Man-Leroy-Daniels-Danced-With-Fred-Astaire-In-The-Band-Wagon. Last accessed 24 January 2018.
55 Michael Rogin, *Blackface, White Noise: Jewish Immigrants in the Hollywood Melting Pot* (Berkeley, CA: University of California Press, 1998), p. 9. Cited in Cavell, 'Fred Astaire Asserts the Right to Praise', p. 69.
56 Rogin, *Blackface, White Noise*, p. 204.
57 Utz McKnight, *The Everyday Practice of Race in American: Ambiguous Privilege* (New York, NY: Routledge, 2010), p. 38.
58 Kelly, 'A Dance of Frenzy, A Dance of Praise', p. 158.
59 Robert Gooding-Williams, 'Aesthetics and Receptivity: Kant, Nietzsche, Cavell and Astaire', in *The Claim to Community: Essays on Stanley Cavell and Political Philosophy*, Andrew Norris (ed.) (Stanford, CA: Stanford University Press, 2006), p. 245.
60 Cavell, 'Fred Astaire Asserts the Right to Praise', p. 69.
61 Ibid., p. 74.
62 Ibid., p. 77.
63 Rothman, 'On Stanley Cavell's Band Wagon', pp. 9–21.
64 Cavell, 'Fred Astaire Asserts the Right to Praise', p. 75.
65 Gooding-Williams, 'Aesthetics and Receptivity', p. 253.
66 Ibid., p. 257. Gooding-Williams spells out the mythical force as fantasy a few pages earlier: '[Astaire is shown] acquiring that blackness through the agency of a "shine" who, by shining his shoes, works a sorcery that disseminates his blackness, as if a priapic Daniels had discharged a second, miniature "shine," a sort of black homunculus, onto the surface of Astaire's footwear' (p. 252).

67 Gooding-Williams, 'Aesthetics and Receptivity', p. 258.
68 We might level a similar charge at Cavell's treatment of homosexuality, which he discusses very little in relation to film but which nonetheless is at the thematic heart of a chapter in *Contesting Tears*: 'Postscript: To Whom It May Concern' draws on metaphors of closeted-ness that what Eve Kosofy Sedgewick refers to as 'homosexual panic' 'is endemic to all and only heterosexual males'. *Contesting*, pp. 151–184.
69 Ibid. It's perhaps instructive to compare Rothman's response to the Bojangles routine with that of the unnamed narrator of Zadie Smith's 2017 novel *Swing Time*: a young woman with a black mother and white father. Having recently lost her job as assistant to a famous pop star, she goes to the Royal Festival Hall to hear an Australian director 'in conversation' and sees a clip from *Swing Time* – 'a film I know very well, I watched it over and over as a child'. She is bored and a bit confused by the discussion of 'pure cinema' as the 'interplay of light and dark, expressed as a kind of rhythm, over time'. Later that evening, after sex, she shows her boyfriend the same clip on her laptop. He is shocked by Fred Astaire's blackface and so is she: 'I'd managed to block the childhood image from my memory: the rolling eyes, the white gloves, the Bojangles grin. I felt very stupid.'
70 Cavell, 'The Incessance and the Absence of the Political', p. 301.
71 Ibid., p. 302.
72 Cavell, *Cavell on Film*, p. 226.
73 Cavell, 'Something Out of the Ordinary', p. 8.
74 Ibid., pp. 8–9.
75 Ibid., p. 9.
76 Cavell, *Cavell on Film*, p. 36.
77 Cavell, *Pursuits of Happiness*, p. 37.
78 Ibid., p. 36.
79 Ibid., p. 41.
80 Cavell, 'Something out of the Ordinary', p. 10.
81 Ibid.
82 Ibid., p. 21.
83 Ibid., p. 17.

84 Ibid.
85 Ibid., p. 19.
86 Ibid., p. 25.
87 Kelly, 'A Dance of Frenzy, A Dance of Praise', p. 163.
88 Cavell, 'The Incessance and the Absence of the Political', p. 307.
89 Cavell, 'Fred Astaire Asserts the Right to Praise', p. 67.
90 See especially, 'Philosophy and the Arrogation of Voice', in *A Pitch of Philosophy: Autobiographical Exercises* (Cambridge, MA: Harvard University Press, 1994), pp. 1–53, and 'The Philosopher in American Life', in *In Quest of the Ordinary: Lines of Skepticism and Romanticism* (Chicago, IL: Chicago University Press, 1988), pp. 3–27.
91 For more on this topic see Standish in conversation with Cavell, 'Stanley Cavell in Conversation with Paul Standish', in *Journal of Philosophy of Education* 46/2 (2012), especially pp. 158–160. Also Stephen Mulhall, *Stanley Cavell's Recounting of the Ordinary* (Oxford: Oxford University Press, 1994), especially pp. 69–74.
92 Cavell, *Little Did I Know*, p. 6.
93 Naomi Scheman, 'A Storied World: On Meeting and Being Met', in *Stanley Cavell and Literary Studies*, Richard Eldridge and Bernard Rhie (eds.) (London: Continuum), p. 92.
94 Kelly, 'A Dance of Frenzy, A Dance of Praise', p. 163.
95 Cavell, *Philosophy the Day after Tomorrow*, p. 151.
96 Scheman, 'A Storied World', pp. 104–105.
97 Kelly, 'A Dance of Frenzy, A Dance of Praise', p. 166.
98 Moi, *Revolution of the Ordinary*, p. 18.
99 Stanley Cavell, *Disowning Knowledge: In Six Plays of Shakespeare* (Cambridge: Cambridge University Press, 1987), p. 5.
100 Cavell, *The Claim of Reason*, p. 20.
101 Cavell, 'The Future of Possibility', p. 29.
102 Ibid., p. 30.
103 Ibid.
104 Cavell, 'Fred Astaire Asserts the Right to Praise', p. 78.
105 Ibid., p. 81.
106 Ibid., p. 82.

107 Cavell, *Pursuits of Happiness*, pp. 1–2.
108 Ibid., p. 7.
109 Cavell, *Cities of Words*, p. ix.
110 Cavell, *Little Did I Know*, p. 442.
111 Zadie Smith, 'Foreword', in *Feel Free* (London: Penguin, 2018).
112 Daniele Rugo, *Philosophy and the Patience of Film in Cavell and Nancy* (London: Palgrave, 2016), p. 30.
113 Cavell, *Must We Mean What We Say?*, p. 229.
114 Cavell, *Philosophy the Day after Tomorrow*, p. 261.
115 Robert Sinnerbrink, *New Philosophies of Film* (London/New York: Bloomsbury, 2011), see especially p. 155.
116 Gillian Rose, *Love's Work: A Reckoning with Life* (New York, NY: New York Review Books, 2011).
117 Cavell, *Little Did I Know*, p. 84.
118 See for example pages 111 and 261 of *Philosophy the Day after Tomorrow*; 'Ugly Duckling, Funny Butterfly', and various sections of *Little Did I Know*.
119 Cavell, *Little Did I Know*, p. 539.
120 Andrew Klevan, 'Guessing the Unseen from the Seen: Stanley Cavell and Film Interpretation', in *Contending with Stanley Cavell*, Russell Goodman (ed.) (Oxford: Oxford University Press, 2005) pp. 118–139.
121 Cavell, *Pursuits of Happiness*, p. 13.

Postscript

1 Stanley Cavell, 'Seasons of Love: Bergman's *Smiles of a Summer's Night* and *The Winter's Tale*', in *Cavell on Film*, William Rothman (ed.) (Albany, NY: SUNY Press, 2005), p. 195.
2 Ibid., pp. 194–195.

Bibliography

Author's note: While most of the works listed below feature within the preceding pages of this book, I have included some – including works by Cavell himself but also by other authors – that do not. My intention is for this bibliography to serve not just as a list of references but also as a useful reading list for those interested in reading more of and about Cavell. The list is not exhaustive – there are other works less pertinent to the matter of film in Cavell's work, and given the rate at which scholarship on the topic is growing, I have undoubtedly missed some more recent contributions to the field. All the books and articles have, however, informed my project in one way or another, and I am grateful to the authors.

Works by Cavell

'The Claim to Rationality: Knowledge and the Basis of Morality' (PhD diss., Harvard University, 1961).

Must We Mean What We Say? A Book of Essays (New York, NY: Charles Scriber's Sons, 1969; Cambridge: Cambridge University Press, 1976; updated version, 2002).

The World Viewed: Reflections on the Ontology of Film (New York, NY: The Viking Press, 1971).

The Senses of Walden (San Francisco, CA: North Point Press, expanded edition, 1981 [original edition 1972]).

'What Becomes of Things on Film?', Philosophy and Literature 2/2 (Fall, 1978), pp. 249–257.

'Epistemology and Tragedy: A Reading of *Othello*', Daedalus 108/3, 'Hypocrisy, Illusion, and Evasion' (Summer 1979), pp. 27–43.

The World Viewed: Reflections on the Ontology of Film (Cambridge, MA: Harvard University Press, enlarged edition, 1979).
The Claim of Reason: Wittgenstein, Skepticism, Morality, and Tragedy (Oxford: Clarendon Press, 1979; Oxford: Oxford University Press, 1982).
Pursuits of Happiness: The Hollywood Comedy of Remarriage (Cambridge, MA: Harvard University Press, 1981).
'Politics as Opposed to What?', *Critical Inquiry* 9/1, 'The Politics of Interpretation' (September 1982), pp. 157–178.
Themes out of School: Effects and Causes (San Francisco: North Point Press, 1984; Chicago, IL: University of Chicago Press, 1988).
Disowning Knowledge: In Six Plays of Shakespeare (Cambridge: Cambridge University Press, 1987; updated 2003 to *Disowning Knowledge: In Seven Plays of Shakespeare*).
In Quest of the Ordinary: Lines of Skepticism and Romanticism (Chicago, IL: Chicago University Press, 1988).
This New Yet Unapproachable America: Lectures after Emerson after Wittgenstein (Chicago, IL: University of Chicago Press, 1989).
'Naughty Narrators: Negation of Voice in Gaslight', in *Languages of the Unsayable: The Play of Negativity in Literature and Literary Theory*, Sanford Budick and Wolfgang Iser (eds.) (New York, NY: Columbia University Press, 1989), pp. 340–377.
Conditions Handsome and Unhandsome: The Constitution of Emersonian Perfectionism (Chicago, IL: University of Chicago Press, 1990).
'Response to Tania Modleski', *Critical Inquiry* 17/1 (Autumn 1990), pp. 237–244.
A Pitch of Philosophy: Autobiographical Exercises (Cambridge, MA: Harvard University Press, 1994).
Philosophical Passages: Wittgenstein, Emerson, Austin, Derrida (Oxford: Blackwell, 1995).
Contesting Tears: The Hollywood Melodrama of the Unknown Woman (Chicago, IL: University of Chicago Press, 1996).
'Epilogue: The Investigations' Everyday Aesthetics of Itself', in *The Cavell Reader*, Stephen Mulhall (ed.) (Oxford: Blackwell, 1996), pp. 369–389.
Emerson's Transcendental Etudes (Stanford, CA: Stanford University Press, 2003).

Cities of Words: Pedagogical Letters on a Register of the Moral Life (Cambridge, MA: Harvard University Press, 2004).

'Responses', in *Contending with Stanley Cavell*, Russell Goodman (ed.) (Oxford: Oxford University Press, 2005).

Cavell on Film, William Rothman (ed.) (Albany, NY: SUNY Press, 2005).

Philosophy the Day after Tomorrow (Cambridge, MA: Harvard University Press, 2006).

'The Future of Possibility', in *Philosophical Romanticism*, Nikolas Kompridis (ed.) (London/New York, NY: Routledge, 2006), pp. 21–31.

'The Incessance and the Absence of the Political', in *The Claim to Community: Essays on Stanley Cavell and Political Philosophy*, Andrew Norris (ed.) (Stanford, CA: Stanford University Press, 2006), pp. 263–317.

Little Did I Know: Excerpts from Memory (Palo Alto, CA: Stanford University Press, 2010).

Writing on Cavell

Boudreau, Kristen, 'The Haunting of History: Emerson, James, and the Ghosts of Human Suffering', in *Stanley Cavell, Literature, and Film: The Idea of America*, Áine Kelly and Andrew Taylor (eds.) (London: Routledge, 2013), pp. 80–95.

Braudy, Leo, 'Review: *The World Viewed* by Stanley Cavell', *Film Quarterly* 25/4 (Summer 1972), pp. 28–29.

Butler, Rex, 'Stanley Cavell', in *Film, Theory, Philosophy: The Key Thinkers*, Felicity Colman (ed.) (Durham, NC: Acumen, 2009), pp. 145–153.

Carroll, Noël, 'Review: *Pursuits of Happiness*', *Journal of Aesthetics and Art Criticism* 41/1 (1982), pp. 104–107.

Conant, James, 'An Interview with Stanley Cavell', in *The Senses of Stanley Cavell*, Richard Fleming and Michael Payne (eds.) (Lewisburg, VA: Bucknell University Press, 1989), pp. 21–72.

Constable, Catherine, 'Seeing Lucy's Perspective: Returning to Cavell, Wittgenstein and The Awful Truth', *New Review of Film and Television Studies* 9/3 (2011), pp. 358–375.

Crary, Alice and Sanford Shieh (eds.), *Reading Cavell* (New York, NY: Routledge, 2006).

Dahl, Espen, *Stanley Cavell, Religion, and Continental Philosophy* (Bloomington, IN: Indiana University Press, 2014).

Danto, Arthur, 'Review: Philosophy and/as Film and/as If Philosophy', October 23 (Winter 1982), pp. 4–14.

Devereaux, Mary, 'Neighbouring the World: Movies as a Subject for Philosophy', in *The Senses of Stanley Cavell: The Bucknell Review* 32/1 (1 Jan 1989) (Lewisburg: Bucknell University Press, 1989), pp. 186–199.

Eldridge, Richard (ed.), *Stanley Cavell* (Cambridge: Cambridge University Press, 2003).

Fischer, Michael, *Stanley Cavell and Literary Skepticism* (Chicago, IL: University of Chicago Press, 1989).

Fischer, Michael, 'Using Stanley Cavell', *Philosophy and Literature* 32/1 (April 2008), pp. 198–204.

Fleming, Richard and Michael Payne (eds.), *The Senses of Stanley Cavell: The Bucknell Review*, 32/1 (1 Jan 1989) (Lewisburg, VA: Bucknell University Press, 1989).

Forrester, Katrina, 'Review of Stanley Cavell, *Little Did I Know: Excerpts from Memory*', *Cambridge Literary Review* 2/5 (Summer 2011), pp. 153–174.

Giordano, Lara K., 'Cavell, Secularism, Cinema: The Politics of The World Viewed', *Constellations* 23/4 (2016), pp. 536–547.

Gooding-Williams, Robert, 'Aesthetics and Receptivity: Kant, Nietzsche, Cavell and Astaire', in *The Claim to Community: Essays on Stanley Cavell and Political Philosophy*, Andrew Norris (ed.) (Stanford, CA: Stanford University Press, 2006), pp. 236–262.

Goodman, Russell (ed.), *Contending with Stanley Cavell* (Oxford: Oxford University Press, 2005).

Gould, Timothy, *Hearing Things: Voice and Method in the Writing of Stanley Cavell* (Chicago, IL: University of Chicago Press, 1998).

Hanson, Karen, 'Being Doubted, Being Assured', in *Images in Our Souls*, Joseph H. Smith and William Kerrigan (eds.) (Baltimore and London: The John Hopkins University Press, 1987), pp. 187–201.

Kelly, Àine, '"Stylists in the American grain": Wallace Stevens, Stanley Cavell and Richard Rorty', *European Journal of Pragmatism and American Studies* 2/2 (2010), pp. 211–223.

Kelly, Àine and Andrew Taylor (eds.), *Stanley Cavell, Literature, and Film: The Idea of America* (London: Routledge, 2013).

Kenny, Anthony, '"Clouds of Not Knowing", Review of *The Claim of Reason* by Stanley Cavell', *Times Literary Supplement* (18 April 1980), p. 449.

Klevan, Andrew, 'Internalising the Musical: *The Band Wagon* (1951)', in *Film Moments*, Tom Brown and James Walters (eds.) (London: BFI), pp. 11–14.

Klevan, Andrew, 'Notes on Stanley Cavell and Philosophical Film Criticism', in *New Takes in Film-Philosophy*, Havi Carel and Greg Tuck (eds.) (Basingstoke: Palgrave Macmillan, 2011), pp. 48–64.

Kompridis, Nikolas (ed.), *Philosophical Romanticism* (London/New York, NY: Routledge, 2006).

Krauss, Rosalind, 'Dark Glasses and Bifocals, a Book Review', *Artforum* 12/9 (May 1974), pp. 59–62.

Kreisler, Harry, 'Stanley Cavell Interview: Conversations with History', Institute of International Studies, University of California Berkeley. Transcript: http://globetrotter.berkeley.edu/people2/Cavell/cavell-con1.htmlVideo:https://www.youtube.com/watch?v=eIIKqEl8xEw

Laugier, Sandra, 'The Ethics of Care as a Politics of the Ordinary', *Literature and Theology* 25/2 (June 2011), pp. 217–240.

Macarthur, David, 'What Goes without Seeing: Marriage, Sex, and the Ordinary in *The Awful Truth*', *Film-Philosophy* 18 (2014). Special Section on Stanley Cavell, pp. 92–109.

Melville, Stephen, 'Oblique and Ordinary: Stanley Cavell's Engagements of Emerson', *American Literary History*, 5/1 (Spring 1993), p. 172.

Modleski, Tania, 'Letter to the Editor', *Critical Inquiry* 17/1 (Autumn 1990), pp. 237–238.

Modleski, Tania, *Feminism without Women: Culture and Criticism in a 'Postfeminist' Age* (London and New York: Routledge, 1991).

Moi, Toril, 'The Adventure of Reading: Literature and Philosophy, Cavell and Beauvoir', *Literature and Theology* 25/2 (June 2011), pp. 125–140.

Moi, Toril, *Revolution of the Ordinary: Literary Studies after Wittgenstein, Austin and Cavell* (Chicago: University of Chicago Press, 2017).

Morgan, Daniel, 'Stanley Cavell: The Contingencies of Film and Its Theory', in *Thinking in the Dark: Cinema, Theory, Practice*, Murray Pomerance and R. Barton Palmer (eds.) (New Brunswick, N.J.: Rutgers University Press, 2016), pp. 162–173.

Mulhall, Stephen (ed.), *The Cavell Reader* (Cambridge, MA/Oxford: Blackwell University Press, 1996).

Mulhall, Stephen, *Stanley Cavell: Philosophy's Recounting of the Ordinary* (Oxford: Oxford University Press, 1998).

Read, Rupert and Jerry Goodenough, *Film as Philosophy: Essays on Cinema after Wittgenstein and Cavell* (Basingstoke/New York, NY: Palgrave MacMillan, 2005).

Rhu, Lawrence, *Stanley Cavell's American Dream: Shakespeare, Philosophy, and Hollywood Movies* (New York, NY: Fordham, 2006).

Rodowick, David N., 'An Elegy for Theory', *October* 122 (Fall 2007), pp. 91–109.

Rodowick, David N., *The Virtual Life of Film*, (Cambridge, MA: Harvard University Press, 2007).

Rothman, William, 'Cavell on Film, Television and Opera', in *Stanley Cavell*, Richard Eldridge (ed.) (Cambridge: Cambridge University Press, 2003).

Rothman, William, 'On Stanley Cavell's Band Wagon', *Film-Philosophy* 18 (2014). Special Section on Stanley Cavell, pp. 9–21.

Rothman, William and Marian Keane, 'Toward a Reading of *The World Viewed*', *Journal of Film and Video* 49 (Spring/Summer 1997), pp. 5–16.

Rothman, William and Marian Keane, *Reading Cavell's The World Viewed: A Philosophical Perspective on Film* (Detroit, MI: Wayne State University Press, 2000).

Rugo, Daniele, *Philosophy and the Patience of Film in Cavell and Nancy* (London: Palgrave, 2016).

Rushton, Richard, *The Reality of Film: Theories of Filmic Reality* (Manchester: Manchester University Press, 2010).

Saito, Naoko, 'Awakening My Voice: Learning from Cavell's Perfectionist Education', *Education Philosophy and Theory* 36/1 (2004), p. 87.

Scheman, Naomi, 'A Storied World: On Meeting and Being Met', in *Stanley Cavell and Literary Studies: Consequences of Skepticism*, Richard Eldridge and Bernard Rhie (eds.) (London: Continuum), pp. 92–105.

Sesonske, Alexander, 'The World Viewed', *The Georgia Review* 28/4 (Winter 1974), pp. 561–570.

Shaw, Daniel, 'Stanley Cavell on the Magic of the Movies', *Film-Philosophy* 21/1 (2017), pp. 114–132.

Shuster, Martin, 'The Ordinariness and Absence of the World: Cavell's Ontology of the Screen – Reading *The World Viewed*', *Modern Language Notes* 130/5 (2015), pp. 1067–1099.

Smith, Joseph and William Kerrigan (eds.), *Images in Our Souls: Cavell, Psychoanalysis, and Cinema* (Baltimore, MD: Johns Hopkins University Press, 1987).

Standish, Paul, 'Stanley Cavell in Conversation with Paul Standish', *Journal of Philosophy of Education* 46/2 (2012), pp. 155–176.

Stewart, Garrett, 'The Avoidance of Stanley Cavell', in *Contending with Stanley Cavell*, Russell B. Goodman (ed.) (Oxford: Oxford University Press, 2005), pp. 140–156.

Trahair, Lisa, 'Being on the Outside: Cinematic Automatism in Stanley Cavell's The World Viewed', *Film-Philosophy* 18 (2014). Special Section on Stanley Cavell, pp. 128–146.

Wolfe, Cary, 'Alone with America: Cavell, Emerson, and the Politics of Individualism', *New Literary History* 25/1 (Winter 1994), pp. 135–157.

Related Philosophical Texts

Austin, J.L., *How to Do Things with Words*, Second Edition (Cambridge, MA: Harvard University Press, 1975 [1962]).

Austin, J.L., *Philosophical Papers* (Oxford: The Clarendon Press, 1979 [1961]).

Cavarero, Adriana, *For More than One Voice: Toward a Philosophy of Vocal Expression* (Stanford, CA: Stanford University Press, 2005).

Collinson, Diane and Kathryn Plant, 'Wittgenstein', in *Fifty Major Philosophers* (Oxford: Routledge, 2008), pp. 211–225.

Culler, Jonathan, 'Bad Writing and Good Philosophy', in *Just Being Difficult? Academic Writing in the Public Arena*, Jonathan Culler and Kevin Lamb (eds.) (Stanford, CA: Stanford University Press, 2003), pp. 43–67.

Ehrenberg, Philip, 'Perfectionism' [blog post], available at https://dnrodowick.wordpress.com/author/phehrenberg/

Emerson, Ralph Waldo. 'Circles', in *The Portable Emerson* (London: Penguin Classics, 2014), pp. 226–236.

Faloni, Matteo, 'Perfectionism and Moral Reasoning', *European Journal of Pragmatism and American Philosophy* 2 (2010), pp. 85–100.

Foucault, Michel, *The Care of the Self* (London: Penguin, 2009).

Heidegger, Martin, 'The Age of the World Picture', in *The Question Concerning Technology and Other Essays* (New York, NY: Harper & Row, 1977), pp. 115–155.

Kierkegaard, Soren, *Either/Or, Volume 2*, trans. Walter Lowrie (ed.) (Princeton, NJ: Princeton University Press, 1944).

Longworth, Guy, 'John Langshaw Austin', *The Stanford Encyclopedia of Philosophy* (Spring 2017 Edition), Edward N. Zalta (ed.), available at https://plato.stanford.edu/archives/spr2017/entries/austin-jl/

Murdoch, Iris, *The Sovereignty of Good* (London: Routledge, 2001).

Rawls, John, *A Theory of Justice* (Cambridge, MA: Belknap Press/Harvard University Press, 1971).

Rose, Gillian, *Love's Work: A Reckoning with Life* (New York, NY: New York Review Books, 2011).

Thoreau, Henry David, *Walden, Or Life in the Woods* (Princeton, NJ: Princeton University Press, 1974).

Wittgenstein, Ludwig, *Tractatus Logic-Philosophicus*, trans. D.F. Pears and B.F. McGuiness (London: Routledge and Kegan Paul, 1961 [1921]).

Wittgenstein, Ludwig, *Philosophical Investigations*, trans. G.E.M. Anscombe, Third Edition (Oxford: Blackwell, 1978), p. 187.

Related Film Texts

Affron, Charles, *Star Acting: Gish, Garbo, Davis* (New York, NY: E.P. Dutton, 1977).

Barthes, Roland, 'Leaving the Movie Theatre', in *The Rustle of Language*, trans. Richard Howard (New York, NY: Hill and Wang, 1986), pp. 345–346.

Bazin, Andre, 'Ontology of the Photographic Image', in *What Is Cinema?*, trans. Hugh Gray (Berkeley: University of California Press, 1967).

Braudy, Leo and Marshall Cohen (eds.), *Film Theory and Criticism: Introductory Readings*, Fifth Edition (New York, NY/Oxford: Oxford University Press, 1999).

Clayton, Alex, *The Body in Hollywood Slapstick* (Jefferson, NC/London: McFarland, 2007).

Creed, Barbara, 'Film and Psychoanalysis', in *The Oxford Guide to Film Studies*, John Hill and Pamela Church Gibson (eds.) (Oxford: Oxford University Press, 1998).

Doane, Mary Ann, *The Desire to Desire: The Woman's Film of the 1940's* (Bloomington, IN: University of Indiana Press, 1987).

Downing, Lisa and Libby Saxton, *Film and Ethics: Foreclosed Encounters* (Abingdon and New York, NY: Routledge, 2010).

Durgnat, Raymond, *Films and Feelings* (Cambridge and London: The MIT Press, Faber and Faber, 1967).

Durgnat, Raymond, *Durgnat on Film* (London: Faber and Faber, 1976).

Dyer, Richard, *Teachers' Study Guide 1: The Stars* (London: BFI Education, 1979).

Frampton, Daniel, *Filmosophy* (London, Wallflower Press, 2006).

Gledhill, Christine, 'History of Genre Criticism: Introduction', in *The Cinema Book*, Third Edition, Pam Cook (ed.) (London: BFI, 2007), pp. 252–259.

Glitre, Kathrina, '"The Same, But Different": The Awful Truth about Marriage, Remarriage and Screwball Comedy', *Cineaction* 54 (2001), pp. 2–11.

Handyside, Fiona, 'Words for a Conversation: Speech, Doubt and Faith in the films of Eric Rohmer and Mia Hansen-Løve', *Studies in French Cinema*, forthcoming.

Hilgers, Thomas, *Aesthetic Disinterestedness: Art, Experience, and the Self* (Oxford: Routledge, 2016).

Kaplan, E. Ann, 'The Case of the Missing Mother': Maternal Issues in King Vidor's *Stella Dallas*', *Heresies* 16 (1983), pp. 81–85.

Klevan, Andrew, *Disclosure of the Everyday: Undramatic Achievement in Narrative Film* (Trowbridge: Flicks Books, 2000).

Klevan, Andrew, *Film Performance: From Achievement to Appreciation* (London: Wallflower, 2005).

Klevan, Andrew, *Barbara Stanwyck* (London: BFI/Palgrave Macmillan, 2013).

Metz, Christian, *Film Language: A Semiotics of the Cinema* (New York, NY/Oxford: Oxford University Press, 1974).

Modelski, Tania, *Feminism without Women: Culture and Criticism in a 'Postfeminist' Age* (London: Routledge, 1991).

Mullarkey, John, *Refractions of Reality: Philosophy and the Moving Image* (London: Palgrave Macmillan, 2009).

Neale, Steve, 'Comedy', in *The Cinema Book*, Third Edition, Pam Cook (ed.) (London: BFI, 2007), pp. 270–276.

Panofsky, Erwin, 'Style and Medium in the Moving Pictures', in *Film*, Daniel Talbot (ed.) (New York, NY: Simon and Schuster, 1959), p. 31.

Perez, Gilberto, *The Material Ghost: Films and Their Medium* (Baltimore, MD: Johns Hopkins University Press, 1998).

Perkins, V.F., *Film as Film: Understanding and Judging Movies* (Boston, MA: Da Capo Press, 1993 [1972]).

Perkins, V.F., *The Magnificent Ambersons* (London: BFI, 1999).

Ray, Robert, *The ABCs of Classic Hollywood* (Oxford: Oxford University Press, 2008).

Rogin, Michael, *Blackface, White Noise: Jewish Immigrants in the Hollywood Melting Pot* (Berkeley, CA: University of California Press, 1998).

Rothman, William, 'Pathos and Transfiguration in the Face of the Camera: A Reading of *Stella Dallas*', in *The 'I' of the Camera: Essays in Film Criticism, History and Aesthetics* (Cambridge: Cambridge University Press, 1988), pp. 85–94.

Rothman, William '"Why Not Realize Your World?" Philosophy Scholar William Rothman Interviewed by Jeffrey Crouse', *Film International* 9/6 (2012), pp. 62–73.

Sarris, Andrew, 'Notes on the Auteur Theory in 1962', *Film Culture* 27 (Winter 1962–3), pp. 1–8.

Sarris, Andrew, *You Ain't Heard Nothin' Yet: The American Talking Film, History & Memory, 1927–1949* (New York, NY/Oxford: Oxford University Press, 1998).

Schmerheim, Philip, *Skepticism Films: Knowing and Doubting the World in Contemporary Cinema* (London: Bloomsbury, 2015).

Shumway, David R., 'Screwball Comedies: Constructing Romance, Mystifying Marriage', in *Film Genre Reader III*, Barry Keith Grant (ed.) (Austin, TX: University of Texas Press, 2003).

Sinnerbrink, Robert, *New Philosophies of Film* (London/New York: Bloomsbury, 2011).

Sinnerbrink, Robert, 'Re-enfranchising Film: Romantic Film-Philosophy', in *New Takes in Film-Philosophy*, Havi Carel and Greg Tuck (eds.) (Basingstoke: Palgrave Macmillan, 2011), pp. 25–47.

Sinnerbrink, Robert, *Cinematic Ethics: Exploring Ethical Experience through Film* (London: Routledge, 2015).

Thomson, David, *Movie Man* (New York, NY: Stein and Day, 1967).

Toles, George, *A House Made of Light: Essays on the Art of Film* (Detroit, MI: Wayne State University Press, 2001).

Wheatley, Catherine, *The Ethic of the Image* (Oxford: Berghahn, 2010).

Williams, Linda, 'Something Else besides a Woman: *Stella Dallas* and the Maternal Melodrama', *Cinema Journal* 24/1 (Autumn 1984), pp. 2–27.

Wilson, George M., *Narration in Light: Studies in Cinematic Point of View* (Baltimore, MD: Johns Hopkins University Press, 1986).

Other Texts

Brooks, Peter, *The Melodramatic Imagination: Balzac, Henry James, Melodrama and the Mode of Excess* (New Haven, CT: Yale University Press, 1976).

Frye, Northrup, 'The Argument of Comedy', in *Northrop Frye's Writings on Shakespeare and the Renaissance*, Troni Y. Grande and Garry Sherber (eds.) (Toronto: University of Toronto Press, 2010).

Ibsen, Henrik, *A Doll's House, The Wild Duck, Lady from the Sea*, trans. R. Farquharson Sharp and Eleanor Marx-Aveling (London: Dent, 1958).

James, Henry, 'The Art of Fiction', in *Longman's Magazine* 4 (September 1884).

McKnight, Utz, *The Everyday Practice of Race in American: Ambiguous Privilege* (New York, NY: Routledge, 2010).

Novotny, Fritz, *Painting and Sculpture in Europe, 1780–1880 (Pelican History of Art)* (New Haven, CT: Yale University Press, 1971).
Phillips, Siobhan, *The Poetics of the Everyday: Creative Repetition in Modern American Verse* (New York, NY: Columbia University Press, 2010).
Smith, Zadie, *Feel Free* (London: Penguin, 2018).

Index

Adam's Rib (Cukor) 105, 110, 112–13, 125–7, 131–2, 170, 193, 195–6
'Adventure of Reading: Literature and Philosophy, Cavell and Beauvoir' (Moi) 221
Agee, James 9
American Beauty (Mendes) 26
American transcendentalism 141, 179
Andrews, Ellie 150
Anton, Paula Alquist 181
Antonioni, Michaelangelo 7, 31, 64, 216
Aristotle 182, 184–5
Arnold, Matthew 138–9, 182, 185, 248
Astaire, Fred 225–37, 240, 245–6
Augustine 185
Austin, John
    on being sure and certain 41
    on challenges of philosophy 36
    influence on Cavell 6–7, 31–2
    on knowing and believing 40
    on locutionary act 39
    neologisms 37
    new mode of philosophical criticism. 43
    ordinary language philosophy 48
    'Other Minds,' 39
    performative utterances 28, 38
    as philosopher of language 30
Awful Truth, The (McCarey) 21, 105, 109, 111–12, 114, 116, 120–1, 124, 128, 131–2, 145
Ayer, A.J. 239

Badiou, Alain 97
Band Wagon, The (Minnelli) 15, 225–31, 233–5, 244
Baudrillard, Jean 97
Bauer, Nancy 22

Bazin, Andre 1, 9, 23, 67–70, 73–4, 76, 78
Beast in the Jungle (James) 224
'Behaviour' (Emerson) 53, 151
'Being Doubted, Being Assured' (Hanson) 96, 153
'Being on the Outside: Cinematic Automatism in Stanley Cavell's *The World Viewed*' (Trahair) 73
Benjamin, Walter 9, 246
Bergen, Candice 113
Bergman, Ingmar 2, 7, 24, 64, 173, 251–2
Bergman, Ingrid 181, 216
Berndle, Lisa 181
Bettinson, Gary 22
Birds, The (Hitchcock) 26, 216
Birth of Tragedy, The (Nietzsche) 8
Bisset, Jacqueline 113
Blackface, White Noise: Jewish Immigrants in the Hollywood Melting Pot (Rogin) 231, 283 n.55
Blackmur, R.P. 8
Bogart, Humphrey 75
Bonner, Amanda 170
Boyer, Charles 6
Braudy, Leo 11, 13, 18, 20, 23
Bringing Up Baby (Hawks) 105, 111–12, 127, 133, 171, 269 n.36
Brooks, Peter 148, 273 n.32
Burke, Kenneth 8
Butler, Rex 15, 22, 57, 115, 205

Cage, John 58
Cagney, Jimmy 76–7
'Calm: On Terrence Malick's *The Thin Red Line*'(Critchley) 22
Capra, Frank 22, 26, 51, 55, 104, 133
Carel, Havi 218, 223

Carroll, Noël 20, 258 n.38
Cavarero, Adriana 175, 276 n.91
Cavell, Benjamin 7
Cavell, David 7
Cavell, Rachel 7
Cavell, Stanley
  about gender 126–32, 149–53
  account on *The Awful Truth* 21
  adolescence 6
  'Aesthetic Problems of Modern Philosophy' 42
  analytic models 19
  anglicization of name 6
  'Art of Fiction, The' 224
  'Avoidance of Love, The' 47, 58, 103, 217
  'Being Odd, Getting Even' 142–4
  childhood 5–6
  Cities of Words: Pedagogical Letters on a Register of the Moral Life 10, 20, 27, 61, 64, 113, 135, 138–9, 181–6, 191, 193, 195, 197, 205, 213, 247
  Claim of Reason, The 12–14, 40
  college life 6
  'Concluding Remarks Presented at Paris Colloquium on *La Projection du Monde*' 64
  Conditions Handsome and Unhandsome: The Constitution of Emersonian Perfectionism 16, 27, 138–40, 193, 206–7
  Contesting Tears: The Hollywood Melodrama of the Unknown Woman 5, 10, 15, 27, 64, 112, 114, 135, 137–9, 144–6, 148, 151, 155, 169, 176–9, 181–3, 187–8, 192, 196, 202, 217, 224–6, 235, 238, 241, 252
  Conversations: The Journal of Cavellian Studies 18
  Disowning Knowledge in Six Plays of Shakespeare 15, 199, 257 n.27
  encounter with Austin 6–7
  'Ending the Waiting Game: A Reading of Beckett's Endgame' 58
  'End of Myths, The' 215
  essays on *The Band Wagon* 227, 235
  feminists, view on 15
  film criticism 218–25
  film ontology 67–70, 76
  on film readings 245–6
  first engagement with film 10
  'Fred Astaire Asserts the Right to Praise' 232
  Future of Possibility, The 216, 244
  good film, definition 209–10
  Good of Film, The 188
  idea of photographs 67–70
  'Ideas of Man and the World in Western Thought' (teaching course at Harward) 7
  'Incessance and the Absence of the Political, The' 113
  'Knowing and Acknowledging' 98
  on Knowledge and Morality 138
  'Knowledge and the Basis of Morality' 193
  1954 *La Strada* 31
  Letter from an Unknown Woman 203–4, 224
  Little Did I Know (autobiography) 8, 213, 218, 241
  marriage, conception of 103–14, 116–19, 127–8
  marriage with Cohen 7
  marriage with Schmid 7
  'A Matter of Meaning of It' 43, 58
  on mechanism or automatism 73–85
  on melodramas 5, 15, 22, 137–8, 143–50, 153, 155, 158–63, 167–9, 171–5, 180–1, 187–8, 192, 196, 201, 203, 210, 217, 245
  on moral reasoning 191–7

'Moral Reasoning: Teaching from the Core' 211
'Music Discomposed' 43, 58
Must We Mean What We Say? 10, 27–8, 31–2, 41–3, 48, 58, 66–7, 90, 98, 103, 115, 169, 215, 222, 237
'Opera and the Lease of Voice' 177
'Opera in (and as) Film' 57
ordinary language philosophy 67, 114
passionate utterances 235–45
perfectionism, notion of 139, 183–91, 194–6, 201, 207–10, 213, 247
'Philosophy the Day after Tomorrow'. 194, 213, 225, 239, 251
Pitch of Philosophy, A 137, 173, 176, 178, 241
popular criticism 12–14
Psychoanalysis and Cinema: The Melodrama of the Unknown Woman' 150
Pursuits of Happiness: The Hollywood Comedy of Remarriage 10, 15, 20, 25, 27, 48, 64, 92, 102, 104–6, 108–10, 112, 115, 119, 132–5, 138, 142, 145–6, 157, 159, 170, 178–9, 182–3, 188, 192, 199, 217, 221, 224, 238, 246, 248, 252
In Quest of the Ordinary: Lines of Skepticism and Romanticism 141, 199, 253, 260 n.35
quoting Freud 112
Rachel (daughter) 7
'Recounting Gains, Showing Losses: Reading *The Winter's Tale*'. 199
on remarriage comedies 24, 102–3, 105, 107, 109–11, 113, 116–20, 123, 126, 129–32, 135, 138, 144–8, 154, 157, 168, 170–1, 188, 190, 192–3, 195, 197–8, 201–2, 204–5, 212, 244–5, 252
on same sex marriages 195
scepticism 85–90, 96, 100, 104, 109, 115, 130–1, 149, 151, 203
on Shakespearean tragedy 103–9
'Something out of the Ordinary' 225, 227, 229, 236–7
subject matter, approaches to 14–15, 21, 68, 86, 134, 247
as teacher and friend 208–12
teacher's praise for *Hold Back the Dawn*'s review 6
Themes out of School 12
'Thought of Movies, The' 56
'Ugly Duckling, Funny Butterfly: Bette Davis and *Now, Voyager*' 158
vision of love 215–18
on Western existentialism 80
'Words for a Conversation' 115
World Viewed: Reflections on the Ontology of Film, The 3, 10–11, 13, 21, 23, 27, 31, 52, 56, 59, 61–2, 64–7, 69–70, 72–9, 81, 83, 88–9, 91, 96, 100–2, 133–4, 138, 140–1, 154, 252
writing for friends and strangers 245–50
writing style 12–13, 19
Cavell on Film (Rothman) 11, 21, 26
Chaplin, Charlie 24, 31, 82
Charisse, Cyd 226
Chazelle, Damien 16
Children's Hour, The (Wyler) 64
Cinematic Ethics (Sinnerbrink) 22
Civil Rights movement 17
Claim to Community, The (Norris) 236
Clair, René 31
Clément, Catherine 175
'Cogito Ergo Film: Plato, Descartes and *Fight Club*' (Bauer) 22

Cohen, Cathleen (Cavell's second wife) 7
Cohen, Marshall 23
Colbert, Claudette 117–18, 132
Coleman, Ronald 2
Collinson, Diane 34
Constable, Catherine 128–9, 172, 196, 270 n.74
Contending with Stanley Cavell (Goodman) 22
Cooper, Gary 54, 68, 152–3
Cordova, Jeff 228
Critchley, Simon 22
Cukor, George 20, 105, 113, 126, 174, 197
Culture and Anarchy (Arnold) 139

Dallas, Stella 167, 177, 181
Daniels, Lee 231–2
Danto, Arthur 217–18
Davis, Bette 155–8
Day at the Races, A (Marx Brothers) 48
de Havilland, Olivia 6
Deleuze, Gilles 15, 18–19, 37, 83, 189
Derrida, Jacques 15
Descartes, René 8, 22, 53, 57, 79, 82, 86, 142–3, 198
Dexter, C.K. 244
Dialogues on Natural Religion (Hume) 8
Doane, Mary Ann 149, 158, 161, 275 n.61
Doll's House, A (Ibsen) 139, 145, 273 n.24
Dover Beach (Arnold) 248
Downing, Lisa 189
Dr Jekyll and Mr Hyde 2
Duck Soup (Marx Brothers) 48
Dunne, Irene 120
Duras, Marguerite 216
Dyer, Richard 76

Ehrenberg, Philip 279 n.84
Eisenstein, Sergei 9, 64, 88
Eldridge, Richard 21

Eliot, George 185
Eliot, T.S. 8
Emerson, Ralph Waldo
  conformity and self-reliance, ideas 139, 142–3, 155, 192
  '*Contesting Tears*' case studies 27, 135, 178
  and Deeds 53–4
  Film Studies context 22–3, 249
  influence on Cavell 14, 16, 20, 110, 139–45
  moral perfectionism 183–5, 188, 191, 195–7, 200, 205, 207
  ordinary language philosophy 102
  ways of thinking 174, 179, 182, 211
Empson, William 8
European cinema
  new waves 64
  post-war productions 64
Everyday Practice of Race in America (McKnight) 231, 283 n.57
Existenz (Cronenberg) 97

Faloni, Matteo 185, 277 n.11
Fellini, Federico 7, 31, 44–6, 58, 64, 81
Feminism without Women (Modleski) 159, 176, 274 n.57
Fight Club (Fincher) 97
Film, Theory and Philosophy: The Key Thinkers (Butler) 22
Film as Philosophy: Essays in Cinema after Wittgenstein and Cavell (Read and Goodenough) 22
film-going vs film-viewing 91
  ordinary practice 62–3
  reading, comparison 65
Film Theory and Criticism (Cohen) 23
Fire Sermon (Quatro) 95
Fischer, Michael 11, 255 n.12
Fontaine, Joan 181
Forrester, Katrina 3, 254 n.3
Foucault, Michel 15, 19, 184
Fox Movie Theatre 5
Frankfurt School 19

French, Marilyn 162
Freud, Sigmund 112, 139, 148, 152, 155, 182
Fried, Michael 80
Friedrich, Caspar David 78
Frye, Northrop 105, 118

Gable, Clark 76, 110, 118, 132
Garbo, Greta 24, 63, 153–6
Gaslight (Cukor) 150, 158, 172–4
Gilbert, P.F. 32
Glitre, Kathrina 127–9, 270 n.71
Godard, Jean-Luc 7, 26, 64
Goodenough, Jerry 22
Gooding-Williams, Robert 232, 234–6, 283 nn.65–6
Goodman, Paul 8
Goodman, Russell B. 11, 22, 255 n.14
Gosling, Ryan 16
Gould, Timothy 11–12, 256 n.17
Graduate, The (Nichols) 64
Grant, Cary 111–12, 116, 120, 127
Gray, Hugh 9
Great Depression 5
Great Expectations (Dickens) 244
Groundhog Day (Ramis) 26
Groundwork of the Metaphysics of Morals (Kant) 2, 8
'Guessing the Unseen from the Seen: Stanley Cavell and Film Interpretation' (Klevan) 22

'Habitual Remarriage: The Ends of Happiness in *The Palm Beach Story*' (Klawan) 22
Hail, Mary (Godard) 26
Hamlet (Shakespeare) 139, 187
Handyside, Fiona 203
Hanson, Karen 96, 153
Harding, Ann 2
Hawks, Howard 105, 112–13, 127, 189
Hearing Things: Voice and Method in the Writing of Stanley Cavell (Gould) 12
Hedren, Tippi 216

Hegel, Georg Wilhelm Friedrich 80, 83, 185, 190
Heidegger, Martin 19–20, 80, 82–3, 142, 185, 207, 220, 265–6 n.57
Hepburn, Katherine 2, 111, 116, 125
Hilgers, Thomas 71, 264 n.28
Hiroshima, Mon Amour (Resnais and Duras) 216
His Girl Friday (Hawks) 105, 112–13, 127, 189
Hitchcock, Alfred 26, 89, 215
Hold Back the Dawn (Leisen) 6
How to Do Things with Words (Austin) 38

I Am a Fugitive from a Chain Gang (LeRoy) 2
Ibsen, Henrik 20, 23, 139, 145, 147, 182, 185, 209, 273 n.24
Images in Our Souls (Smith) 149–50, 153
Interpretation of Dreams, The (Freud) 139
It Happened One Night (Capra) 104, 110, 112, 117, 127, 132–4, 145
It's a Wonderful Life (Capra) 22

James, Henry 185, 224

Kant, Immnauel 8, 20, 80, 83, 182, 184–5, 190, 194, 201, 237, 240, 246
Kaplan, Ann 161
Keane, Marian 21, 66, 69, 79, 95
Keaton, Buster 24, 31, 91–2
Kelly, Áine 20, 231, 234, 242–3
Kelly, Grace 216
Kenny, Anthony 13, 256 n.23
Kerrigan, Willaim 151, 273 n.33
Kierkegaard, Søren 19, 31, 80, 83, 207
King's Row 2
Klawan, Stuart 22
Klevan, Andrew 22, 29–30, 54, 101–2, 119, 123, 167–8, 218,

223–5, 227, 250, 258 n.1,
  259 n.5, 268 n.20, 282 n.49
Kompridis, Kompridis 219–20
Kracauer, Siegfried 23, 69
Kramer, Stanley 88
Krenek, Ernst 58
Kuhn, Thomas 7

Lacan, Jacques 15
Lady Eve, The (Sturges) 104, 110, 112,
  127, 131, 165, 171, 191
La La Land (Chazelle) 16
La Sirène du Mississippi (Truffaut) 88
La Strada (Fellini) 44, 81
Laugier, Sandra 225
L'Avventura (Antonioni) 216
Levinas, Emmanuel 19
Locke, John 8, 80, 83, 182
Lombard, Carole 2, 63
London Review of Books, The 48
Lord, Tracy 170, 244
Lost Horizon 2
Luther, Martin 8

MacArthur, David 100, 102, 121,
  268 n.12
Macbeth (Shakespeare) 43
Machiavelli, Niccolo 8
Mamoulian, Rouben 154
Marx, Karl 80, 83, 96
Marx Brothers 47–51, 116
Matrix, The (Wachowski) 97
McCarey, Leo 105, 124, 131, 172
McKnight, Utz 231, 234
Meditations (Descartes) 8, 57
Melville, Stephen 11, 256 n.16
Mendes, Sam 26
Metz, Christian 71, 76, 149, 264 n.29
Mill, Stuart 8, 139, 172, 182, 190, 194
Milton, John 117
Minnelli, Vincent 15, 225, 228–30
Mitchell, James 226
Modleski, Tania 15, 149, 158–61,
  176–7, 183, 234–6, 238,
  274 n.57

Moi, Toril 218, 221–3, 225, 243, 281
  n.24
Monkey Business (Marx Brothers)
  48, 50
Moore, G.E. 19
Morgan, Daniel 23, 69, 83, 255 n.10,
  264–265 n.42
Mr Deeds Goes to Town (Capra) 26,
  51, 55, 152, 174
Mulhall, Stephen 13–14, 21–2, 98,
  107–8, 110, 119, 123, 153,
  156–7, 184, 186, 192, 205,
  256 n.19, 272 n.12, 285 n.91
Mullarkey, John 67
Muni, Paul 2, 76
Murdoch, Iris 221

Neale, Steve 105, 269 n.26
New Critics 11, 44
New Historicism 15
*New Philosophies of Film: Thinking
  Images* (Sinnerbrink) 22
New Takes in Film Philosophy (Carel
  and Tuck) 218
Nichols, Mike 64
Nietzsche, Friedrich 8, 19–20, 80,
  142, 182, 185, 192, 196, 237
Night at the Opera, A (Wood) 26,
  49–50
Norris, Andrew 236
'Notes on Stanley and Philosophical
  Film Criticism' (Klevan) 218,
  223
'Notes on the Auteur Theory' (Sarris) 9
Notorious (Hitchcock) 216
Novak, Kim 216
Now, Voyager (Vidor) 63, 137–9, 150,
  155–8, 169, 176, 192

Office, The (Tim) 95
On the Aesthetic Education of Man
  (Schiller) 182
On Liberty (Mill) 8
'On Stanley Cavell's Band Wagon'
  (Rothman) 233

On the Subjection of Women (Mill) 139
'ordinary language criticism' (Moi) 218, 221
Othello (Shakespeare) 72, 144
'Other Minds' (Austin) 39

Palm Beach Story, The (Sturges) 22, 105
Panofsky, Erwin 8–9, 23, 67–9
Pennies from Heaven 209
Perkins, V.F. 223
Peter Ibbotson 2
Philadelphia Story, The (Cukor) 20, 105, 110–13, 117, 127, 139, 170, 196–7, 244
Philosophical Investigations (Wittgenstein) 25, 33–4, 51, 188
Philosophical Romanticism (Kompridis) 219, 255 n.7
photography 67–8, 75, 82, 102
  mechanical basis 86
  painting vs 70, 78
Picasso 70
Plant, Kathryn 34
Plato 139, 142, 182, 186, 198, 200
Polanski, Roman 64
Preface to the Letter of St. Paul to the Romans (Luther) 8
Prince, The (Machiavelli) 8
Psycho (Hitchcock) 88–9

Queen Christina (Mamoulian) 154

Ramis, Harold 26
Rawls, John 113, 182, 185, 188, 205
Read, Rupert 22
Reading Cavell's The World Viewed: A Philosophical Perspective on Film (Rothman) 21
Reagan, Ronald 2
Republic (Plato) 139, 186
Resnais, Alain 7, 64, 216
Rich and Famous (Cukor) 113
Richards, I.A. 8
Richardson, Tony 72

Robinson, Bill (Bojangles) 233
Rodowick, D.N. 18, 76, 85, 209, 257 n.34, 257. n 34, 264–265 n.42, 266 n.70
Rogin, Michael 231
Rohmer, Eric 26, 182, 197, 199, 201–3, 208, 279 n.64
Rose, Gillian 249
Rosemary's Baby 64
Rosen, Michael 88
Rothman, William 11, 21–2, 26, 66, 69, 79, 95, 111, 132, 135, 161, 177–9, 209, 233–4, 257 n.29, 275 n.62
Rousseau, Jean-Jacques 206
Routledge Companion to Film and Philosophy (Rothman) 22
Rushton, Richard 22
Russell, Bertrand 19, 257 n.31
Ryle, Gilbert 32

Saito, Naoko 212
Sarris, Andrew 9
Saxton, Libby 189
Scheman, Naomi 242–3, 285 n.93
Schiller, Friedrich 182
Schoenberg, Arnold 58
Second Treatise of Government (Locke) 8
Second World War 17, 83–5, 215
Senses of Walden, The (Thoreau) 10, 140, 266 n.61
Sesonske, Alexander 72, 264 n.31
Seven Year Itch, The (Wilder) 105
Shakespeare, William 16, 23, 31–2, 43–5, 57–8, 72, 79, 102–3, 105, 107–8, 118, 139, 144–5, 147, 154, 169–70, 182, 187, 197, 199, 202, 209, 268 n.24
Shaw, Daniel 69
Shaw, George Bernard 182, 185
Sherlock Junior (Keaton) 91–2
Ship of Fools (Kramer) 88
Shuster, Martin 80–1, 85, 265–6 n.57, 266 n.61

Sinnerbrink, Robert 12–13, 22, 114, 160, 164–8, 188–9, 193, 196, 208–9, 218–20, 248, 256 n.21, 256 nn.23–24, 269 n.41
Smiles of a Summer's Night (Bergman) 2, 7, 10, 216, 251–3, 255 n.7
Smith, Joseph H. 149, 151
Smith, Zadie 215, 247, 284 n.69
'Something Else Besides a Woman: *Stella Dallas* and the Maternal Melodrama' (Williams) 161
Stage Door 2
Stanley Cavell: Philosophy's Recounting of the Ordinary (Mulhall) 22
Stanley Cavell and Literary Skepticism (Fischer) 11
Stanley Cavell (Eldridge) 21
Stanwyck, Barbara 112, 116, 161, 165, 167–8, 181
Stella Dallas (Vidor) 20, 158–61, 163, 166–7, 175–7, 222, 244, 275 n.61
Stewart, Garrett 11–12, 14–16
Stewart, James 116
Studies in Hysteria (Breuer and Freud) 155
Sturges, Preston 23, 104–5
Sublett, John (John Bubbles) 233
Sullavan, Margaret 2
Swing Time (Stevens) 233–4, 284 n.69

Tale of Winter/Conte d'hiver (Rohmer) 26, 182, 197
Taming of the Shrew, The 127, 170
Theory of Film (Kracauer) 23, 69
Theory of the Leisure Class (Veblen) 139
Thompson, Bob 6
Thoreau, Henry David 10, 16, 20, 27, 31, 53, 110, 140–2, 145, 174, 207, 272 n.12
Three Comrades 2
To Be or Not to Be 2

To Catch a Thief (Hitchcock) 215–16
Tom Jones (Richardson) 72
Tractatus Logico-Philosophicus (Wittgenstein) 2, 32–4
Tracy, Spencer 2, 125
Trahair, Lisa 73–4, 83, 91, 264 n.35, 265 n.54
Treatise of Human Nature, A (Hume) 2
Truffaut, François 64, 88
Tuck, Greg 218, 223
Turner, J.W. 78

Une Femme Mariée (Truffaut) 88

Vale, Charlotte 155–8, 181
Veblen, Thorstein 139
Vidor, King 20, 137, 166
Vietnam War 17

Wachowski, Lana 97
Wachowski, Lilly 97
Warne, Peter 150
Warren, Robert Penn 8
We're Going on a Bear Hunt (Rosen) 88
What Is Cinema? (Bazin) 9
What Is Film Theory? (Rushton and Bettinson) 22
White, Morton 6–7
Wilder, Billy 105
Williams, Bernard 7
Williams, Linda 161–7, 169, 178
Winterset 2
Winter's Tale, The (Shakespeare) 2, 15, 107, 127, 198–9, 251–2
Wittgenstein, Ludwig 19–20, 22–3, 25
  frictionless ice 118
  human body, emphasis on 151
  imagined duck-rabbit 25, 238
  influence on Cavell 19, 23, 25, 29, 31, 140–1
  ordinary language philosophy 26, 32–7, 39–40, 43–4, 47–8

on pain 97, 101
perfectionism, concept 185, 207–8
plain view 213, 223
publicness of language 90
Wölflinn, Heinrich 8
Women's Room, The (French) 162
Wood, Sam 26
Wordsworth, William 141

World Viewed: Reflections on the Ontology of Film (Cavell) 3, 10–11, 13, 21, 23, 27, 31, 52, 56, 59, 61–2, 64–7, 69–70, 72–9, 81, 83, 88–9, 91, 96, 100–2, 133–4, 138, 140–1, 154, 252
Wyler, William 64

Žižek, Slavoj 15, 97

www.ingramcontent.com/pod-product-compliance
Lightning Source LLC
Chambersburg PA
CBHW070016010526
44117CB00011B/1598